Hi, my name is Mike Copeland and I am a writer. I've put together a collection of my favorite humor lifestyle articles from the past five years in a book entitled Alive and Kickin'. Even if you'll never read it, the highlly artistic, beautifully decorated cover will make the perfect Toilet Tank Book. Here's what readers are saying about my literary masterpiece:

"If a toilet tank book is something to read while you're sitting on the crapper I'll take two."
—*Mike Mooney, Softball Teammate*

"I hope everyone buys Mike's book. It's not very good, but he owes me $40.00."
—*John Macholz, Mike's Neighbor*

"Mike must have had a great proofreader and editor, because he almost never went to class and always copied my homework."
—*Burt Harris, Fraternity Brother at Cal State Northridge*

"That was the funniest book I've ever read. I laughed so hard I wet my pants."
—*Ekim Dnalepoc, Mike's Best Friend*

"A toilet tank book? That's brilliant! I wish I would've thought of that because a book on my life would be much more entertaining than Mike's silly ramblings."
—*Floyd Killen, Legendary Lead Singer of Floyd's Ordeal*

"If my dad sells a lot of books he promised to buy me a horse. He better not be lying."
—*Hannah Copeland, Mike's Daughter*

"I would rather read all seven Harry Potter books than Mike's stupid book. Wait, he mentioned me in his acknowledgements? I take back what I just said."
—*Mitzi Copeland, Mike's Sister*

"Alive and Kickin' is a wonderful read. It has action, adventure, romance and a really cool Soduku puzzle. To be honest, I never read it."
—*Dana Kruger, Mike's Book Club Friend*

"Oh sure, you can write a book, but do you ever vacuum the carpet, fold laundry or cook dinner? I don't think so."
—*Julie Copeland, Mike's Wife*

"Dad wrote a book? On what?"
—*Claire Copeland, Mike's Daughter*

"Alive and Kickin' had nothing to do with martial arts. That's false advertising. What a rip off!"
—*Craig Nunn, a Close Personal Friend of Mike's Wife*

Raoul –

always stay

alive & kickin'

Best Wishes,

Mike Graham

alive & kickin'

Sideways Views
from an Upright Guy

Michael S. Copeland

ABOOKS
Alive Book Publishing

ISBN 978-0-9857367-0-5 Paperback
ISBN 978-0-9857367-1-2 E-Book

Library of Congress Control Number: 2012942005

Library of Congress Cataloging-in-Publication Data

LC control no.: 2012942005LCCN
permalink: http://lccn.loc.gov/2012942005
Alive & Kickin': Sideways Views from an Upright Guy
/ Michael S. Copeland.
Edition: 1st ed.
Published/Created: Alamo, CA: Advanced Pub. LLC, 2012.
Description: p. cm.
ISBN: 9780985736705 (pbk. : alk. paper)
       9780985736712 (ebk. : alk. paper)

Printed in USA by Advanced Publishing LLC
ALIVE Publishing Group
3200 A Danville Blvd.
Suite 204
Alamo, California 94507
www.alivebookpublishing.com

DEDICATION

This book is dedicated to Julie, Hannah and Claire.
You are my everything!

TABLE OF CONTENTS

FOREWORD

My introduction to Michael Copeland came by way of the first article he submitted to me at *ALIVE Magazine*, in late 2006 or early 2007. As I recall, his submission was quite formal—neatly typed, double spaced with a well conceived cover letter attached. He noted, quite properly, that he was an experienced writer, with several of his works having appeared in a few other magazines. I read Mike's article and decided that it wasn't the best fit for *ALIVE*; an emailed rejection letter was Mike's introduction to Eric Johnson.

At this point I will offer a tip to aspiring writers—while persistence is a virtue some editors consider annoying, some of us appreciate it and consider it an indication of a writer's backbone. The relationship between writers and editors can be delicate, and if a writer gives up after only one or a few rejections, it's doubtful they will ever see their work in print, much less see it as a regular feature in some periodical.

Of course Mike didn't give up. He worked-up submission number two which became the beginning of a series of what is now some fifty-plus feature articles in *ALIVE Magazine* over the past five years—the fruit of which you hold in your hands. Not only has Mike developed a healthy immunity to rejection letters, his writing has developed to where it is an integral part of what makes *ALIVE Magazine*, alive!

The full measure of Mike's accomplishment in *ALIVE &
Kickin'* can only be realized when you understand the level of
talent, discipline and hard work required to come up with
different article ideas, month after month. As you will see, Mike's
subtle approach keeps it fresh and fun, as the smile he brought
to my face each month will soon be yours.

As best selling author and columnist for *The New Yorker,*
Malcom Gladwell says in his preface of, *What the Dog Saw,*
"Good writing does not succeed on the strength of its ability to
persuade. It succeeds or fails on its ability to engage you, to make
you think, to give you a glimpse into someone else's head..."
This book is successful because it does all of these.

Writers have different reasons for doing what they do. Some
are after commercial success or professional accolades. Some are
hoping to "make their mark" by creating what they hope will
someday be considered classic literature.

When Mike first suggested *ALIVE & Kickin'*, I asked him why
he wanted to publish his work as a book. He replied that he had
a dual purpose; he wanted to create something for others to enjoy
and he wanted to create something dedicated to his family—
a legacy of sorts for his children.

As to purpose one, Mike's work has always received high
praise from countless *ALIVE* readers over the past five years, so I
know *ALIVE & Kickin'* is right on target. As to purpose two,
Mike's family can and should be proud of him. I know I am.

Eric Johnson

ACKNOWLEDGEMENTS

I wish to thank the following people for all their support, encouragement and love. Julie, my wife, who has the tolerance of a saint and a great sense of humor. My daughters, Hannah and Claire who have provided me with inspiration and motivation every day of their lives. Thank you to my publisher and boss at Alive Magazine, Eric Johnson. Eric gave me an opportunity, a voice and is a wonderful mentor. Thanks to my proofreading team of Julie Lewis, Julie Copeland and my late father-in-law, Lou Warshaw. You've caught mistakes, typos and grammatical errors that I never would. Appreciation also goes out to my buddies, Rob Price, Brian Ke ly, Burt Harris, Jason Allen, John Killen and Derek Sousa whose wit, sarcasm and humor have always challenged me intellectually and creatively. I would also like to thank Barbara Slater, John Macholz, George Papageorge, Blake Chauvin, Jim Ludwig, Wendy Butler, Peggy Warshaw, Mitzi Copeland, Cathy Tisa, Christine Skilling, Steve Caltagirone, Christina Doell and Mike Mooney. I call these people my "feedback friends" because they let me know if my subject matter and content are on target or way off track. Finally, thank you to anyone who is reading this book. If it weren't for you, this book would probably be considered a published diary and boy, wouldn't that be sad.

I

HOLIDAY MAGIC

I have very fond memories of the holidays growing up. That time from Halloween through New Year's was magical as a kid. As soon as school started in September, my friends and I started planning our Halloween costumes and Trick or Treat route. Thanksgiving always meant family, food and football and Christmas was utter euphoria. No school, visiting Santa, opening presents and chugging gallons of egg nog. As adults, my wife and I have always tried to create that festive seasonal joy for our daughters, especially as a dual holiday (Christmas/Hanukkah) family. Julie has always decorated the house in theme, we enjoy entertaining with our friends and we're not half bad cooks. These articles are just a small glimpse into a few of the enchanting holiday times, past and present.

1 What am I going to be for Halloween?
My Annual Halloween Conundrum

Halloween has always been one of my favorite holidays, right up there with Christmas, Easter, 4th of July, Thanksgiving, Valentine's Day, Father's Day and Arbor Day (who doesn't like planting trees?). What's the biggest difference between Halloween and all other holidays of lesser fun? On Halloween you are required to wear a costume. Costumes are cool. If you can find just the right apparel and accessories a good costume can transform a person into anything or anyone that they might want to be for a night. That last sentence kind of sounds like I'm talking about cross dressing, not that there's anything wrong with that. As much as I like and take pride in my annual costumes, every year it's the same question: What am I going to be for Halloween? It doesn't matter that I'm 49 and stopped Trick-or-Treating when I was a kid (23), there's still a lot of pressure to find just the perfect costume.

> *I'm going to be a cowgirl cause I already got all the stuff.*
> *Boots, hat, vest and a bandana. Wanna see?*
> —Lauren B. Age 9, Danville

When I was a youngster, my mother made most of my costume decisions. Cry as I might, she just wouldn't buy into my ideas of serial killer, big time wrestler or adult film star. So, despite my protests, I wore all the traditional classics; pirate, cowboy, caveman, toilet paper mummy. During those adolescent years, when money was tight because dad was dressing up as a degenerate gambler every weekend during football season, I was convinced to wear dirty old clothes and tell people I was bum or a hobo. Sadly, a lot of neighbors just thought I was too lazy to dress up. Today, it's not politically correct to pretend to be a homeless person, but isn't hoboness really just a lifestyle choice?

Isn't a hobo just a businessman who got tired of the nine-to-five grind in a bad economy and took to traveling the country utilizing our elaborate train system (by way of an empty freight car)? Truthfully, I can't tell you the last time I saw a hobo, but I'm sure they are still out there.

> *I might be Captain America. Did you know his shield can*
> *cut through metal and protect you from bullets?*
>   —Carter L., Age 7, Danville

High school had its ups and downs when it came to dressing up for All Hallows Eve Night. As a freshman, you certainly didn't want to stand out or appear dorky showing up for a Pumpkin Walk that may never actually happen. You could find yourself standing all alone on one of the school's tennis courts in a wicked cool matador costume while others mock you. Tears of pain don't just bounce off a spandex bull-dodging suit like you might think—they stain. Damn those chess club pranksters! It was different when our sophomore glee club dressed up as the cast of Grease. Unfortunately, I drew Sandy as my character. Hells Angels was the theme our junior year and we were bad ass. That was until we ran into some actual Hells Angels at the mall and they made us strip down to our underwear and walk home—three miles—and it was raining. Finally, my senior year rocked! Me and my boys dressed as the members of the rock band KISS. It's just tough to look very "swag" in 11 inch platform shoes and runny demon make-up. By the end of the night, I just looked like a teenage San Francisco drag queen.

> *Guess what I'm going to be... he's from Star Wars, he's on*
> *the dark side and he's Darth Vader.*
>   —Jake A. Age 6 ½, Pleasanton

College brought all kinds of new and exciting costume ideas even though every Halloween frat party I ever attended, during my four...five...okay, six years of collegiate bliss, had a "Pimp and Hooker" theme. Not that I'm complaining. Fortunately there are a lot of television pimps to draw inspiration from for costume ideas; there was Huggy Bear from the series *Starsky and Hutch*, Rooster was a main character on *Baretta* and let us not forget Prime Time Neon Dion Sanders of the Dallas Cowboys whenever he appeared on a pre-game show before *Monday Night Football*. Fortunately, I still had my 11 inch Kiss platform shoes and a slick burgundy crushed velvet smoking jacket to get me into character. My signature line was, "back off sucker before I cut you." The co-ed ladies-of-the-night loved my protective dark side.

> *I'm going to be a princess because I like them and want to be one. And that is the costume mommy bought me from Costco.*
>
> —Madison O., Age 5, Danville

In my bar hopping early 20s, it was one super hero costume after another. Superman, Spiderman, Aquaman, Captain America, Captain Shots, Captain Drunk Guy and my favorite, Captain Hit On Every Girl In the Bar. That was the year I met my wife.

As a married man and now father, I find myself tending toward a more conservative costume. There's the ever popular, Plastic Surgeon (a lot of women want a second opinion), the sexy youth soccer coach (Mustangs provide us with the hunkiest Nike dry fit coaching shirts) and the fan favorite, parish priest (if you don't mind listening to people confess their sins—and I don't). Of course it really doesn't matter what costume I wear because it is 100% guaranteed to embarrass my daughters (Ages 12 and 14). We've been invited to the same family friend's party for years and each year as they get older I become unexplainably more embarrassing. There's nothing I can wear that won't mortify them if their friends are within a three mile radius. Now my strategy is just to achieve maximum shock value. Male cheerleader, Studio 54 Roller Disco Superstar and Tooth Fairy are my "go to" costumes whenever they've been misbehaving or disrespectful.

> *I think I'm going to be a cheerleader because I like*
> *cheerleaders and cheering is fun.*
> —Nadia L., Age 7, Danville

But alas, I'm back to where I started. What am I going to be for Halloween this year? To dress as a local magazine writer would just drive the neighborhood women crazy and if I were to suit up as an anonymous member of the underground protest group Anonymous I might draw unwanted attention to myself. I could always be an Indian, construction worker, policeman or one of the other members of the Village People. I respect firemen way too much to pretend to be a fireman. No one would buy me as a professional athlete, unless I dressed up as a member of the Pro Bowlers Tour. Apparently it looks like life has finally come full circle and I'm destined to bring back the pirate, cowboy or caveman. My mother would be so happy. Although given the current economy and present state of commercial real estate, hobo might not be a stretch. Don't be surprised if I ring your doorbell and ask for candy. I'm old school that way.

> *I have no idea what I'm going to be! What are you*
> *going to be?*
> —Michelle C., Age 9, San Ramon

2 The Turkey Doesn't Have It So Bad
Tales of Dysfunctional Family Thanksgivings

I love Thanksgiving. What's not to love? There's food, festivities, football, family and friends and who doesn't love a four day weekend? Living in the Bay Area, the weather is usually good, and because so many people travel this time of year the roads are usually traffic free and I'm all about the cheesy holiday TV specials? Yet, on the Monday following Thanksgiving, to hear some of the family horror stories coming from the people I work with, the guys at the gym and the parents at our kid's elementary school, I'm thinking the turkey doesn't have it so bad.

Let's start with the food. Preparing a Thanksgiving dinner is stressful. If the Turkey and fixings aren't perfect (and perfect is the enemy of good) you might as well chuck it all out the window and order a pizza. Whether you Roast, BBQ or deep fry the bird, if it's the least bit dry you better know the Heimlich maneuver because someone's going to make "the face" as they pretend to choke down Turkey Jerky. But for the sake of argument let's assume the turkey does turn out tender and moist, then there's the simple task of coordinating the complicated preparation and delivery of a few other tasty treats to round out the feast, such as stuffing, mashed potatoes and gravy, corn nibblets, warm rolls, cranberry sauce, a greed salad, green beans and perhaps candied yams or sweet potatoes. Let's not even get into desert, because if not for Marie Calendars the rate of Thanksgiving Day Hari-Kari would be off the chart. Granted, women are usually the one's that bear the responsibility of preparing the meal because candidly if men were responsible for preparing the meal there wouldn't be a meal. So, thank you ladies

When I referenced festivities above, I mean it's now become a week long celebration. Why is it that the kids are out of school the entire week instead of just the Thursday thru Sunday like we were back in the olden days? Festivities at the Casa de Copeland include everything from house cleaning to the Thanksgiving Eve run to In-and-Out Burger (you can't believe how many people crave a double double the night before a major holiday). Sadly, not being able to sleep-in on a non work weekday is a bummer because there's additional house cleaning and food prep to get done. Truthfully, feeling like a waiter/bartender/valet/coat check girl in your own house is second only to the post meal clean up which includes washing dishes you didn't even know you owned. Please let us not forget the unexpected house guest staying the night for alcohol related reasons. Good times.

Of course, we always look forward to the traditional Thanksgiving Day football games featuring the Detroit Lions in the morning and the Dallas Cowboys in the afternoon. Unfortunately, both of these teams have sucked over the last ten years and the game is usually a blow-out shortly after opening kick off. At least it's the game is something to stare at in lieu of making conversation.

That brings us to family and friends. While it's nice to bring loved ones together it's impractical to think that all of life's problems will miraculously disappear for the purpose of enjoying a holiday together. Grandpas love telling everyone how everything was better in his day, when he and his pilgrim buddies had the first Thanksgiving dinner with the native American Indians. Grandpa's memory is slipping a little. The Mother-in-law can't resist the urge to subliminally criticize their daughter-in-law's clothes, table setting, housekeeping, cooking, parenting (pick anyone that applies) while the daughter-in-law does her best to resist the urge to reach for a knife. Cousins are often good for telling hilarious prison stories from past holidays spent in lock up and the cornucopia of adolescent kids are either fighting, get into some kind of inappropriate mischief behind closed doors or stinking up the bathroom right before it's time for everyone to wash their hands. Dad's just can't want to impart life lessons relating to tasks as brain numbing as the proper way to carve the bird. Finally, most siblings are either jealous, competitive or condescending. Close friends are often invited to participate because friends are the family we pick (pick to defuse a potential family disaster). When you're someone's guest at a holiday function it's reassuring to observe first hand that yours is not the only dysfunctional family that has a hard time holding it together. I've even heard tell that occasionally someone (or everyone) may over indulge in alcohol. I know…hard to believe, but that's traditionally when the real drama begins.

Even the four-day holiday is overrated because all we do is eat, watch bad football and visit overcrowded malls, movie theaters and restaurants. Yes, restaurants, because by Saturday we'll eat anything other than more turkey leftovers. By Sunday, we start getting depressed about how much work lies ahead getting the house ready for Christmas.

If all the holiday misadventures I've heard over the years are true, and I have no reason to believe their not, then I'm surprised more people don't skip Thanksgiving. Just treat it like another Thursday. Pick up a rotisserie chicken and a box of Mac and Cheese, watch *Gray's Anatomy* on TV and be done with it. Maybe, just maybe, it's not quiet as bad as some people make it out to be and all things considered, there is an awful lot to be thankful for each year. On the other hand, maybe the Turnkey doesn't have it so bad.

If the above rhetoric hits close to home, take comfort that Thanksgiving only happens once a year. Howver, be advised that Christmas shopping now starts at Midnight.

3 Why Thanksgiving is a Guy's Favorite Holiday

Thanksgiving is a holiday every guy can appreciate. Food, football, more food, family, social drinking and, did I mention, food? Virtually any guy can appreciate the history, the sentiment and the festivities behind the true meaning of the holiday, but if pressed, most guys would admit they typically associate Thanksgiving with eating. Even the early settlers, who attended the first recorded Autumn Harvest Feast in 1621, were focused on the food. English Colonist John Smith, Captain John Woodlief and current U.S. Senator/Presidential candidate John McCain undoubtedly shared such gastronomic atrocities from across the pond as Shepherd's Pie, Pasties, Yorkshire pudding and Bangers and Mash. At the same table, the Native Americans likely introduced our Pilgrim pioneers to such culinary delights as BBQ turkey, corn on the cob, cranberry sauce, Pillsbury crescent rolls and candied yams with deliciously baked golden brown marshmallow topping. Not much has changed. My buddies, who represent a random sampling of guys, reluctantly assisted me with their unique views of our favorite guy holiday. Needless to say, food was a recurring theme.

> *Thanksgiving is all about the food in my family.*
> *The whole day is focused around eating. When I was*
> *a kid I asked my mom why we didn't eat like this every day.*
> *My mom asked why I didn't give thanks for my blessings*
> *every day? Moms can be so tough.*
> —Dino M, 36

We attended a Thanksgiving dinner at a distant cousin's house that included every adult putting $5.00 in a kitty. When you entered the house you had to immediately weigh yourself. The person that put on the most weight by the end of the night won the pot.

—Brian L., 38

It probably isn't a major revelation that a large majority of guys enjoy eating; hence, guys enjoy Thanksgiving. Not just the succulent pleasure of our traditional turkey and fixings, but the ingestion of virtually anything that slides across the dining room table, coffee table or kitchen counter. From cheese whiz on crackers as an appetizer to pumpkin pie with whipped cream for dessert, we'll eat ham, yams, clams or Spam if it's presented on a serving tray. A guy doesn't feel truly satisfied unless he's put on between 10 and 15 pounds over the 4-day extended weekend. I've been known to start with a traditional Double-Double from In-and-Out Burger on Thanksgiving Day eve (it's tradition), then to chow down like an underweight sumo wrestler tying to bulk up over the next 72 hours. Although our goal isn't to eat ourselves sick with an odd assortment of turkey leftovers including turkey sandwiches, turkey soup, turkey pudding and turkey toothpaste, that's just typically the end result. And being guys, we will attempt to balance the excessive calorie intake by working out, typically beginning with a series of invigorating naps.

I try to get to the gym at least once during the holiday week end. Assuming I'm going to ingest approximately 1,000,000 calories, I make it my mission to burn off at least 150 calories on the treadmill.

—Blake C., 48

Before a guy can eat even think about eating it must be determined where, exactly, the holiday will be spent. Most guys I know don't mind hosting Thanksgiving at their houses because that means we don't have to travel. As anyone who has ever hosted a TGDM (Thanksgiving Day Meal) knows, the days leading up to the big event are filled with cooking, cleaning and decorating the house. At least that's what my wife tells me. I just try not to use the downstairs guest bathroom on that particular Thursday. Hosting the annual holiday usually means the extended family is coming over. I'm not going to use the line that families are the friends you don't get to pick, but while everyone has the best intentions, holidays can also bring out the worst in families. It's a gamble. A little too much wine from a box and things can go from good to ugly faster than it takes to snap a wishbone.

> *With four kids between the ages of 7 and 13, Thanksgiving is the only weekday of the year when we all get to sit down and have dinner together... unless of course Christmas or Easter happens to fall on a Tuesday.*
> —Rob P., 40

> *I'm at the point where I don't mind making mindless conversation with relatives I only marginally like and see only once a year.*
> —Dave B., 41

> *If we go somewhere for Thanksgiving and the host says dinner is at 4:00 I want to be seated at the table with food on my plate by 4:01. I might have re-thought my invite if I knew we were going to sit around and make small talk for 3 hours. I hate it when I'm too full of nuts, chips and alcohol to properly gorge myself.*
> —J. Blazy, 48

Thanksgiving Day is a wonderful opportunity for a guy to give thanks. Thanks for his family's health, happiness and good fortune. Unless he happens to be living off of his retirement, in which case he probably lost a fortune over the last couple of months. Truthfully, I am thankful for a lot of things in my life, not the least of which is that I don't work in the banking industry. Given the current housing market, I'm thankful I'm not a mortgage broker or a residential real estate agent. I am a commercial real estate agent and that industry has been kicked in the groin too but that's another topic for another article. I'm also thankful that I'm not an ice road trucker or crab fisherman in the Bering Strait. Those jobs look really hard. I think we're all thankful that we don't work for the Oakland Raiders. Truthfully, most guys are just thankful to have a job. It's all about providing for our family and in this wild economy, that is something not as easy as it once was.

> *I'm not sure how many American families still try to spend a small amount of time expressing thanks and appreciation for the good things in their lives, but I hope that some still do.*
> —Jim F., 77

> *In 1970, I spent my first Thanksgiving away from my family on the DMZ in Vietnam. During the holidays I always think about our military personnel doing service in other countries. We should all be thankful for their sacrifices.*
> —Ben S., 60

The perfect Thanksgiving Day also includes a little football. This year, take the Cowboys straight up and go with the underdogs on the Lions game. Of course, I'm not advocating gambling. In between the countless hours of gridiron viewing, there's nothing a guy likes more than throwing the old pigskin around on a crisp, autumn day. As kids growing up, a lot of us can remember gathering in the street with our neighbors for the annual "Turkey Bowl" touch football game before dinner. Now, as parents, a lot of guys try to carry-on the tradition with our children. Sure it's sad when one of the youngsters gets hurt and runs into the house crying, but if she would just learn to catch a tight spiral, accidents like these wouldn't happen.

> *I loved getting together with the friends and family for the annual Turkey Bowl flag football game at our local park. Even after I moved out and went away to college, we still got together the morning of Thanksgiving Day for years. I once broke my nose during a game and missed dinner entirely because I was in the ER.*
>
> —Patrick M., 50

The rest of the weekend can be spent in a variety of productive guy ways. While most guys will do anything to avoid watching a parade or going shopping, we aren't opposed to getting a few household chores accomplished. Putting up the outside Christmas lights the day after Thanksgiving has almost become as much a tradition as sending our women folk to the mall. When we're not lying on the couch watching TV most guys I know will try get out to see a movie, maybe walk the dog or play a board game or two with the kids. I've even been known to take the family bowling.

> *My wife and her mom can literally shop from 6 am to 6 pm on the day after Thanksgiving. I don't go for fear of looking weak. Once my daughter starts attending this female family ritual, my son and I will attempt to get out and play golf with the other 9,000 Tri Valley dads left on their own.*
>
> —Jeff B., 38

A real guy, a "guy's guy," likes Thanksgiving for so many reasons. We treasure those four days off from work, not shaving, playing video games with the kids, raking leaves, getting Christmas ornaments down from the rafters, catching up with the neighbors, staying up late watching our DVR shows, sleeping in, reading the newspaper in our pajamas, surfing questionable websites and just hanging out with the family. Christmas, Valentine Day, the 4th of July and Halloween all have their place but Thanksgiving is a true "guy holiday." Did I mention there's also lots of food to eat?

4 How Can it Be Thanksgiving?
I Still Have Halloween Candy Left

For most parents, once the kids are back in school, Halloween is upon us in the blink of an eye. Halloween is followed all too quickly by Thanksgiving, Hanukkah/Christmas and New Year's Eve. While the fall/winter holidays can be a joyous season, it can also be a time of chaos, exhaustion and weight gain. This is the time of year that a certain, Miss Jenny Craig, loves. She, and her multi-billion dollar-a-year weight loss company, know all too well that Halloween night through New Year's Day is when a majority of the people on this planet tend to pack on the weight. It's a humanistic hibernation ritual whereby we store up our food reserves for a long winter of inactivity. That's what J. Craig is counting on. From Snickers bars to pumpkin pies, Christmas cookies to Champagne parfaits, Jenny and her competitors at Weight Watchers, Nutrisystem and countless other weight loss programs are licking their chops (metaphorically speaking) hoping we Americans continue to load up on the calorie-rich holiday treats the way we traditionally do. Our inability to say no to any sprinkle covered holiday delicacy guarantees these weight loss empires that they will be rolling in dough (no pun intended) when their target market demographic initiates their #1 New Year resolution... lose weight. That iron-will determination historically lasts until Valentine's Day, but it's all the diabolical Ms. Craig, et al, need to get us worked up, signed up, suited up and weighed up...er... in, all thanks to holiday overindulging.

Every year, I resolve to lose weight. I've come to realize that if you are what you eat I need to eat a skinny woman.
— Stacy Hallissey, Age 43

31

Just pay attention to the latest round of weight loss TV commercials, assuming you're not up getting a snack when there's a break in the TV action. Queen Latifah, Marie Osmond and Valerie Bertinelli are competing to see who can portray the hottest cougar as a form of subliminal advertising to entice women to lose weight. Kirstie Alley was part of this well crafted marketing campaign until she fell off the wagon and resumed eating her way through the Scientology Kraft Services break room. While I admire Marie Osmond for her physical transformation, especially having had seven children, she lost my respect when she collapsed during a *Dancing With The Stars* episode. It was probably from starving herself. On the other hand, Miss Bertinelli hasn't looked this enticing since I first fell in love with her in 1976 as she played the part of the beguiling youngest daughter, Barbara Cooper, on *One Day At A Time*. Thanks to her divorce from Eddie Van Halen, Val (as I like to call her) has rededicated herself to health and fitness and now she's popping up on talk shows and magazine covers wearing little more than a tiny white bikini. Wowzer!

Even the guys are getting into the weight loss action as evidenced by former sports stars such as Dan Marino, Don Shula, Mike Golic, Boomer Esiason, Charles Barkley and Tommy Lasorda, all slimming down for a taste of that mad weight loss advertising cash. Unfortunately, no one gives a rip about washed up athletes losing weight.

Most grocery and drug stores, for which I will include Target and Walmart in this category, have entire isles dedicated to dietary supplements. There are powders, vitamins, drinks, gels and pills lining the shelves to assist people with their constant fight with their metabolism; aka will power and snack cravings. The diet centers are usually strategically located adjacent to the Hostess snack isle. On a recent undercover investigative reporting mission, I observed shoppers purchasing everything from pre-packaged low calorie meals, to appetite suppressants and high colonics, all in an attempt to drop a few pounds. Since I'm currently carrying an extra 20 lbs. on my Calvin Kline underwear model frame, I'm as guilty as anyone in need of a little appetite suppression assistance. While I've never met a cookie I could resist, I draw the line at the high colonic hydrotherapy fad. There's no way I'm introducing my insides to an intestinal water park ride just to drop the equivalent of a Nestle Toll House cookie.

Now that the holidays are upon us, it will be virtually impossible for many of us to fight the overpowering feast of delectable temptations coming out way. Sadly, I've decided to just give in. That's right, it's going to be food hedonism at my house from Oct. 31st through Jan. 1st. Please don't bother coming over if you're not planning to bring a cornucopia shaped caramel popcorn ball or a Rice Krispie menorah treat. I'll be sampling every decadent goodie I lay my eyes on before going cold turkey beginning January 1st. Actually, I love eating cold turkey sandwiches (with cranberry sauce and Cheetos) while I'm watching bowl games and parades, so rehab might not be so bad.

> *I lost roughly 50 lbs. this year. Unfortunately, trying to balance healthy eating habits and the festivities of the holiday season might be impossible. I'll probably just cave in to temptation and start up again after the Super Bowl.*
> —Scot Wilson, Age 50

Halloween: Is it possible to eat your weight in candy? I'll let you know. Seriously, my wife is to blame for my poor Halloween eating habits. Every year she anticipates that we'll get about 1000 more Trick-or-Treat visitors then we actually do. She buys enough candy to feed all of the kids in Transylvania because we would be perceived as bad neighbors if we ran out of bite size candy. Inevitably, we have half a dozen ghosts and goblins that ring our door bell and I end up consuming my 600th bag of mini

M&Ms by mid-November. Being a responsible father, I also take it upon myself to limit the sugar intake of my own children by eating a majority of the candy they've collected. This prevents cavities and the risk of childhood obesity. Distressingly, I have so many fillings in my mouth that I set off the metal detector whenever I fly, but the good news is I've been pre approved as a contestant on *The Biggest Loser* next season.

Thanksgiving: What would the Pilgrims say if they knew we had taken their traditional day of giving thanks, not to mention the magnanimous gesture of our Native American Indian friends who were willing to host this inaugural event, and turned it into an all day food orgy? Thanksgiving Day morning typically begins with me enjoying a Starbucks Pumpkin Pie Frappuccino as I disembowel the turkey. Coincidently, the day usually ends with me wiping pumpkin pie crumbs off my chin as I waddle off to bed. The rest of the weekend is dedicated to resting up before the next meal. Does watching football on TV qualify as exercise? It's almost like I do a sit-up every time I strain to get off the couch. Can I get some gravy with my pumpkin bread?

Hanukkah/Christmas/Kwanzaa: Regardless of your religious preclusion, most of us will be praying to the Scale God once this glutinous consumption of holiday treats has passed. Pity those of us who celebrate more than one of these traditional ceremonies because I carry both Catholic and Jewish guilt while I chow down on an ample supply of Christmas cookies and Rugelah. The upside is I don't need any additional padding to fit into my Santa suit. When you add work related office parties to the family and friend gatherings you have a recipe for disaster and I'm not talking about the red and green deviled eggs. Please don't bring up my collection of inappropriate photocopies document ing my every widening rear end (aka junky junk in my Badonkadonk) from the last eight office holiday blowouts.

New Year's Eve: Don't let anyone tell you that alcohol doesn't have any calories. There are 210 of those bad boys in just one of Oprah's Pomegranate Martinis. Most of the calories consumed by the average American suburban dad and mom on New Year's Eve are liquid calories. There's spiked cider, warm toddies, holiday themed cocktails, neighborhood spirits and spiked eggnog. Wisely, at my house we try not to eat too heavy on NYE. We usually avoid a formal sit down dinner in favor of appetizers, hor d'oeuvres, finger foods and a TGI Friday's sampler platter. It's so much healthier to simply snack during a night of merriment than to try and prepare a big meal with all the fixings.

> *My New Year's Eve party menu begins with a Captain and Coke at happy hour, followed by an evening of wine, shots and champagne. I also like to cap off the night with an Irish coffee. Then there's Bloody Mary's on New Year's Day morning and a 12 pack of beer while watching college football games.*
> *I probably should try to eat a little something*
> —Craig Nunn, Age 51

The holidays are a time for love, laughter and embracing traditions. We attend parties, host family gatherings, sing carols, share recipes, exchange gifts and enjoy cheesy holiday television specials. As parents and responsible adults, we should try and set a good example for our children. Everything in moderation is never a bad motto to embrace. Let's collectively, as a region, agree to monitor our candy intake this Halloween, avoid going back for seconds and thirds at Thanksgiving, pass on the 24 days of cookies in December and never, ever "drink in the New Year." If you still find that you're overwhelmed and feel like you might need some assistance, go ahead and call Jenny Craig. She's probably waiting for your call.

5 A Visit with Santa
The Do's & Don'ts of a Traditional Holiday Experience

Tell any kid in America that you're taking them to see a heavy set, jolly, elderly gentleman with white hair, wearing a red velvet suit, who has a garage full of hobbits and mythical flying pets in his back yard and you might get a call from the police or Child Protective Services before you even get to the car. A child's visit with Santa Claus can be either a wonderful holiday tradition or a disaster, depending on the youngster and the Santa in question. It's safe to say most children love to visit St. Nick, but sadly for some it can be a good idea gone terribly wrong which will require years of counseling to erase the emotional scars brought on by this traumatic experience. Luckily I have some dos and don'ts that should eliminate the potential risk and ensure a joyful yuletide outing.

When you visit Santa, he is nice and he gives you prizes.
—Bailey, age 6

When visiting Santa at any one of the Bay Area malls, galleries, outlet centers or mega department stores, expect a three to five hour wait in line. While the wait can certainly heighten your child's anticipated meeting with the bearded bearer of presents, it can also lead to a screaming meltdown that the elves and Mrs. Claus will be able to hear way up at the North Pole. Additionally since candy canes aren't technically a meal or nutritional supplement, DO plan to bring snacks or pack a lunch. DON'T try to be the first family in line when the doors open because that would mean getting up at 4:30 in the morning just to wait out in the cold for the store's early bird opening hour of 6:00 am. Another helpful hint includes bringing a lap top computer so your tikes can work on their gift list. When the "big guy" finally spouts the famous line, "and what would you like this year?" your little one should be ready to roll through 40-50 items like an auctioneer at a 4-H pig and chicken sale.

I like Santa to hear my list from me.
—Tyler, age 5 ½

Anyone who has ever seen holiday movies such as *Miracle on 34th Street, A Christmas Story* or *Elf* knows different Santas react, well, differently. My daughters actually think Santa has numerous brothers and cousins who help out during the holidays but as with any family, there's strife. The delusional "real" Santa is usually a retired gentleman who enjoys the tradition of the holiday and genuinely wants to create a magical moment for the children that visit. Next, there's "part time job" Santa. This is the miserable guy in his 30's or 40's looking to supplement his income. After leaving his crappy day job, the only "fulfilling" opportunity he's looking for involves sitting on his butt for long periods of time. He's cranky, impatient and often takes more bathroom breaks than someone with IBS. Lastly there's college kid Santa. He's always inexplicably smiling, doesn't quiet fit in the suit and will occasionally CRUNK dance with the female high school elves. Even though the kids might question Santa addressing them as "little dude," his legitimacy is often overlooked due to the overall enjoyment of the interaction. DO go to a venue that uses the FBI, ATF and CIA to do background checks on their Santa applicants. DON'T offer Santa a medicinal mistletoe treat.

That's not the real Santa at the store, the real Santa is too busy.
—Susie, age 7

Sadly, while the Santa you choose to visit may be the second coming of the real thing, there's no guarantee that your child will see it that way. I've seen kids run screaming, up a down-moving escalator, to avoid sitting with the giant, ho, ho, hoing guy in the winter wonderland display. It's an experience similar to the first Disneyland trip. There are those children who love seeing the characters come to life and can't wait to hug, nuzzle or babble joyful words of endearment. On the other hand, there are those boys and girls who think that oversized, over-stuffed, over-stimulated characters in bright colored clown outfits are scarier than Freddie Krueger from *Nightmare on Elm Street*. Group Santa in with Barney, Big Bird, Mickey Mouse and the Easter Bunny and gauge your child's receptiveness before dropping the fruit of your loins off in what could be perceived as the bogeyman's lap. DO introduce the tikes to Santa if they are emotionally ready for the whole experience, DON'T play Fear Factor with your little one's psyche.

> *I don't like to talk to Santa because I'm shy so I just write to him.*
>
> —Sarah, age 6

When my sister and I were kids we visited a place called *Santa's Village* nestled off highway 17 in pristine Scotts Valley. While the month of December was a festive time in this oasis of the Santa Cruz Mountains, the rest of the year it looked like some freaky adult rest stop for truckers looking to kill time during the up or down leg of a cross country long haul. Santa's Village offered rides (spinning hot chocolate cups), a petting zoo with baby reindeer (aka goats), cute cafes, like Sugar Plum Bistro (with delicious reindeer burgers) and the surreal experience of visiting Santa and Mrs. Claus at their pre-Christmas hideaway. My parents told us that this is where Kris Kringle came to "fatten up" and relax before the big day, but by the time I was 16 or 17 that story was starting to raise a few questions, such as: where, exactly, was the naughty and nice list? what elf was in charge of the other elves toy production? and, wasn't the highest and best use for this prime piece of real estate single family homes or an

R&D park? Alas, that's what eventually happened. Santa sold out for top dollar to a development company and Santa's Village was gone forever. DO sell when the market is hot, DON'T build a theme park with limited seasonal appeal.

> *When I was little I visited Santa every year, but I didn't expect him to actually bring me what I asked for since I was Jewish and celebrated Hanukkah.*
> —Julie, age 46

I'm all about tradition and the magic of the holiday season. I have very fond memories of sitting on Santa's lap as a child and telling him that I was a good boy before politely asking him for a remote controlled car, BB gun, football or subscription to *Maxim* magazine. OK, that was just last year, but the point is, I was ready for the whole Santa experience. Over the years, I have seen way too many holiday pictures (from those overpriced photo packages that every Santa's workshop offers) of children with terrified facial expressions, or worse yet, the shot of some toddler crying, screaming or pulling away from a frustrated Santa. Parents need to realize there's no rush and it's acceptable to wait another year before pushing for the, "you gotta visit Santa if you want him to bring you presents," trip.

DO make this a happy and loving holiday season. DON'T get on Santa's naughty list.

Christmas Magic
Male/Female - Point/Counterpoint
(with Dione Travis)

It's safe to say that as men and women, we anticipate, process and reflect upon a majority of life's experiences differently. I never thought this would include the holiday season, specifically Christmas, but apparently it does. I have found that to many women, the Christmas season is a chaotic but enchanting time full of sugar plum fairies, eggnog toddies and caroling. On the other hand, many men view the holiday as just a lot of added commotion to our otherwise comfortable routines. My friend, Dione Travis and I, have come up with a male/female, point/counterpoint account of the Yuletide celebration.

Dione: I'll admit it. I'm one of those annoying people who absolutely adores Christmas. I love everything about it. I love the glow of twinkling lights. I love the over-the-top displays people set up in their front yards. I love little girls in velvet dresses and little boys pulling at their itchy shirt collars. I love the Christmas carols they pipe into the mall. I even secretly love it that the stores start breaking out the Christmas displays in October. Or is it September now? I cry buckets over "It's a Wonderful Life" every single time I see it. I love Christmas because it's MAGICAL. If I stop for a moment and quietly take it all in, Christmas can turn me right back into a six-year-old who is completely wowed by all the spirit of the season.

Mike: I'll admit it—I'm one of those annoying people that simply tolerates Christmas. Don't get me wrong, I'm not Ebenezer Scrooge or the Grinch. The tradition, the parties, the family time, the television specials and the look of joy on my daughters' faces on Christmas morning are all wonderful, but it's all the other stuff leading up to the birthday of Jesus that drives me a little crazy. The over-the-top displays people set up in their front yards; the cutesy outfits we have to buy the kids and the sappy holiday music that is piped into stores are all just too much for me. It infuriates me that the stores break out their Holiday displays in October, or is it July now. I think *It's a Wonderful Life* is the cheesiest movie ever made. The studio should do a remake of that flick using my favorite actor, Dwayne "The Rock" Johnson, and add a little holiday action. Christmas has its magical moments but it's just become way too commercialized for me. Whatever happened to that innocent time, back when I was six (or thirty one) years old, and all I wanted in the world was for Santa to bring me a Schwinn Stingray bike?

Dione: Here's what I didn't know as a kid: All that magic—it takes a whole lot of work to make all that magic happen. Long hours, late nights, stress up the ying-yang. I had no idea what was happening behind the scenes. I remember coming home from school to find that the house had been transformed into a delightful Christmas wonderland. But it never occurred to me the number of trips my mom took up and down the attic ladder, arms loaded with heavy boxes of decorations, or the swearing she might have done while untangling the big mess of lights. I remember the huge mound of perfectly wrapped presents that always seemed to appear out of nowhere, but I never considered the hours my mom might have spent fighting the crowds at the mall or the late nights she spent agonizing over her sewing machine to create the perfect wardrobe for my sneezing *Bless You Baby Tender Love* doll.

Mike: If we all got back to simpler times I think everyone would agree that the magic would still happen with a lot less effort and ying-yang stress. When I was little, we made construction paper link-chains and typing paper snowflakes. All we needed was scissors, paper, some tasty paste and the house was transformed into an enchanted winter wonderland. We imperfectly wrapped presents in old shoe boxes with cheap Thrifty

Drug Store wrapping paper and a bow we saved from the previous year or a recent birthday. The To/From tag was taped on. We decorated our tree as a family with hand-me-down ornaments and homemade toilet paper roll creations consisting of glue, felt and glitter. Most years we put up our outside lights, but it was usually just one strand along the front of the house. As for Christmas morning, I was happy if I got a new camouflage outfit for my *Bless You Tender Love GI Joe Killing Machine* action figure.

Dione: Don't get me wrong, I willingly signed up for this job because I want the same kind of magic for my kids that I had as a child. And mostly, I love doing it. I love the thrill of picking exactly the right gifts for the people I care about. I love decking the halls with boughs of holly. I love baking dozens of cookies. But man, it's stressful and it's a whole lot more work than I ever could have predicted. I also had no idea that when I signed up for this gig, that I would pretty much be doing it all by myself. I'm basically a one-woman show while somehow my husband still manages to take credit for a huge part of it.

Mike: Don't get me wrong, I want my kids to get the holiday high so I willingly contribute to this excessive behavior. As a progressive metro-sexual male, I don't even mind buying a present, going to the tree lot, visiting my family and taking time off from work. I do seem to recall that when I was a kid my mom did most of the work. Women today have it so much easier. The new generation dads take on a lot of the responsibility. We usually start with creating the front yard Santa's Village display (complete with every outdoor display item our wife's picked up the previous after Christmas sale) and it ends with us taking down and cleaning up the dried out, needle dropping, fire hazard tree. I'm not saying that my wife doesn't do a majority of the actual tasks, for which I give her ample credit, but I help.

Dione: I'm not sure I'll ever forget last Christmas Eve. It was close to midnight, after most everyone had gone home and the rest of the family had finally gone to bed. I was finishing up the dishes when my husband came and put his arms around me and said, "Well, we did it. We pulled off another Christmas!" He added, "How 'bout we go to Maui next year instead of going through all this stress?" I didn't have time to fantasize about a relaxing Hawaiian getaway because I was too busy self-righteously analyzing the "we" part. WE pulled it off? WE?

Okay let's see:

I took 608 digital photos of the kids in their adorable matching outfits to get one perfect shot for the Christmas cards that I ordered, addressed and mailed.

I hauled 14 boxes of decorations down from the attic and decorated the tree and house from top to bottom.

I baked 468 Christmas cookies, including a few dozen snot-covered ones with my daughter's kindergarten class.

I built and decorated one gingerbread house with two sugar-wired children.

I built and decorated one three-story Barbie house by following a 42-page instruction manual.

I spent two hours waiting in line with two bored children in order to get one two minute visit with the cranky mall Santa.

I painstakingly chose, bought and wrapped ALL the gifts for friends and family, including year-in-review scrapbooks for the grandparents, and personalized photo calendars for all the relatives with every birthday and anniversary carefully noted.

I planned the menu for Christmas Eve, bought and prepared all the food and cleaned the house from top to bottom in preparation for the arrival of our family.

And I took 218 photos to commemorate the event.

Meanwhile, my husband;

Hung three strings of lights on the outside of the house.

Remembered the morning of his office Christmas party that he needed a white elephant gift and asked ME if I could figure something out and wrap it real quick.

Made sure everyone's drink glass stayed full and also carved the meat on Christmas Eve.

After he gave me his little speech on how stressful all of this had been for US, HE went to bed while I stayed up to finish cleaning up the Christmas Eve destruction and make Santa magic happen. This included filling my own Christmas stocking because HE almost always forgets and I didn't want to have to hurt HIM when my five year old would, no doubt say upon seeing my empty stocking, "Mommy must not have been very good this year."

Mike: Last Christmas Eve, after everyone had gone home or off to bed, I finishing watching Letterman and then I too put my arms around my wife (once she was finished cleaning the kitchen and arranging all of "Santa's" presents around the tree) and said, "Well we did it. We pulled off another Christmas." Come to think of it she did give me a funny look as she stormed up to bed. I assumed she just didn't want to watch Conan. Maybe next year I'll suggest something like Maui, only given this economy it's going to be more like a day at the Santa Cruz Boardwalk, but I digress. Shouldn't the holidays be a time to relax even for the parents? I do like to think that I held up my share of the work, so let's see last year;

I suggested we use that picture from Easter for the holiday card because the kids looked so cute all dressed up in those pastel outfits.

I brought a few boxes of ornaments in from the garage and who put the star on top of the tree? Big Daddy, that's who!

I ate approximately 468 Christmas cookies.

I offered to build a Gingerbread house in the back yard where her parents could stay during their next visit.

I took the electric scooter out of the box and if I could've found the directions I'm sure I wouldn't have had to call the neighbor on Christmas morning to help us set it up.

I planned the menu. She probably doesn't remember me asking, "Honey do you want to cook a Prime Rib or Turkey this year honey?"

I offered to wrap gifts but she said I went too fast and didn't always cut the paper the right size. Does she really think anyone notices how pretty the wrap job is?

I raked some leaves and didn't use the downstairs bathroom for a week.

I took a few pictures (from my cell phone) but I won't touch that stupid video camera. I don't even know how it works.

I'll have you know that being the bartender is not an easy job. There's a lot of responsibility and somehow I always get over-served.

Meanwhile my wife;

Did lots of stuff too. So much stuff that it would take up every page in this magazine if I listed it all.

After we finally get to bed, assuming my Joe Boxer Mistletoe lounge pants aren't a hit, I usually sneak downstairs to add a few surprise gifts around the tree and fill mommy's stocking with gift cards and Honey-do coupons. It's important that Santa recognizes "nice" mommies too.

Dione: It has occurred to me that Mrs. Claus had undoubtedly been working her butt off all this time while her husband has been getting all the glory, flying around the world gorging his jolly self on cookies and milk. There's truth in the old saying that a woman's work is never done, but our day is coming.

Mike: You poor misguided woman. Mr. Kringle, aka Santa Clause, deserves sainthood status because he's got an incredibly tough gig. He works from a home office, has thousands of employees with so much seniority he can't fire anyone and his wife is a partner in the company. It's a safe assumption that he and the little woman view the holidays differently from the North Pole too. I would love to hear their point/counterpoint arguments.

The Lost Art of Caroling
A Spin on Holiday Song Classics

This has been one of the toughest years in recent memory. We have been faced with a tremendous rise in unemployment, the military conflict in the Middle East and Adam Lambert not winning American Idol. On a more local level, the housing market is still sluggish, our school system lacks funds and our professional sports teams are abysmal. Perhaps a return to simple core values would help turn the tide. Simple, little pleasures, such as family dinners, game nights and holiday caroling could be just what our country needs to get our economy (and attitude) back on track.

I can't recall the last time I went caroling during the holiday season. People just don't carol like they once did, back in the olden days. While we love to watch our kids perform at multicultural holiday school functions, as adults we just don't embrace caroling the way our parents, grandparents and every resident at Rossmoor Leisure World in Walnut Creek did when they were young. We've all seen the old black and white movies, (*It's a Wonderful Life, Miracle on 34th Street, A Christmas Carol*), and admired how those folks caroled. Anytime there was a group of people gathered together at a holiday party, office function or neighborhood gathering, a festive song usually broke out. Fortunately, there was always someone who could play the piano beautifully and was well versed in songs like *Silent Night* or *Oh, Come All Ye Faithful*. One of my co-workers does play the bass in a Goth metal band, but that's not likely going to cut it if I feel like singing *Jingle Bells* in our reception area.

Maybe the older generation's willingness to break into song had something to do with their lack of music listening options. Unless you went down to the Copacabana to see Ricky Ricardo, tuned in Sinatra on the Zenith radio, or fired up some Andy

Williams records (vinyl LPs and 45s) on the old phonograph, it was hard to hear a good holiday song. Today, I just ask my kids to download Coldplay's version of *Joy to the World* to my iPhone and I'm humming myself silly while working out at the gym in my candy-cane print, striped unitard.

Don't get me wrong, I love the classic holiday songs (not to mention the claymation television specials). Perhaps, if someone (me) took the time to re-work a few of the traditional holiday carols, it might give them just enough of a contemporary edge to catch on with the younger generation. We've seen aging musical artists such as Elton John, Madonna and Tim McGraw team up with popular rap and hip hop artists like Justin Timberlake, Eminem, Rihanna and Lil Wayne to create a more appealing sound to target the music buying demographic of mid-teen boys and tweener girls. That's exactly what this holiday season needs: people embracing the lost art of caroling again. It might be just the ticket—start the New Year with a smile on our faces and a song in our hearts—and good things will happen.

After spending hours locked in a dark closet, with only a strand of twinkling lights to provide illumination, I had an epiphany. In an attempt to capitalize on several topical issues, I've reworded a few of our beloved, feel good classic holiday songs to inspire people to carol. Feel free to hum along as you read my poetic stylings:

JaMarcus the Raiders QB
(Sung to Rudolph the Red Nosed Reindeer)

JaMarcus the Raiders QB
Couldn't complete a single pass
and if you watched on Sundays
it was obvious why the team was in last (place)
All of the Seahawk players
made him fumble and called him names

Coach Cable wouldn't let poor JaMarcus
Play in any divisional games
Then one losing Bronco game
Al Davis came to say
JaMarcus with your arm so weak
Won't you drive the bus this week
Then all the players loved him
and the Raiders finally won a game
JaMarcus the new bus driver
You'll be in the Greyhound Hall of Fame

Let it Mend (sung to Let It Snow)
The economy this year is frightful
bankruptcy ain't so delightful
Next Year we'll all have money to spend
Let it mend, let it mend, let it mend
The stock market doesn't show signs of stopping
bio fuel and solar energy is popping
I got a hot stock tip from a friend
let it mend, let it mend, let it mend
When everyone goes back to work
How I'll love seeing all that glee
We'll go back to the good old days
of giving gifts like they were free
My attitude has gone from bad to good
and my dear I feel it should
I've got Tequila and a reason to blend
Let it mend, let it mend, let it mend

Arnold the Governor
(Sung to Frosty the Snowman)

Arnold the Governor, was a jolly happy soul
with muscled frame and charming wife
and state deficit with a mighty whole
Arnold the Governor, is a fairy tale they say
He tried his best, but made a mess
but the Terminator he once did play
There must have been some magic in that
$3,000 designer suit he wore
for when they placed it on his back
he owned the senate and assembly floor
Oh, Arnold the Governor
was Mr. Universe back in the day
he knew he could and probably would
star in Kindergarten Cop Part II - the play
Thumpidy thump thump
thumpidy thump thump
Look at Arnold run
Thumpidy, thump thump
Thumpidy, thump thump
Politics wasn't really any fun

The Swine Flu Song
(Sung to The Dreidel Song)

I have some flu like symptoms
I picked them up today
I have is a temp and coughing
Swine flu I do display
Oh sicky, sicky, sicky
I'll feel better in 5-7 days
who knows if it's the real thing
but, Swine flu I do display

Ok, so maybe I'm no John Mayer or Taylor Swift, but let's see them craft a holiday song that incorporates timely social issues such as news, politics, medicine and sports. I'm like a modern day Bob Dylan. No one appreciated his early word-smithing genius, and now, unfortunately, no one can understand what he's saying. I bet Bob Dylan carols, albeit in some gravelly mumble-type fashion.

Caroling may be just what our nation needs to rise like a Phoenix out of the ashes of this brutal economy. Embrace the joy of the season, at the top of your lungs, and let's all bring caroling back into fashion. It's a grassroots movement, but one that I hope will promote some old-school peace on earth and goodwill to man. It sure worked for the Fox television series *GLEE.* That's my favorite show.

Now, pass me the eggnog and hand me my scarf and mittens, because me and the family are hitting the mean streets of Blackhawk for some yuletide, non-religion-specific caroling. Happy Holidays!

8 If I Was Santa

Santa is The Man! Everyone loves that jolly, present bringing, sleigh driving, reindeer flying, carol singing, list reviewing, letter reading, stocking stuffing, cookie eating, ho-ho-hoing, red suit wearing, giant elf-of-a-man.

By all outward appearances, Santa would seem to have a charmed life. He is loved by billions, has a palatial mansion located on sprawling estate (just like David Duffield), is married to his one and only love and successfully portrays the captain of industry as CEO of a prosperous business. However, look a little deeper and you might see a man struggling through midlife crises.

Being adorned by the entire world has its challenges — just ask Justin Bieber. You're constantly hounded by fans and paparazzi, your every embarrassing guffaw is caught on video and replayed on YouTube the same day, and I haven't even mentioned the celebrity stalkers.

Santa's sweet pad is located on the North Pole. The North Pole! Not real convenient if you need to get to Safeway, B of A, Starbucks or Baja Fresh. Does Comcast even service the North Pole?

When it comes to the ladies, I don't want to be the one to say Santa's got a wandering eye, but face it, he is a man. They don't just make up songs like, *I Saw Mommy Kissing Santa Claus.* There's no question that he loves Mrs. Claus, but women throw themselves at him, all in the hopes that he'll stuff their stocking with something special.

Finally, running a year round, multi-line manufacturing operation with worldwide distribution has got to be stressful. Think of the procurement issues. Just think of the workers comp and HR nightmares connected with hundred-year-old elf employees.

Granted, Santa is one cool cat, but don't let overly envious until you've walked a mile in his red and white Uggs.

We can all agree that Tim Allen turned in an Oscar worthy performance portraying Kris Kringle in *The Santa Clause* movie trilogy, but what would any of us do if we got to try on the big red suit and take on the job of Santa for a day? I, for one, would keep tradition alive. For instance, I would maintain a rigidly strict Naughty and Nice list. There has got to be consequences if you're going to go off the deep end and have a meltdown during the year. Kids, are you reading this? Accountability means rewarding the nice kids and totally blowing off the naughty kids. Here's a quick N&N list off the top of my head.

Naughty: Charlie Sheen, Tiger Woods, Jesse James, the entire Lohan family, politicians (Republicans and Democrats), mean people and terrorists.

Nice: Chilean miners, every player, coach and front office person connected with the San Francisco Giants, Bono, Bill and Melissa Gates, teachers and every person serving in our armed forces.

> *If I was Santa, I would make more public appearances throughout the year so everyone believed in me. Children's imagination is important, but sometimes you have to meet people.*
> —Izzy S. 12, Danville

> *If I was Santa, I would breed Rudolf. We could use more flying reindeer.*
> —Tiffany R. 49, Danville

If I was Santa, I would patent the Reindeer powered sleigh. How long will it be before Toyota is cranking out hybrid sleighs at the Nummi plant in Fremont and taking all the credit for another environmentally efficient, aka, "Green" breakthrough?

Santa has been using magic dust, reindeer poop and simple lift versus thrust antler aerodynamics for years and he deserves some recognition for that alternative energy discovery. The intellectual property rights alone could go for hundreds of millions of dollars. Not to mention, imagine the value of stock options if he put together a VC backed start-up company and went the IPO route.

If I was Santa, I would spread the holiday out. Hanukkah has the right idea utilizing eight nights. We should make Christmas at least a week which would give Santa more time to deliver all those presents. One night to hit every house in the world is stretching it a bit thin.

—Lisa W. 50, Walnut Creek

If I was Santa, I would make sure every child had a present under the tree even if they didn't have a tree.

—Christina D. 33, San Ramon

If I was Santa, I would wipe out everyone's debt. It would be so nice to begin Christmas morning with a financial clean slate.

—David R., Danville

If I was Santa, I would learn how to fly like a superhero so that I could give the reindeer a water and food break once in a while on Christmas Eve.

—Jessica F. 11, Danville

If I was Santa, I would wrap a Victoria Secret model up and place her under Matt's tree.

—Matt M. 26, Danville

If I was Santa, I would bring the Raider fans a Super Bowl victory. Santa was obviously paying attention to Giant's fans last year seeing how he just delivered San Francisco a World Series.

—Dave B. 44, Walnut Creek

If I was Santa, I would deliver family members to all military service men and women who aren't able to be home with their family during the holidays because they are protecting our country and freedom!

—Julie L. 40, Dublin

If I was Santa, I might start thinking about a pre-season conditioning program. Much like the National Football League with all of their off season mini-camps and organized team activities (OTA's), Christmas has become so huge that you've got to arrive at camp in shape. Chances are, the North Pole probably has a 24 Hour Fitness facility. I would hire a personal elf trainer to set up a cardio and weight training program that would allow me to shed some weight, shape and tone. I would even be open to taking a yoga class or two. After that, I would start modifying my diet to reduce the carbs and high caloric goodies such as hot chocolate with whipped cream, fruit cake and egg nog. Having Santa-like proportions myself, I've recently made the same commitment to health and fitness. Hey, maybe we could be work out partners.

> *If I was Santa, I would go on a diet. He's not a big as those people on The Biggest Loser show, but if he keeps eating cookies he might be one day.*
>
> —Olivia P. 12, Danville

> *If I was Santa, I would shave off my beard. Men don't really have beards anymore and it makes him look really old.*
>
> —Nicole C. 11, Danville

If I was Santa, I would bring Lou Wolfe, the A's owner, the MLB rights to move his team to San Jose. I would also distribute coal to everyone in our legal and political systems.

—Gabe A. 40, Alamo

If I was Santa, I would make a few changes to my toy making facility, simply to be more efficient. What's the old saying; if you're not getting ahead you're falling behind. I'm not saying Mr. Clause doesn't know his stuff, I'm simply suggesting he might consider hiring a consulting firm to perform a needs analysis of his overall operation. In today's tech-friendly business environment, he might find that logistic software and/or outsourcing is the way to go.

Oh, who am I kidding? Santa is doing just fine. He's the man behind the magic of the holiday season. Keep doing what you're doing, Saint Nick, and if it's not too much trouble, would you bring me a new bike. I've been real good this year. Just ask Eric Johnson, my editor at Alive.

9   Occupy North Pole

If you read my last article, *Another Election Year*, in the November issue of Alive Magazine, you would know that I'm not overly political. I am proud to be an American citizen and I do exercise my right to vote, but it's not like I would ever join a call center movement and interrupt your dinner hour with a courteous reminder to support my candidate or vote down a referendum. In the past, I was never one to protest. While I whole-heartedly believe that protests have their time and place, I'm just not a joiner—that is, until me and my bowling group of dads decided to drive to the North Pole and "Occupy" Santa's Workshop. It's not that we have anything against Santa or Mrs. Claus; we were just caught up in the moment.

We got our idea from Occupy Wall Street ("OWS"). OWS, as most everyone knows, is a people-powered movement that began on September 17, 2011 in Liberty Square in Manhattan's Financial District, and has spread to over 100 cities in the United States and over 1,500 cities globally. OWS is fighting back against the corrosive power of major banks and multinational corporations over the democratic process, and the role of Wall Street in creating an economic collapse that has caused the greatest recession in generations. The movement is inspired by popular uprisings in Egypt and Tunisia, and aims to expose how the richest 1% of people are writing the rules of an unfair global economy that is foreclosing on our future. (I got that from their website *www.occupywallstreet.org).*

I would be lying if I told you we have enacted some altruistic global movement to liberate the working class elves, to determine if Santa's monopoly on Christmas has made him a billionaire, or to expose the NYSE symbol "SWS" as Santa's Workshop. From what I've seen, the elves seem to be pretty merry. Santa runs his operation as a Not for Profit and SWS is actually a failing solar company headquartered in Sunnyvale. Granted, the folks at PETA might have something to say about the cruelty of making reindeer fly, but to a man, our group of super athletic suburban dads agreed that if we could fly, we would gladly pull Santa's rig.

Can you imagine a bunch of premium-jean-wearing-dad's, from the I-680 corridor, pulling Santa's sleigh? Santa might yell out, "On Blackhawk, On Diablo, go Crow Canyon and Round Hill." No, the truth is, me and my boyz were just looking for something different to do during our holiday break and a trip to the North Pole sounded cool. No pun intended.

The occupations around the world are being organized using a non-binding consensus-based decision-making tool known as a "people's assembly." We don't even know what that means. This process of organizing your local community and bring awareness to social injustice makes sense and it's sure popular, but I've heard many people verbalize that a great majority of the occupy participants just seem to be on the "encampment bandwagon." I'm not saying that our Occupy North Pole was well thought out, but we certainly wern't going to cause trouble. We actually did have a "hidden agenda." We wanted to see how the toys were made.

For my entire lifetime, I've heard about Santa's Workshop. Who doesn't know about the "naughty and nice" list, Rudolph the Red-Nosed Reindeer and Frosty the Snowman? It wasn't too hard to convince sixteen beer drinking suburban dads to take a little road trip for the good of mankind. I also promised them we would stop at In-N-Out Burger. Ultimately, what got my brothers to jump in their SUVs and begin the 13,000 mile journey from Danville to the North Pole, was that I promised anyone that accompanied me that they get to a case of eggnog beer from the North Pole Brewery.

After a rather long drive, our occupation began once we set up our tent city and began making protest posters. Slogans such as; *Less than 1% of the world has Mistletoe, Jingle Bells the Government Smells* and, *Frosty is Cold Blooded,* seemed harmless enough. Truth be told, we were just hoping to get some face time with Mr. Kris Kringle and enjoy the hot chocolate dispensing fire hydrants. If we could score a University of Santa's Workshop hoodie and a candy cane foam finger, the trip would be considered a success.

To no one's surprise, Santa didn't appreciate our occupation. He came out a few times and told us to go home because he was busy working on the time challenges of delivering presents to the seven billion people that now inhabit the earth.

Sometime after our beer buzz wore off, and the ten thousandth elf thrown snowball rained down on the Occupy NP wiener roast, we decided to pack it in and head home. It's not that we didn't believe in our cause...wait, what was our cause? No, our occupy movement ended when we realized that we could be more effective at home, being solid familymen during the holidays. Not to mention, it was so cold, we were freezing our "bowling" balls off.

Santa reminded us that the holidays are a time for family, not fighting...or something like that. The Jolly One is usually munching cookies and mumbles a lot. Maybe next year, we'll Occupy Arizona during baseball's Spring Training, or Occupy San Diego with the kids (the zoo, Sea World and LEGOLAND) for spring break. One day, I would like to Occupy Maui or Orlando during the summer. I just hope my wife doesn't expect me to Occupy Michigan (the in-laws) for Thanksgiving next year or you'll really hear me protest.

II

NEW THINKING
ABOUT NEW YEARS

The New Year provided me with the opportunity to do a variety of articles on resolutions without calling them all resolution pieces. I believe that we're all entitled to a fresh start and what better time to start than January first. Resolutions aren't for everyone, especially me, so I try to motivate myself with goals and objectives disguised as resolutions.

10 My New Year's Resolutions
The Subtraction by Addition Concept

Every year around this time, a majority of us make a conscious effort to quantify those things in our lives that we would like to change, improve or, at the very least, revise in a positive way, with the start of a new year. This is commonly called our New Year's Resolutions. Maybe it's the desire to find a new job or lose weight and get in shape by working out more. A lot of us want to spend more time with our family, complete home improvement projects or perhaps find a new relationship. I've known friends that wanted to take classes toward an advanced degree, get back to their church or pursue a long lost hobby. Raise your hand if you have ever made a list of life-altering New Year's resolutions to vigorously attack as of January 1st, or maybe January 2nd because who can really start the year off on the right foot when you're hung over, eating leftover pigs in a blanket while watching 12 parades and 27 college football bowl games on TV? At least that's how I traditionally celebrate New Year's Day. However, this year I've got a list of resolutions and if I can miraculously find where I put it (probably under the broken Christmas ornaments and empty Champagne bottles), I'll be ready to set into motion, plans for a better me in the New Year.

After years of falling short of my intended goals, evidenced by the fact that I have neither washboard abs, a lucrative sports management business or jillions of dollars in disposable cash, I have decided to go with a "subtraction through addition" approach to my resolutions this year. For everything I take away I'm going to add something in return just to balance the Zen playing field of life. If you relate this concept to other areas of life, it's like reducing the brown spots and weeds in your lawn by fertilizing and watering it more. I think I may be on to something.

Health and Fitness: My first resolution is to have more energy and lose 10-15 pounds (subtraction). Obviously that means I'll need to eat better and work out more (addition). So with the subtraction through addition strategy I plan to consume more Red Bull (at least a 6-pack daily) and Rice Crispy treats (because they are light, tasty and made from good ingredients—cereal is nutritious). Unless I miscalculate, if I'm constantly snacking and wired on caffeine I'll likely not need to eat three sizable meals a day. Additionally I'll be joining a bowling league and increasing my fantasy sports involvement to include NASCAR and golf. We can all agree that the sport of bowling is a rare combination of stretching, yoga and cardio, while online gambling promises to keep my heart rate up.

Career: While most of us like what we do for a living, who doesn't have a dream job? I've always wanted to be a roadie for Def Leppard, to coach of the Bud Light Woman's Beach Volleyball team, or be the quality control taste-tester for See's Candy. Assuming those jobs are taken by more qualified individuals, I've decided my second resolution is to work smarter not harder at my primary job by finding a way to be more productive in my lead generation (addition) thereby subtracting the amount of time I actually need to spend at the office. My plan is to triple my business solicitation emails to include family, friends and my existing client base. The subject line reading, "How would you like to help me make more money?" I feel relatively certain that the average individual doesn't receive nearly enough mass distributed emails related to network marketing. My email is all about reducing my personal debt (subtraction) and doing nothing for the person on the other end, except to put a strain on their bandwidth (addition). Life is about helping your fellow man, so send me a sales lead.

Family: I truly believe that I'm a good father, but what dad wouldn't like to spend more time with his kids? The problem is

I'm loaded down with too many tasks around the house. Hence, to afford myself more quality time with my girls (addition) it is essential that I reduce my list of household chores (subtraction). Initially, I will be getting my daughter's matching-pink, push lawn mowers for Christmas. It's impractical to expect an eight and ten year old to use a gas powered mower, plus the exercise will be good for them. I'm confident that me telling the girls, by taking over the landscape maintenance around our house they'll be helping the environment (saving baby seals in Alaska), there's no way they can turn me down. Additionally, they'll be taking out the garbage, emptying the dishwasher and walking the dog, all in order to get more, meaningful interaction with dad.

Brain Power: Every year I promise myself that I'll read more motivational books, enroll in a class or two and watch more educational television programming, but this year I'm going to do it by adding a broader definition to the term "self help." For instance, motivational books are, by definition, books that motivate you to do something. John Gresham motivates me to not commit a crime and get sent to death row. Steve Martin's recently published autobiography should motivate me to be funnier. Magazines such as *FHM* or *Maxim* might motivate me to do all kinds of new things that I'm sure my wife would appreciate. Reading problem solved. As for taking a class, I've been thinking of taking a memory class so I can remember where I left my car keys/TV remote/kids allowance/etc. This kind of knowledge is critical for everyday success and transportation. Finally, there's educational programming, which wasn't a problem when the kids were younger and there was a daily ritual of *Mr. Rodgers, Sesame Street* and *Barney*. All of those PBS programs are very educational. Today my idea of educational television is watching the medical procedures on *House* or re-runs of *Scrubs.* I guess we could always watch the History Channel if there's something cool on, like a Moon landing or Earthquake stuff. So another resolution will be to spend less time watching *Glee, The Office* and *Mad Men* and more time viewing smart TV shows like what's on the Discovery Channel and Nat Geo Wild.

There are, inevitably, other aspects of my life that I will attempt to improve throughout the year, but I think I might be onto something with this subtraction through addition concept. I'm not sure the notion of spending less time at church is going to fly simply by saying that I'll be talking with the big guy upstairs a little more often, but this — by + is a work in progress. The important thing is to acknowledge that we all have things in our lives that we can work on to make us better people. It's like a 12 step program where the first step is admitting there's a problem. My problem, like many people, is I don't often succeed in accomplishing my New Year's resolutions. However, this year I feel good not only about my goals, but my strategy. Although I've reduced the number of actual resolutions, I plan to spend more time focused on the objectives I've outlined. Subtraction by addition may just make this the best year ever.

11 A Positive and Optimistic New Year

By and large, I think most of us would rather be positive and optimistic than negative and pessimistic. It's obviously more encouraging and hopeful to see the glass half full as opposed to half empty. It's simply more uplifting to interpret the weather forecast as partly sunny as opposed to chance of rain. Pick the cliché, but we do have a choice as to how we view life? Being positive and optimistic has got to have more upside than being negative and pessimistic. Granted, the tendency of many of us (including the media) is to focus on the worst case scenario, especially given the overwhelming global obstacles we're currently facing. However, I'm planning to buck that trend and go against the norm because my 2009 New Year's resolution is to be more positive and optimistic; not just about the economy, but about everything. I'm vowing to see the forest through the trees and the light at the end of the tunnel. Let's hope it's the Caldecott Tunnel.

I'm finally excited about a New Year's resolution. I'm inclined to believe that if I have a positive attitude and maintain an optimistic outlook, it might be just the start of good times ahead. What's the downside? If we all start at home, spread it through the neighborhood and then take it to work, school, the gym, our churches and community functions, what's the worst that could happen? So what if people think I'm a little eccentric (nutty) or a bit "out there" (nutty)! What if people actually adopted this positive movement and it spread across the country? I think this is how Tony Robbins got started and he's amassed something close to a bazillion dollars in self help books, tapes and seminars. My resolution is free.

I'm going to start by declaring that the economy can't get any worse, it can only get better. The new and improved me maintains that the economy has hit rock bottom and will begin to turn around by mid year. My C+ in Econ 101 taught me enough to know that every economy has down cycles. We're too great a nation not to eventually recover. We've seen government bail outs, massive layoffs, corporate bankruptcies, stock market volatility, fluctuating oil/gas prices, a meltdown in the mortgage industry, the possible demise of the Big Three U.S. auto makers… and has anyone checked the price of milk lately? The American economy hasn't taken a butt kicking like the one it experienced in 2008 since the Great Depression. If my 401K were a durable good, like soap or toothpaste, it could be bought at the Dollar Store. We could walk around in t-shirts that read, "the economy sucks," but wouldn't it be more productive to simply work hard, cut back, budget our personal finances and have faith that the road to economic recovery begins with small steps? That's going to be my approach. I might even make bumper stickers and t-shirts that read, I'm on the Road to Recovery. (Hopefully everyone will understand that I'm referring to economic recovery and not an addiction).

Next, I'm going to give our new president a chance. I may have voted Republican but as an American I'm going to get behind our new president and pull for his success. The fact of the matter is, Barack Obama is our new Commander-in-Chief and he has a colossal job ahead of him. Had McCain won he would've been up against the same domestic challenges, but with added opposition coming from a Democratic House and Senate. President-elect Obama is a passionate leader with innovative ideas. It's too easy to say we're going to be over taxed, under militarized and governed into a Socialistic society. Let's give the guy a chance. He has inherited a mess. Let him establish his cabinet, take office and get his feet wet. I recently spoke with a relative who lives in Illinois and they loved this guy when he was working exclusively for their state. Apparently, Senator Obama established a lot of innovative social programs within the State and plenty of people prospered. I'm all about helping people and personally prospering. Don't worry Mr. President, I've got your back.

We are all painfully aware that our local housing market has been pummeled. That's the bad news. But the good news is, we still live in the greatest area on earth. Where else can you have such easy access to the opportunities that we do living right here in the I-680 corridor? We're a little over an hour away from the Pacific Ocean, the Sierra Nevada Mountains are less than a three hour drive and San Francisco, one of the most beautiful cities in the world, is virtually in our backyard. We have access to colorful historical sites, renowned universities, easy-to-navigate freeways and efficient public transportation, a world class wine region, an incredible climate and a variety of entertainment destinations. Whether your tastes are theatre, museums, movies, concerts or professional sporting events, we have it all right here. I love living in the Tri Valley for all of the reasons I just described and there's no doubt in my mind that it's only a matter of time before the value of my house will appreciate itself back to what I paid for it.

Getting back to the subject of professional sports, our local franchises have really let us down the last few years. It's tough to be a loyal fan considering how pitiful the Giants, A's, Warriors, Raiders and 49ers have performed. Granted, the San Jose Sharks have done pretty well, but let's be honest…it's hockey. Unless you're a Canadian ex-patriot it's hard to fully appreciate a sport none of us played as kids. On the other hand, we've all shot a few hoops, threw the old pigskin around and probably played Little League or SRVGAL softball. We have to be positive and believe that any of our pro sports teams are just one season away from getting back into the playoffs. If I was the Bay Area General Manager, I would get our baseball teams pitching and a power hitter, the football teams both need new ownership, a proven head coach, better defensive players and a game breaking receiver. Finally, the Warriors need an established big man. There, problem solved. I'm ordering my play-off tickets tomorrow.

We've all heard about global warming and we realize our environment is in serious trouble. Al Gore's documentary, *An Inconvenient Truth,* was a very compelling movie a few years ago, but is his New Year's resolution to be more optimistic and positive? I don't think so. Maybe our polar ice caps are melting and the rain forests are disappearing (blah, blah, blah), but I'm tired of hearing about how bad things are without a plan to improve the situation. I'm optimistic that the people of this world can alter their bad habits and institute change. The Earth will take one tiny step toward a healthier tomorrow, once we stop using aerosol hair spray and start recycling our Aquafina water bottles. The arctic region is bound to eventually get a little snow, senior housing developments have already slowed down in most rain forest regions and our air quality will get progressively better, once everyone is driving a Prius. Let's do it for the kids.

Finally, I don't think there's any way that the Dow Jones could ever get under 1,000 points, but if it does I'll have three words for my financial planner; buy, buy, buy.

Positivity and optimism are serious drugs. Try a little and you inherently want more. A positive and optimistic person can either be the life of the party or someone you want to strangle. I personally don't see myself shuffling around the office singing "Gray skies are gonna clear up, put on a happy face," anytime soon, but I do plan to lose the negative, depressed, defeatist attitude. Optimism breeds optimism. If we start embracing a more positive, optimistic outlook on life, the better our chances are of modifying the general public's perception of the challenges we face and how to resolve them. Like I said earlier, what have we got to lose? Let's all start the New Year on a positive note.

12 I Resolve to Fulfill My New Year's Resolutions

Maybe, because it's the year 2010, I feel a responsibility to raise the level of my game when it comes to New Year's Resolutions. It's hard to believe that it was just nine short years ago that we thought the world's economy, or at the very least our home and work computers, might experience a meltdown of epic proportion as a result of the Y2K apocalypse. Fortunately, that little millennium snafu never came to be. Unfortunately, the bottom did eventually fall out of the financial markets, in late 2008.

Come to think of it, I have been having trouble with my PC when surfing websites such as Craigslist, Facebook and Suburban Swingers.com. Perhaps we were just off by a few years and it was actually Y210K? I will admit that I'm also more than a little concerned about this new movie, 2012. In my experience, Mayan predictions aren't anything to trifle with and the end of the world is a pretty significant premonition. Oh well, that's two years away, lets just focus on the here and now, 2010.

For the past couple of years, I've relied on the traditional classics when it comes to my New Year's resolutions. My goals and objectives tended to center around losing weight, being a more involved parent, attending church, working harder, communicating more regularly with friends and relatives, community efforts such as giving blood or other bodily fluids, and of course, to stop beating my pets. I don't physically abuse them mind you, but occasionally I am sarcastic and condescending to them. Just the cats that is—the dog and I get along fine.

If I were to revamp this traditional resolution list, it's got to be more accomplishment oriented. There's got to be an action plan, not just a mission statement behind my resolutions. Knowing this, please feel free to follow along as I lay out the groundwork for a happy, healthy and prosperous new year.

I resolve to be a better father, if it's possible to be better than perfect. I'm only kidding. I know there's always room for improvement. I could be more patient. I tend to raise my voice after just the 8th time making a simple request of my daughters. Next year, I'll wait until the 9th request. I could also be more understanding of "tween" girl issues such as vampire love, procrastination, texting, hair/clothes/shoe styles, mumbling, slouching and the intense dislike of sisters.

I shouldn't be so offended when, despite the countless hours spent driving, attending, coaching and cheering at their various activities, that they would rather stuff iPod buds in their ears than actually have a conversation with their father. Life lessons, advice, quality time = BORING, at my house. I hope my tears don't fry the computer keyboard. This year, I'm determined to reconnect with the demon seeds I've spawned and be a better Daddy.

I resolve to be a better husband, if it's possible to be better than perfect. I'm only serious. I cook, I clean, I mow, I watch what I eat and workout to make myself desirable. I... I... Ok, I don't actually do any of those things, but I could, I mean I will. Marriage is a two-way street and lately I've been letting someone else drive. We all know that marriage takes work. Unfortunately a lot of us have jobs that also require that we work. After I put in a long day at work-work I don't have the energy to come home and put in another couple of hours relationship work. Marriage work requires more effort than real work. It's emotionally draining and doesn't pay as well. I'm not saying that relationship work doesn't have it perks (wink, wink, nudge, snicker), but last I checked, there's only 24 hours in the day, and as you know from past articles, I need my "me" time. This year, regardless of the conflicts and my own limitations, I am determined to reconnect with my beautiful, wonderful wife and be a better domestic partner.

I resolve to take better care of myself. I'm not implying that I could transform my 47 year old desk jockey body into one of those Werewolf boys in the *New Moon* movie, but there's certainly room for improvement. After trying the crazy diets, the boot camps, Bikram Yoga, spin classes, *Dancing with the Stars* Home Edition and the high colonics, I'm convinced the "well balanced" approach is the only tried and true method for maintaining good health and fitness. I'm confident that if I initiate a daily regime of healthy eating, 8-10 hours of nightly sleep and exercise with Wii Fit, in time I'll feel good about wearing a Speedo at the beach again. This year, I'm determined to live a less deep-fried lifestyle.

I resolve to take no medicine that has side effects worse than my illness. If the prescription or over-the-counter medication could cause blindness, deafness, muteness, open sores, migraine headaches, paralysis or impotence then I refuse to swallow it, inhale it, drink it or secrete it! I don't care if I have teenage facial acne, double vision, start growing hair on the bottom of my feet and crave the taste of human blood, the medication prescribed can't be the cause of a more serious aliment such as, oh I don't know…death. This year, I'm determined to read the packaging for possible side effects before trying to feel better.

I resolve to be a better writer. I'm well aware that my writing style is amateurish and sophomoric, often relying on "bathroom" humor for laughs. In fact, a recent poll determined that most of my articles are actually read in the bathroom. I acknowledge that I tend to be a little wordy, not knowing when to end one sentence and begin another, but that could be considered a style and not a deficiency of the content…oh, I'm doing it again. I'm also not a very strong proof reader. Candidly, I don't know if anyone actually reads the monthly drivel I put out. There hasn't been a lot of reader feedback. I don't know why I even bother. Would anyone even notice if I took up some other creative hobby, such as pottery or gardening? If only there was a health-club-like studio for all of us "artsy folks" living along the I-680 corridor, where we could drop-in and spend a few hours channeling our creative energy into tangible goods. That would be cool. This year, I'm determined to put more thought into the content of my writing... or take up needlepoint.

I resolve to generate additional income by opening up a health-club-like creativity studio for all the artsy folks living along the I-680 where they can drop in, and for $50 an hour, pursue their creative desires. We'll offer classes in pottery, gardening, needlepoint and magazine article writing (with an emphasis on sophomoric bathroom humor pieces). As depressed as commercial real estate is in the Tri-Valley, I shouldn't have any trouble finding a vacant retail space with storefront entry. I'll find someone to negotiate a sweet deal for me. There's got to be at least one landlord out there willing to trade stock options for rent. This year, I'm determined to supplement my income (never ruling out multi-level marketing as an option).

I resolve to dress better and pay attention to my overall hygiene at work. Somehow Casual Friday became Casual Everyday. While it used to be acceptable to sport Dockers and a Polo Shirt on the last workday of the week, I may have recently crossed the line. Last week, I wore my wife's Victoria Secrets bathrobe and UGG boots to an inner office Power-Point presentation. Granted I looked "hot," but my boss still wrote me up... for being late. On those Friday's before a long holiday weekend, I often took the liberty of not shaving, brushing my hair or applying cologne...or deodorant. Apparently, the term "going green" doesn't apply to one's teeth. This year, I'm determined not to scare off clients or co-workers with my impersonation of a UC Berkeley tree sitter.

Finally, I resolve to fulfill my New Year's Resolutions. It would be easy to stick my chest out and brag to my bowling group about my resolutions list. I'm relatively certain that most of those guys didn't make a list of New Year's Resolutions. They would rather sit about and mock me. They are so jealous of my bowling abilities, my good looks and my celebrity status. At least that's what my mom tells me. I bet no good Carl and Damon and Marc and Jeff and Tommy and Craig... note to self, add stop being so competitive with guys in the bowling group to next year's resolution list. Where was I? Oh yea, Resolution + Action Plan + Execution = Results.

A resolution is by definition a thing determined upon, decision as to future action, a formal statement of determination by an assembly. If I truly resolve to change my life by accomplishing my resolutions, I could move mountains. Isn't that what Brett Farve did? Look at him. This year is going to be the best year ever, and 2011 will be even better than that. I resolve to bring up my game and live life to the fullest for the next two years.

I might as well since the world is going to end in Twenty Twelve. Just ask a Mayan.

13 Finding the Meaning of Life in the New Year
Learning to Appreciate Simple Pleasures

Since the beginning of time, people have prophesized about the meaning of life. What is the point of our existence? How does one find purpose? Is inner peace obtainable? Why didn't I invent Facebook? The question is as simple as it is complex. Ultimately, it would seem logical that we all desire a certain amount of joy and happiness in our lives. Whether your spiritual inspiration is Freud, Nietzsche, Mandino, Budda, Yoda or Zuckerberg, our search can be a lifelong journey or enlightenment can be just a paragraph away. Who knew I was so deep, right?

During my pursuit of enlightenment, both spiritual and intellectual, I have recently unlocked the meaning of life. How? Where? When, you might ask? Let's just say I attend the church of common sense on a regular basis and this epiphany came to me several weeks ago. Not being one to selfishly hoard a hidden treasure such as this, my New Year's gift to all of my readers (both of you) is sharing this profound, yet oddly uncomplicated, secret. Ready? Are you sitting down? Life is about the pursuit of happiness and happiness can be found by appreciating simple pleasures. Simple pleasures can be found each and every day in every aspect of our lives, if we just take the time to acknowledge them when they occur.

No one person lives life attending a non-stop party filled with attention, adulation and admiration, but we all have simple pleasures that fill our heart and recharge our emotional battery. No amount of money, fame, career success, recognition, good health, sports accomplishments, religious purity or sexual conquests can sustain a person for a prolonged period of time. However, if one embraces the simple pleasures, these flashes of joy and contentment add up to a lifetime of happiness.

Relationships: No relationship is perfect and every relationship has its challenges. Regardless how your relationship is defined; friendship, dating, betrothed, civil union, partners, a married couple, roommates, co-parents or estranged exes, the key is to appreciate the simple pleasures. Too often, young couples expect the honeymoon to never end and are disappointed or disillusions if there are days, weeks or months of strife. A more rewarding approach may be to focus on the simple pleasures that bring you moments of joy. My wife appreciates when I unload the dishwasher or do the grocery shopping. I, on the other hand, enjoy when we read the Sunday paper on the back patio or when I find my favorite new songs uploaded on my ipod. My worst day at the office can be erased if she greets me with a supportive hug when I arrive home. Our simple pleasures include walking the dogs, going to the movies or enjoying a nice bottle of wine. Neither of us it perfect and at times we seem disconnected, but we do our best not to take each other for granted as that's a simple pleasure, in and of its own.

Parenting: Being a parent is hard and I don't recall getting an instruction manual when we left the hospital's maternity ward. Babies cry too much, toddlers toddle too busy, tweens whine too much and teenagers are too moody, rebellious and prone to making bad decisions. However, parenting can also be the greatest job in the world, if you take time to appreciate the simple pleasures. Contrary to popular belief, in affluent communities the latest, greatest or most expensive next big thing isn't what makes a child happiest. A child will likely respond most favorable when a parent is involved, engaged and invested. Holding hands with my daughters is still precious. Hearing usually combative sisters laugh and giggle warms my heart. I love when they're beaming with pride as the result of bringing home a good grade or accomplishing some athletic feat. I especially like our conversations right before bed time. If I died tomorrow, my heart would be filled with the memories of the simple pleasures we've shared.

Some of my fondest memories I have as a child are of simple pleasures spent with my parents. I remember wrestling with my father in the back yard of our house, seeing my mom's smile whenever I donned my Cub Scout uniform and the comforting, reassuring hugs the both dolled out whenever I was sad or down.

Career: In a perfect world, we would all win the lottery and either not have to work or be allowed the privilege of pursuing the career we choose, not the one we've fallen into. What's the old saying? Do what you love and you'll never work a day in your life. Sadly, most of us do what we do because it's either too late to change careers or the career we want wouldn't pay the bills. So what choice do we have except to find that simple pleasure in our Monday through Friday, nine to five routine? If you're the boss (owner, manager, supervisor or chief) isn't it rewarding when an underling accomplishes a task or completes a project to your satisfaction? It's especially rewarding if you've trained this energetic, enthusiastic, eager-to-please employee to succeed. At the same time, if you're a workerbee, you'll undoubtedly agree how nice it is to get praise or recognition from your superior. Closing a sale, providing great customer service, addressing a company need, concern or problem can be incredibly rewarding, if you recognize your own contribution as a productive member of the team. When you apply yourself and do your best, you'll be surprised how fulfilling work can be, thanks to recognizing the simple pleasures your role plays within the organization.

The end of the year is a chance to re-evaluate where we are and where we want to be over the next twelve months. The New Year brings everyone a new beginning; a chance to reinvent ourselves. This year, my lone resolution will be to truly appreciate life's simple pleasures. If we learn to appreciate the simple pleasures in life, we can assuredly enhance our level of happiness as we endure our suburban existence. I may not have invented Facebook, but I may just post this life altering mantra for all my friends to read.

14 My New Year's "To Do" List

My one and only resolution of the New Year was to not write a magazine article about New Year's Resolutions. I'm one for one so far and feeling good. As I near my 50th birthday, I've determined that New Year's Resolutions aren't for me anymore. I find resolutions much too be daunting and cumbersome; almost a sad car trip to failureville. However, there are a few things I would like to accomplish in the calendar year 2012. My intentions are to tackle them as a "To Do" list for the coming twelve months so I can check off my completed tasks as I go along, much like my weekend "Honey do" lists. Unlike the weekend list of chores and errands, my New Year's To Do list won't start with pick-up dog poop in the backyard.

TO DO:

1) Make More Money. Currently I'm experimenting with a high end Canon Laserjet copier, but if that doesn't work I'm thinking there's got to be a counterfeiters website. Error! Hyperlink reference not valid. Then again, I could simply work harder at my day job or supplement my income with a paper route.

2) Get Out and Vote. It's our responsibility to vote as United States citizens. The question isn't, should I vote? but, who do I vote for? Do I give President Obama another four years or should I back the yet to be named (Newt or Mitt) Republican candidate? Decisions, decisions, decisions.

3) Read More. I'm currently reading *The Hunger Games* trilogy by Suzanne Collins. I previously finished *The Girl with the Dragon*

Tattoo trilogy by Stieg Larsson. I must like trilogies. Reading is good. It makes me smarter. I'll likely mix in the occasional biography, autobiography or book about our national geography. A "graphy" trilogy.

4) Write Another Screenplay. Sadly my first screenplay, entitled, *Allen and Allen,* about two brothers who are dysfunctional partners in a San Francisco law firm forced to work together in a desperate attempt to rescue their mother from a vengeful psychopath, didn't sell. Obviously, I need to spend another 1000 hours coming up with a new storyline that has more commercial box office appeal. Maybe I'll go indie and write a script that could be made on a shoestring budget by a couple of theater arts majors from Cal State East Bay, instead of one needing a major motion picture studio budget, complete with a killer Craft Services catering spread.

5) Commune with Nature. With Mt. Diablo right here in our own backyard, seriously...a few of our friends have homes that abut Mt. Diablo. In their case, that oversized hill is "right in their own backyard." We're also a short drive from Lake Tahoe, the Pacific Ocean, Yosemite, and even Pinnacles National Monument. With so many outdoor options, why do I spend so much time in front of the television and computer?

6) Appreciate the Arts. By "arts" I mean mostly music. With the worldwide music domination by Apple and all things "i", we purchase music a song at a time. I do miss buying CDs, and before that, record albums, cassettes and eight track tapes. Granted, it did seem a little wasteful to listen to ten mediocre tracks, just to hear the one or two songs you really wanted. This year I'm going to learn out to navigate iTunes all by myself and

expand my playlist. Don't get me wrong, I might go to a museum, too. I do like looking at pretty pictures.

7) Be More Romantic (with my wife). I'm pretty sure I'm about as romantic as any Alamo/Danville/San Ramon husband. I bring home flowers, I write love notes, I cuddle, we listen to Kenny G music, but I know I could do more. At least that's what my wife tells me. Starting with Valentine's Day, it's going to be an ongoing Tunnel of Love at my house.

8) Get in Shape. Last year I lost 20 pounds and ran a marathon. It would now appear that I found what was lost. My annual holiday triathlon training (eating, drinking and napping) now has me ready for hibernation. With my over abundance of back hair, I actually do resemble a grizzly bear. If I ever want to regain my championship belt in the Suburban Dad Fight Club I'm going to have to start training. Wasn't it Brad Pitt in the movie *Fight Club* who said, "The first rule of Fight Club is to never talk about Fight Club?" Darn it! Does that mean I'm out? Nonetheless, I'm going to start my training right away.

9) Do Not Die. I don't know if I believe in this whole Mayan Calendar thingy, where they say the Earth will be ravaged by a variety of cataclysmic astronomical events on December 21, 2012, but I, for one, will be doing my best to not die this year.

I'm sure I could think of many more motivating and achievable tasks, but I'm getting tired. I need to add, Take Regularly Scheduled Naps, to my list. Oddly, my "To Do" list looks a lot like a list of New Year's Resolutions. Oh well, at least I didn't try and start it on January 1st like all the other knuckleheads. They've probably flamed out and give up already. I'm feeling real good right now.

III

SPRING IS SPECIAL

Spring holidays were a little quieter around our house than the fall and winter extravaganzas. Much less pomp and circumstance went into Valentine's Day, St. Patrick's Day, March Madness, Easter and Father's Day, than say Halloween, Thanksgivng and Christmas. Pastels, lace and paper mache are much more prevalent during these lesser-quality holidays, but no less sentimental. Although these spring holidays carry a little less tradition, less pizzazz and much less expense, they do have their place in my life.

15 The Evolution of Valentine's Day
From the Perspective of an Ever-evolving Male

Valentine, by definition, is a gift or greeting card sent to a friend, relative or loved one on Valentine's Day. That sounds so wholesome, so provincial, so 1800's. "Father, as it is St. Valentine's Day I'll be taking the carriage over to the Van Huggin's estate to deliver my Hallmark greeting card and a box of Russell Stover candies to Miss Rebecca." Perhaps it was that simple at one time, however over the years Valentine's Day, more so than any other holiday, has taken romance to a new level, via commercialization. As an ever-evolving male, Valentine's Day has introduced many different meanings, traditions, contexts, pressures and outcomes over my 45 year existence. How can one day (February 14th) meant to honor St. Valentine, a Christian martyr of the third century A.D., have caused one man so much confusion and strife over the years? you ask. Allow me to present a chronological account of this holiday as experienced by me at different stages in my life hoping only that other men will be able to relate to this bewildering and pressure-filled, international day of love.

The year was 1967; Mrs. Doten's second grade class was working on our red and white construction paper placemat/cardholders in anxious anticipation of our Valentine's Day school party. My biggest decision of that time was whether to give my buddies the Fantastic Four or Topps Baseball Valentine's cards. That was until Mrs. Doten announced that cards were to be given to every member of the class. "Even girls?" I asked. "Even girls," she replied. "With all due respect Mrs. Doten, but by the true definition of the word Valentine (see above) girls do not factor into any of the aforementioned groups," I so eloquently explained in my best, seven-year-old logic. Needless to say Mrs. Doten's "No Child Left Behind" logic prevailed, and at the Red and White Festival we all exchanged gender neutral cards and rock-hard, heart-shaped candies, (obviously invented by pediatric dentists to loosen fillings and chip the teeth of their captive, target market). Now mom's were another story because, technically, they weren't girls; they were, well, moms, and there's not a self respecting boy out there that doesn't want his mother to be touched and overjoyed by his homemade Valentine card.

At my middle school, the teacher in charge of Student Activities instituted a carnation flower fundraiser for Valentine's Day. Discreetly, you could pay $1.00 for a red or white carnation to be delivered to the person of your choice, with a little note attached. Not surprisingly, the object of my affection, Kristy Bollero, was also the object of affection for half the male student body at Issac Newton Graham Junior High and on Valentine's Day she could be seen carrying enough flowers to cover a New Year's Day float. Not to be outdone, the most popular guy, Greg Murphy, collected so many carnations from the Peter Frampton loving 7th and 8th grade girls, that he looked like he had just won the Kentucky Derby. Those of us, not-so-popular students (and math teachers), walked home flowerless and saddened by this twisted spin of an already puberty-confusing holiday.

> *I remember getting Valentine's Day cards in school signed from your Secret Admirer. It was fun if you found out it was someone you liked or a boy you thought was cute but it was always a let down if you found out it was from someone creepy.*
> —Kathy S.

By high school I had finally morphed out of my lonely dork phase. I'm not saying I was Zac Efron from *High School Musical* but I could at least get a date for the big Valentine's Day dance. My *Heart's on Fire Dance* date in 1978 was Katie (last name withheld) who, in classic high school terms, was an uber hot, clarinet playing, band geek. Now anyone who has ever seen the movie, *American Pie,* will tell you those band camp girls are wild.

Of course there's added pressure to having a date on Valentine's Day and that would be figuring out an appropriate gift for the special person. Knowing every girl loves an adorable stuffed animal, I headed down to the Hallmark store at the mall with my $8.00 budget and found the cutest little teddy bear holding a heart that said "Be Mine." Fortunately for me, the store threw in a free card with my generous heart felt purchase. Hallmark, *"when you care enough to send the very best."* Sadly, the day was ruined when Katie gave me the same bear/card combo. You see ladies, guys hate stuffed animals. Katie would've been better off making me a peanut butter sandwich in the shape of a teddy bear. I would've appreciated and enjoyed the sandwich a lot more. As we slow-danced in the school gym, to *Last Dance* by Donna Summer, sadly Valentine's Day 1980 turned out to be our "last dance."

> *My senior year of high school my 21 year old boyfriend (now husband) had a dozen red roses delivered to my first period home room class and I had to carry them around all day. Needless to say I was the envy of every teenage girl and female teacher.*
>
> —Mindy G.

Fast forward to 1984, when a certain college senior and social chairman of the Sigma Chi chapter at Cal State University, Northridge, pulled off the Valentine's Day campus exchange of all Greek exchanges, by securing a mixer with the highly coveted ladies of Kappa Kappa Gamma sorority—more commonly known as the House of Hotties. Unfortunately, my neanderthal fraternity brothers consumed way too much peppermint schnapps (for minty fresh breath) that afternoon, in anxious anticipation of our V-day pajama party themed blow out. By the time the girls showed up, the only sober males to be found at our house were me and our 63 year old house cook, Hank. Needless to say the KKG's were not pleased and they immediately exited the premises in disgust. In a last ditch effort to salvage the night, I immediately overrode the national fraternity by-laws and made Hank an honorary brother. He and I drank pitchers of Killian's Red and ate pink Mac and Cheese with several girls from the CSUN marching band (see band girl comments above) who just happened to live in the apartment complex next door.

> *I hate that stores put up Valentines Day stuff just days after Christmas. Whose buying chocolate two months early? Besides, the best gift is always the card, especially if it's homemade.*
> —Jane D.

When you're an adult and seeing someone special around Valentine's Day, the only suitable gifts are flowers or lingerie. Of course if you're looking for that special, one of a kind gift guaranteed to really touch her heart, try rain water in a wine bottle. Chicks love that sentimental stuff. Oddly, when you get married and Valentine's Day rolls around the only suitable gift is flowers and jewelry along with a nice dinner at your wife's favorite restaurant. I'm not complaining, but Valentines Day has now just become an excuse for me to act like a romantic fool while telling my wife how great she is and how much I appreciate her in a variety of ways. Now that I have two daughters, I also have little Valentine's to focus my attention on. The beauty is, their love is unconditional, although being their mother's girls they always appreciate flowers and jewelry.

> *Regardless whether we dress up for a romantic dinner out or just eat take out in front of the TV after the kids go to bed, we always have champagne on Valentine's day.*
> —Traci B.

This year, as a tribute to Mrs. Doten, I gave everyone in my office (male and female) a Valentine Day card. The men applauded my bravery for coming out of the closet and embracing my alternative lifestyle and the women have a class action sexual harassment suit pending against me. Even though I've evolved over the years, Valentine's Day can still be complicated and confusing.

16 Misfit Holiday Mascots
Why Cupid, the Leprechaun and the Easter Bunny need a Mascot Makeover

When most people think of the holiday season, they instinctively think of the big three; Thanksgiving, Christmas and New Years. That warm, magical and all-loving period of time between the fourth Thursday in November and the first day in January, when families and friends get together to celebrate the glorious, enchanting, heartfelt holidays of the season. It is not unusual for a majority of us to also instinctively think of holiday mascots, as we commemorate these joyous occassions; the Pilgrims of Thanksgiving, Santa Claus for Christmas and Dick Clark for New Year's—er, I mean Father Time (a younger version of Dick Clark)—and baby New Year. The mere thought of these holiday mascots puts a smile on my face. Much like mascots at a sporting event, holiday mascots have entertainment value. Their job is to excite and entertain the crowd, especially the little ones, in addition to wreaking havoc around the venue. Holiday mascots are almost as important as the meaning of the holidays themselves, which is why it is so critical to have an appealing mascot representing your holiday.

Every year, the lunar calendar aligns itself so that Valentine's Day, St. Patrick's Day and Easter Sunday fall within a 45-60 day time period to give us a misfit mascot holiday season. I say misfit because individually, these holidays all have their place in history, folklore and religion, but collectively they are one giant freak fest of odd ball mascots, hell bent on serving us up a heaping helping of food, fun and commercialization. Cupid, a leprechaun and the Easter Bunny each have their place in our hearts, but lets face it, they are not what smart marketing people would pick today as symbols for such high profile, money-generating holidays. In marketing terms, it's time for a mascot makeover.

Valentine's Day will soon be upon us. For greeting card companies, candy makers and florists, this may be the biggest selling day of the year. However, representing the international day of love and romance is a height-impaired, heavy set man-child, wearing diapers or skorts, while brandishing a dangerous weapon (bow and arrows). Cupid was the god of love in Roman mythology and it is commonly believed that he is the child of Venus. I'm surprised some cutting edge, Beverly Hills advertising agency hasn't contracted the actor, Jonathan Lipnicki (the child actor from the movie *Jerry Maguire*) to dress up in a Speedo swim suit while carrying a crossbow to be the celebrity spokesman If I saw a Cupid mascot heading my way in some restaurant or theater, I would try to restrain him until the county's psych services unit arrived. If the brain trust behind Valentine's Day was proactive they would transform Cupid into more of a teen superhero type of mascot. Picture a skater kid about 16, dressed in a fire engine red Under Armour suit, who soars through the air like Torch from the Fantastic Four. Just a brush of the heat vapor from his super speed would be all the love potion unsuspecting mortals would need to enhance the romance. If you think "tweener" girls like the Jonas Brothers, just wait till they meet Cupid Boy.

Being of Irish decent, I feel comfortable picking on the leprechaun used in a majority of St. Patrick's Day advertising, as well as being used by the board of regents at Notre Dame University. The leprechauns depicted are always elderly and diminutive in size, much like an old hobbit or troll. It's not just his age or stature that creeps people out. It's also his outfit, the surly attitude and the whole chasing the pot of gold at the end of the rainbow thing. In Irish mythology, a leprechaun is a type of male fairy said to inhabit the island of Ireland. They usually take the form of old men which enjoy partaking in mischief. According to legend, if anyone keeps an eye fixed upon one, he cannot escape, but the moment the gaze is withdrawn, the leprechaun vanishes. Creepy, right? No wonder Notre Dame University's school slogan is "the fighting Irish" because every other college mascot wants to kick some Leprechaun butt when they play against one of their sports teams. The Lucky Charms breakfast cereal commercials don't help either. It's obviously time to go younger and cooler. Make him 22ish, buff him out like one of our U.S. Olympic male gymnasts (they're tiny too), dress him in a Boston Celtics jersey and teach him to Riverdance. While we're at it, let's get him to share a little bit of that gold he's always hoarding. The little leprechaun dude's popularity would skyrocket if he passed out some gold bling. He would be like a Pimprechaun.

In my opinion, the Easter Bunny went through a transformation years ago but it has turned out drastically bad. First of all, what does a rabbit and chicken eggs have to do with a deeply religious event anyway? Not a darn thing. However that's another article for another issue. While the thought of a sweet and innocent cotton tailed bunny delivering chocolate goodies and colored eggs in pastel colored baskets worked wonderfully, the 6'7" rabbit on steroids who sulks around the mall the weeks leading up to Easter Sunday is another thing entirely. Who needs to sit on and oversized Easter bunny's lap just for a photo op? That's infringing on Santa's territory anyway. Let's kick it old school and get rid of the awkwardly tall kid in the sweaty, smelly, frayed, floppy ear, mall rat suit. Easter is about Easter egg hunts, church, bonnets, lilies and families sitting down for dinners consisting of Honey Baked ham and scalloped potatoes. Even in this high tech age of i…everything, it's time to get back to the cute, cuddly, furry, little, adorable bunny we remember as kids. That's the perfect mascot for such a beautiful and meaningful holiday with longstanding traditions.

Organizers behind our celebrated holidays need look no further than our local sports teams for inspiration. The mascots that fans respond to, thanks to their entertainment value, include "Thunder" with the Warriors, "Oski," the CAL bear and "Sharkey" down in San Jose. On the other hand, the mascots that don't work include Lucille the Seal with the Giants, the A's elephant (can anyone explain the whole pachyderm connection to the Athletics) or the Stanford Tree. Just look at the national marketing success of the USC Trojan, the Phillies Fanatic or the Dallas Cowboy's cheerleaders. At the core of it all a mascot is about marketability. Let's face it, Cupid's, the leprechaun's and big old Easter Bunny's best day's are behind them. Somewhere, there is a place for castoff misfit mascots that are forced into exile. That place, if I'm not mistaken, is Rossmoor Leisure World in Walnut Creek. Regardless, it's time to update our holiday mascots for the sake of the long term marketing and appeal of the holidays they represent. Who's with me?

17 The Fight for February
The Super Bowl vs. Valentine's Day

I'm as romantic as the next guy—not with the next guy, mind you, but compared to other guys. I love my wonderful wife and adore my two incredible daughters. I'm a compassionate brother to my three, extremely high maintenance sisters, and I adore my nieces to pieces. At the same time, I love football. I played football, I watch football and I've even been know to wager on football (only in the states that have legalized gambling of course). I'm also a firm believer that two things can be equally true. I can love the women in my life and I can love football. That's why I'm having trouble coming to terms with the fact that both the Super Bowl and Valentine's Day are scheduled in the month of February this year. For die-hard football fans like me, the Super Bowl is our Valentine's Day. It's the day we don't have to be embarrassed to express our amorous infatuation with the sport that impacts our lives so profoundly. I'm concerned that I couldn't possibly give all my affection to both days, simply because there's only so much love to go around on a per month basis.

In years past, the Super Bowl has taken place at the end of January, two weeks following the conclusion of the AFC and NFC Championship Games. Valentine's Day occurs somewhere in mid-February. I think it's one of those floating dates like Thanksgiving-the second Tuesday of the month, or something like that? Each sacred day has an entire month devoted to itself, without any celestial distractions, and that's the way it should be. The supreme calendar gods who work for Hallmark or Day Timer didn't schedule Halloween and the 4th of July in the same month did they? No! Easter and St. Patrick's Day don't both fall in March, do they? Granted, Christmas and New Year's Day are only a week apart, but they have their own separate months, right? So why all of a sudden do two significant events of such monumental importance, have to crowd each other during a month of the year that already suffers from "day envy," carrying around a mere 28 days (29 in a leap year) when the other months routinely have a robust 30-31 days?

Being the romantic fool that I am (just ask my wife), I look forward to devoting my heart and soul to a designated day of passion, lust and amour, but I like Valentine's Day too. Now that the NFL has moved the Pro Bowl to the week between the league championship games and the Super Bowl, the SB is the climax of a season that goes by way too quickly. Once that game is over, the American public is forced to endure six weeks of college and professional basketball, before baseball's spring training games begin. I'm sure we can all agree that March Madness is an addictive rush, but other than that, a good segment of the country's population (men) go through clinical depression until the Opening Day of Major League Baseball. Thank God for Madden Football on PS3.

Below is a spreadsheet analysis of Valentine's Day versus the Super Bowl, emphasizing the amount of preparation and emotional effort that goes into two distinctly different days of equal status.

	Valentine's Day	Super Bowl
Time:	All day. From a good morning to a "good" night	All day: pre-game, game, post-game
Celebration:	Flowers/gift/card and the appropriate level of amore	Betting pools, shots, a lot of high-fives and chest bumps
Theme:	Red and White	Team Colors
Food:	Dark Chocolate, Milk Chocolate or White Chocolate	Chips and dip, pizza, ribs, nachos, peanuts, popcorn
Beverages:	Expensive wine or inexpensive champagne	Beer, Tequila and Jager
Venue:	Home or fancy restaurant	Raging neighborhood party or wicked fun sports bar
Advertising:	Romantic commercials featuring greeting cards and mall jewelry stores Pass the tissues.	E*Trade commercials featuring baby making online stock trades. One word: hilarious!
Wagering:	It's a safe wager that most guys will screw-up some element of the pressure-filled holiday, but I bet most of us are still hoping to get lucky.	I won $350 last year with the numbers 5 and 8 and my neighbor is still bringing in my garbage cans, thanks to moi taking the Cardinals +6

There's no need to place blame anywhere specific, but I would like to know who is responsible for the scheduling mishap, this programming snafu, this "exhibition of love" calendar confliction? Although the history of Saint Valentine's Day is shrouded in mystery, its origin dates back to 496 A.D. Knowing that this is only the forty-forth anniversary of the Super Bowl (XLIV), V Day obviously has tenure. It looks like Roger Goodell, the Commissioner of the National Football League, needs to spend a little more time with his team of consultants, evaluating his scheduling options for next year's Super Bowl. The first of my many suggestions to the NFL online suggestion box will be the elimination of that worthless bye week.

I believe there should be an annual day to commemorate love, compassion and appreciation for both the special people in our lives and an event of the Super Bowl's magnitude, just not in the same month. Imagine how many men could potentially need time off from work due to emotional exhaustion. Take it from a guy with a lot of love in his heart, there's no reason two prominent day's of worship and devotion need to fight it out in the month of February. The Super Bowl is meant to be played the last weekend of January and that's all there is to it. You're welcome, Mr. Cupid.

18 Admitting My March Madness Addiction

Hi, my name is Mike and I'm a March Madness addict. Maybe addict is too strong a word. Granted, I did participate in 38 separate brackets last year, but does that really qualify me as a bracketaholic? I know a lot of guys that play twice that many. How many brackets should be considered too many, five, ten...thirty-seven? There are no doubt many men reading this right now thinking, "Is there such a thing as too many brackets?" Isn't March Madness just wholesome fun? Playing a March Madness pool is as "All American" as apple pie, blue jeans and government bailouts. Everyone does it, and it's not like I've gambled away the house or anything.

However, due to last year's losses, my kids may have to settle for an AA degree from Chabot/Las Positas Community College, as opposed to a Bachelor of Science from Stanford or CAL. I know what you're thinking: the first step toward recovery is admitting there's a problem.

For those of you who are fun impaired, March Madness is the NCAA men's division one, college basketball championship played annually in, well...March. Since its inception in 1939, people of all ages, races, religions and careers (except bloggers who prefer to play Dungeons and Dragons in their parent's basement) have fanatically charted the progress of the top 64 collegiate basketball teams (65 if you include the play-in game) in the country, as they vie for the title of National Champion. The tournament, aka The Big Dance, takes place over three weeks during the month of March at sites across the United States and has become one of the nation's more prominent sporting events, literally watched by hundreds of millions.

I first caught the bug in 1979 when I saw Magic Johnson, a sophomore at Michigan State, defeat the previously undefeated

Indiana State Hoosiers, led by Larry Bird. It wasn't until college that I first started experimenting with brackets. I resisted for a long time, but ultimately I caved in to peer pressure. All of my friends were doing it and I just wanted to be cool.

California State University Northridge, my alma mater, is not a basketball powerhouse. In fact CSUN has appeared in the NCAA tournament exactly one time. That historic event took place during the 1999 - 2000 season. However, that one invitation generated a CSUN Matador March Madness party, the likes of which have never been seen, before or since, in the San Fernando Valley. But I digress. My troubles started with a harmless fraternity pool, ultimately won by Tom Roukis. Tom pulled Villanova out of his rear end to win it all in 1985. I'm pretty sure Tom didn't know the difference between the tournament's Sweet 16 (teams still alive after the first weekend of play that advance to the regional semi-finals) and his little sister's Sweet 16 (birthday party). My $5.00 buy-in turned out to be the gateway drug to my 24 year March Madness habit.

Before you judge me, first let me give you some history on this adrenaline pumping rush that holds the people of this country in a vice like grip every spring. The NCAA tournament is made up of conference tournament champions from each Division I conference (Pac 10, Big 12, ACC, etc.), which receive automatic bids. The remaining slots are at-large berths, with teams chosen by an NCAA selection committee. The selection process and tournament "seedings" are based on several criteria, including team rankings, win-loss records and PRI data. Inevitably, some teams are invited that perhaps shouldn't have been, and a few deserving teams are left out. Did I mention that Cal State Northridge has only been invited once, while schools such as Duke, UCLA, North Carolina, Kentucky, Arizona and Indiana seem to have someone on the inside looking out for them? I know, digressing again.

All sixty four teams are seeded and placed into brackets. Low seeded teams play high seeded teams (#1 plays #16). The teams which are still alive after the first weekend advance to the regional semi finals (the Sweet Sixteen) and finals (the Elite Eight). The winner of each region advances to the Final Four and those winners play in the National Championship game. It all seems very logical and orderly, but if the #15 seed Richmond Spiders hadn't knocked out the #2 seeded Syracuse Orangemen in the first round of the 1991 tournament, I would be a very wealthy man today.

Did you know that it was H.V. Porter, an official with the Illinois High School Association, who first coined the term "March Madness," to commemorate a basketball tournament back in 1939? It was Brent Musburger of CBS Sports who first used the phrase in conjunction with the college tournament in 1982. I know this because I'm a junkie.

Here are ten interesting facts that you may not know about March Madness...

1.   From 1939-1950 there were only eight teams in the tournament and while the field has expanded over the years, it didn't reach 64 teams until 1985.

2.   UCLA has won the most NCAA basketball championship titles (11).

3.   Only six teams have entered the tournament ranked #1 in the polls and gone on to win the tournament. Only once have all four number one seeds made it to the final four.

4.   Since 1983, the winning team has been given the hardwood floor from the championship venue.

5.   The biggest margin of victory in a championship game was 30 points.

6.   No #16 seed has ever beaten a #1 seed since the field was extended to 64 teams.

7. The term March Madness is a registered trademark.

8. There are 9.2 quintillion (9,223,372,036,854,775,808 to be exact) possibilities for a 64 team bracket.

9. The 1976 Indiana Hoosiers were the last team to go undefeated during the regular season and sweep a tournament.

10. 1942 was the last time Stanford won the tournament and CAL hasn't won since 1959.

On the Monday that the brackets are released, I take all of this pointless crap, er...I mean all of this significant statistical data into account, as I begin my extensive research into executing the perfect bracket strategy. For that one week of the year I don't eat, I don't sleep, I don't even bathe. My wife and kids know not to even talk to me. I spend countless hours reviewing internet post-ings, listening to radio sports talk shows, perusing newspapers from around the country and absorbing ESPN Sports Center expert analyst analysis, to get the most up-to-date input for my brackets.

Studies have been conducted charting the amount of time employees spend (waste) at the workplace, deciphering their brackets during those three weeks in March. Needless to say, there's an unbelievable amount money lost in corporate America during this down time of religious gaming devotion, otherwise known as *March Madness*.

The term "Bracketology" has become recognized in Webster's Dictionary. It is defined as "the process of predicting the field progression of the NCAA post season basketball tournament."

Now as I sit in the basement of my local church working on step seven or eight of my 12 step program, I am finally free of the March Madness demons that have plagued me in the past. My new lease on life allows me to reflect on my past mistakes and focus on my real life priorities.

Of course it's still difficult this time of year to stop from wondering if Valparaiso's up-tempo offense can overcome Marquette's pressing defense, or if Wisconsin's back court height is going to be too much for Michigan's all conference point guard to contend with, should they make it to the next round.

Who am I kidding? I'm jonesing for a bracket. I would risk it all for just one chance to feel the rush, as I slyly pick St. Mary's to be a Sweet 16 dark horse. Alas, I know it cannot be. If I could innocently play just one bracket, I wouldn't have a problem. One bracket always turns into two brackets and then I can't stop. So I now try to just take it one day at a time, as I rely on cigarettes, coffee and meetings to curb my hoops craving.

Our nation's sports-ravaged obsession with the NCAA tournament is, for the most part, harmless. This piece was not meant to downplay the seriousness of real addictions or the recovery process. This analogy is just my way of harmlessly making light of my engrossing participation in an otherwise meaningless and trivial form of entertainment.

The fact that this chaotic event will take place during a period of unparalleled economic duress and political transition, will hopefully prove to be a much needed distraction to the stress-filled challenges we are all facing.

As the always entertaining Dick Vital likes to say, "It's March Madness Baby!"

19 My Father's Day Gift Letter
Gift Giving Ideas for this year's Father's Day

Father's Day has never been about the gift, but somehow it is a noticeable element. As much as I have adored my paper mache pen and pencil holder, numerous paperweights and framed set of handprints, there's only so much wall and desk space at my office. I'm only disappointed that, in these overly health conscious PC times, my kids won't be making me an ashtray like I made my father. There's a long and storied history of children all over the country, of every age, race and culture making or buying their beloved father some less-than-functional trinket to express their undying love and appreciation. Unless I'm wrong, and I don't think I am, Father's Day was created simply to honor father on the third Sunday in June. Ideally, it was a beautiful sentiment to designate one day out of the year to acknowledge a Dad's contributions to the family unit. It never hurts to let the head of the house (my buddy John Macholz says that the wife is the neck that turns the head) know how much his love, caring, support, protection, generosity, encouragement, wisdom, leadership and financial security are appreciated. Although I need as many ego strokes as I can get, I don't really need another ESPN BBQ apron, a pair of "World's Greatest Dad" boxer shorts or camouflage print cargo pants?

Unlike Mother's Day, when gifts are not only expected, but required, and there seems to always be a huge marketing emphasis on taste, quality and decorum. Expense is no issue for Mother's Day. In fact, it is usually recommended that gifts be coordinated by family members. I think protocol states: flowers from a son or youngest child, tasteful outfit from the eldest child (preferably one with fashion sense) and jewelry from the husband are preferred. If there are more than two children, the rest of the litter can make brunch or dinner reservations. Mother's

Day dates back to the Stone Age. In an early episode of the Flintstone's, Fred and Pebbles spent weeks picking out the perfect stone necklace for Wilma. Father's Day, on the other hand, started around 1962—right about the time cigarette companies were looking to expand their product line by marketing a masculine lighter as a suitable gift for Dad.

It wasn't until I had children of my own that I realized my own dear father lied, year after year, when he told me he loved my gifts. The year was 1970. I was 10 years old and in 4th grade. I gave my father a homemade tie rack. I spent days…okay, hours, putting together the perfect RONCO, "do it yourself" Father's Day gift that I purchased at GEMCO. God bless the man because the tie rack was a hunk of junk. I don't think it could have held a bow tie, much less several neck ties, and yet he proudly displayed it on the back of his closet door until I finally moved out of the house. Granted, I would do the same for my children today, but wouldn't it just be easier for all parties involved if the dad simply wrote a letter, a "Dear Santa" type of letter, listing a few, non-monetary, much-desired items that might make the day even more enjoyable, memorable and appreciated?

Dear Son/Daughter or other,
I think we can agree that I have been a very good Dad this year. Despite the numerous long talks, assorted life lessons, necessary groundings, occasional suspensions of your allowance and the periodic repossessions of your assorted electronic gadgetry (Nintendo DS, IPOD, Wii, etc.) I think it's been a pretty 12 months. It was your Mother that instituted the mandatory disconnect to friends via cell, text and internet after 11:00 pm and during church. Granted, I'm sorry about showing up at your school, shouting your name from the parking lot wearing plaid golf pants, a Hawaiian shirt and my cowboy hat while blasting a Huey Lewis and the News song

from Mom's minivan. But that was an isolated incident that I hope can be forgiven.

As much as I have appreciated the amount of thought and effort that have gone into past Father's Day gifts such as the bird house, dried fruit humidifier and the chore coupon book, it's my pleasure to provide you with an assortment of gift ideas that will make this a true "Honor thy Father" day.

1) Let me sit in the back of our Chevy Tahoe on the next family road trip and watch a movie of my choice. You will need to convince your mother to drive. She shouldn't mind though, considering how critical she is of my driving. I can't imagine a more enjoyable way to spend two hours in the car than by putting on a set of head phones while curled up in the backseat with a blanket, watching a good action flick like Scorpian King, Fast Five or Rundown, staring my favorite actor, The Rock. Now you may need to occupy yourself during my PG 13 Rock film festival, but be thankful times have changed, because when I was a kid, we had to play "I Spy," the alphabet game or read a book on every car ride. The olden days.

2) On the weekends, don't make fun of me if I want to wear a tank top and cut off jeans while working in the yard. I know, I know, I'm not the ripped "20 something" guy I once was, but it's my house. Maybe I do have hair growing out of unsightly places, but since I'm both the gardener and the car wash attendant, I should be able to wear whatever is comfortable. Be glad I keep my shirt on.

3) One day a week let me have control of the Comcast cable digital music channel. If my head doesn't explode listening to Hannah Montana and the Jonas Brothers then your head won't explode listing to Journey and Def Leppard. "Lovin' Touchin' Squeezin'" and "Pour Some Sugar on Me" are classics in the rock world, my Disney Channel loving friends.

4) Since I make your lunches every day for school, how about making my lunch one weekend day a month? I would love a peanut butter and mayonnaise sandwich or a ham and grape jelly quasadilla. Heck, I don't care if you give me a left over tuna casserole sandwich with tapioca pudding and a cheese stick. It's all about the effort you put into it. I also think you'll have a new appreciation of how hard it is for me to come up with healthy and appetizing lunches.

5) Give me just one uninterrupted day of using the bathroom. How many times do I just get situated on the commode when someone screams..."DAD," "DADDY," or, "FATHER," I need you right now! I can't so much as crack a magazine before the house paging system goes off, requesting my assistance, attention or response to some minor/major situation.

6) Finally, because I coach SRVGAL softball, Mustang Soccer, volunteer at school and the SPCA, help sell Girl Scout cookies, assist with homework and attend every imaginable show/ production/activity, how about not giving me attitude or grief if I want to play softball, go to the gym, bowl or, heaven forbid, want to play a round of golf with my friends on the weekend. The world won't come to an end if Daddy isn't around for a couple of hours.

That's my list and it won't cost either of you a dime. Thank you for your consideration.
Sincerely,
Dad

I have two wonderful daughters who I love more than life itself. I treasure every moment being their dad. However, if they were to ask themselves, "What would Dad really like this Father's

Day?" they would have already taken the first step in giving me the perfect gift. My reaction will far exceed their expectations. I'm speaking for the greater Dad population when I say, "It's truly not about the gift but the love that goes into it that means the most." Just work with us a little.

IV

SUMMER DAZE

Summer fun and summer vacations are another childhood memory that we try and recreate for our children. I grew up on Dalma Drive in Mountain View, California. It was a blue collar neighborhood filled with alot of kids from colorful families. Remembering that there were a lot fewer electronic stimulants, like none, meant we had to rely on each other and our imaginations for entertainment during our days and hours of free time. Our Play Station was Kick Fall, our X Box was Hide and Seek and our Wii was Kick the Can, Jump the River or Freeze Tag. As a family, we loved traveling and we try to travel as much as possible now. I should probably state that while we love traveling by plane, we are not so fond of the car. My parents subjected my younger sister and me to horrendous cross country road trips armed only with books and a deck of cards. This is a family ritual that I would never subject my daughters to even with all the modern day car traveling amenities we never had such as iPods, portable DVD players and laptops.

20 Summer Vacations
Adventures and Misadventures of my Childhood Summers

When I think of the summer vacations of my youth, the magic always started at 3:00 pm on June 8th. That was the last day of school. Back in the olden days the school year was always September 8th to June 8th—no exceptions. By some cosmic glitch in the calendar of the sun, those days never fell on a weekend so we could religiously schedule those dates into our 12 year PDA (if we had one back then) starting in Kindergarten. When the final bell rang, the chains of academia broke loose and freedom rained on the youthful masses. A heard of mating bison couldn't have stopped me from busting through the door of my classroom into a world of staying up late, sleeping in and no responsibilities. Of course me and every other kid in my neighborhood usually waited until June 10th before uttering the inevitable phrase, "Mom I'm bored, there's nothing to do."

The best part of summer is no school, no tests and no homework.
—Charlie L. age 9

June also meant the conclusion of the little league baseball season. Little league was for ages 9-12, before the days of minors, majors, minors majors and Senior Major Minors. The number of boys that continued playing organized summer league baseball dropped off significantly as they got older, as many gave it up in favor of summer jobs, year round commitments to other sports or to become stoners, but everyone played little league. In our town, every little leaguer still has delusional aspirations of playing pro ball. Our McKelvey Park had a snack bar, PA announcer's booth and a home run fence. If you could "park one" over the fence, you were a stud. My last year of little league, Jay Hines hit 15 bombs in an 18-game season. If that happened today he would be tested for steroids or Human Growth Hormones, but in 1974 he was the king of the park. I loved the glory days of little league, probably because that's when my own baseball career peaked. When we weren't at McKelvey we were usually putting together pick up lob ball games in the streets of our neighborhood. We ate, drank and breathed baseball, and the occasional broken window was just an occupational hazard paid for out of our allowance.

> *I like everything about summer, especially playing sports and video games with my friends.*
> —Logan P., age 10

Summer nights were reserved for various forms of mayhem and mischief; namely hide and seek, door bell ditch and sleepovers. Evenings were triggered when, one by one, we were called into the house for dinner by our crazed mothers, who were crazed because they had been sweating over a hot stove for hours, due to the fact that virtually no one had central air conditioning and no one ate light or healthy. Salads were something you ate before the meatloaf, corn on the cob, bread and mashed potatoes arrived. Once the sun set, a group of a dozen or so boys and girls became children of the night and it wasn't until the old people on the block—today they're known as "empty nesters"—started to complain about the frenzied noise or their door bells being rung continuously for hours without a hint of an actual visitor, that we were finally called in for the night (unless of course we could maneuver a sleepover.) Sleepovers usually meant sleeping outside with a group of buddies in a make shift beach chair fort with no curfew. Since dad and mom rarely stayed up past Carson, this allowed us to sneak out of the backyard for a well orchestrated TP blitz on someone's house.

Summer is great because you get to hang out with your friends and you have so much freedom,
                                              —Elliot B., age 11

Another haunting memory of summer was chores. My dad liked to say, "Being out of school doesn't mean you aren't going to work, young man." To earn money, you had a list of chores to complete every week. Not sissy things, like putting away your CDs/ DVDs or turning off the computer, we had heavy lifting jobs like mowing the lawn...with a push mower, washing cars, pulling weeds, sanding the fence, scrubbing the patio and replacing the TV antenna attached to the chimney, but that last task wasn't added to my list until I was seven. I felt like a chain gang convict, doing time on Dalma Drive.

What summer was complete without the annual road trip car vacation? Name a kid who doesn't enjoy being trapped in the back seat of a car for hours on end with warm air blasting into their face, as his dad winds his way through a series of hairpin mountain passes, with his mom making him eat homemade tuna sandwiches to avoid stopping. I experienced more motion sickness in the back of Dad's Buick than the crab fishermen do on *Deadliest Catch* during a storm with thirty foot swells.

These trips from hell (and I don't think Satan even takes his kids on long car trips) were topped only when we got a car with air conditioning, whereby we were forced to inhale secondhand cigarette smoke for eight hours a day from two parents each with a pack-a-day habit. Coal miners have cleaner lungs than my sister and me. The trip was only worth the pain if we stayed in a hotel with a swimming pool. Back then I dreamt of living in a Holiday Inn with an attached Denny's restaurant. Visiting relatives was always a jip because we didn't get to eat out or swim. Boy I loved a good chicken fried steak and a spritz.

The best part of summer is taking cool vacations with your family.

—Austin C., age 12

Now as I stare at my computer screen or make a sales call in the late afternoon of another hot summer day, I still have flashbacks of sun burns (Coppertone is not sun screen) from a day at Santa Cruz, building a fort in the backyard, waiting for darkness at the drive in, bleacher seats at an A's game and neighborhood pool parties.

My kids wish adults got work off for the summer and frankly, so do I. Reality is we don't, but I do take pleasure knowing that they are swimming, at day camps or enjoying a play date with one of their friends.

Summers are a time of joy for kids, and although the circumstances may be different than mine I'll try to ensure that they have as much fun as I did. Hopefully they'll treasure the adventures or misadventures they encounter along the way.

21 Sizzling Summers
Now and Then

When I reflect back on the sizzling summers of my youth I've come to appreciate that it was a euphoric period of time for anyone who had just been released from the shackles of structured education. However, it was a dramatically different time from the PC summers our children experience today. Granted, there is an underlying truth in the saying, "the older I get, the better I was," when it comes to everything from sports to romance. Yet I have nothing but the fondest memories of growing up when all we had to rely on was our imagination and innovation to fuel countless adventures (both good and bad) during the dog days of summer. So, given the many pleasure filled memories that most of us cherish, why do we as parents feel the need to over schedule, over commit and micro manage how our children spend their free time? Has the world gotten so crazy that we can't just let our kids run free (to a certain degree) for the summer? Why do we feel the need to live their lives for them with a planned daily summer schedule?

For starters, summers have gotten shorter. It's a fact, just ask Al Gore. Back in the 70's and 80's we had a full 12 week break from school. Thanks to global warming today's kids are lucky if they get 2-3 weeks off. Maybe it's actually 10 weeks, but considering the amount of off days they get throughout the school year, it's a wonder they get a break at all during the summer. Nobody's complaining, least of all mothers, but summer vacation used to mean 90 uninterrupted days of staying up late, sleeping in until the crack of 10 (11:30 if both parents worked) and coming up with one crazy idea after another to stave off boredom. Here is a list of sizzling summer activities I've recalled from my childhood in contrast to how today's kids spend their limited amount of free time from mid June to late August, otherwise known as Summer Vacation.

Back in the day, nobody in my neighborhood had a pool in their back yard, which meant our options were limited to either running through the sprinklers or creating our own water world theme park complete with a slip n' slide made out of 2000 Glad sandwich bags and a garden hose. Granted, we often let the water run for eight solid hours and/or killed half the lawn, but hey, it was fun and free (until your parents had to pay the water bill). Today, my two "tween" princesses think the sprinkler fairy magically waters the grass every other morning and the garden hose is for dad to use when he's too cheap to visit Sponges for a $20.00 car wash. If they can't go to "the club" or a real water park, they'll suffer through a 115 degree heat wave before they'll prance around the front yard in their bathing suits. This year I'll be introducing them to new game called, Power Wash the Patio.

When we wanted to play with our friends, we jumped on our bikes and rode to someone's house to see if they were home. My parents wouldn't even let me use the phone to call first, thinking we needed the exercise, fresh air and another way to kill 20 minutes. It didn't matter how many blocks, miles or cities away a friend might live even if we had to ride across a freeway, over train tracks or through a prison chain gang. Having a bike meant you had a mode of transportation to get from point A (home) to point B (not home). I'm almost certain that if we did some type of historical traffic study, experts would find that today's drivers aren't any worse than the drivers of yesteryear. So why do we feel the need to drive our kids everywhere when gas will soon be $23.00 per gallon? I finally put a stop to being a weekend chauffer when my kids wanted a car ride to the house next door.

Neighborhood pick-up games were common place on our block. Everyday we would go door to door to round up enough kids to play Kickball, Over the Line or Jump the River. We even made up games like Water Balloon Dodge Ball. I can remember when my parents simply said, "Be home before dark," just assuming we were somewhere safe in the neighborhood. Today, most of us won't let our kids venture out any further than the front yard unless they have a cell phone and a GPS chip implanted in their shoulder. In another year or two, kids won't even have to leave their house. Instead they'll simply text message each other with instructions on how to access a predetermined web based hide-and-go-seek computer game. Oh wait...that's already happening.

It wasn't a sizzling summer without a few trips to the drive-in. Our family would pile into the station wagon and pull into the outdoor movie theater right around dusk. For those of you under 30, a station wagon was the original SUV. We always found a spot somewhere between the screen and the snack bar/bathroom. Our vehicle was loaded with pillows, blankets, home made popcorn (Jiffy Pop of course) and an Igloo cooler full of real Coke~a~Cola (before diet, decaf or Cherry flavored). My sisters and I played on the cheap playground equipment until it was dark enough for the screen to come to life. Sound could be heard crackling out of the metal audio speakers we hung on the driver's side window rolled exactly ¾ the way up. Of course no one in the car could see very well, the sound was awful, the windows fogged, it was either too hot or too cold, and if we brought friends, there was never enough room. Those were good times. It was usually more educational and stimulating to watch the teenage couples in the adjacent cars. Their action was usually rated NC-17 and much better than the movie being shown. Today, kids have portable DVD players already in their cars. Any trip that lasts over an hour is a rolling drive-in theatre, complete with head sets and a library of recently released flicks. I once got a ticket for tailgating a car because we were trying to watch their movie. True story.

My buddies and I were also big fans of attending summertime Giants and A's baseball games whenever we could talk someone's dad into taking us. No one complained that we were sitting in the bleachers and that the wind chill factor made it 10 degrees below freezing during a night game at Candlestick. We just put on three jackets and wore socks on our hands. Today, thanks to my friends with corporate season tickets, my kids have been able to enjoy games from the very best field level seats and luxury boxes. They've even gotten the Rock Star treatment when they sat in the A's Diamond Level (thanks to a very generous co-worker) but that experience may have ruined my daughters for life. They're officially ball park snobs who will never sit in the upper deck again.

Other memorable sizzling summer experiences from my youth included outdoor sleepovers in homemade forts, setting off firecrackers for the 4th of July, weekdays spent at the local Park and Rec. department, sunburns at the beach, the insufferable road trips in the family car and a heartbreaking summer crush or two. It's a shame to think that our kids won't get to embrace the simple life experiences we had because the world has become so complicated, and we've reduced their free time and freedom. Most kids today are overcommitted with scheduled activities such as swim team, summer school, camps (church, scout, music, sport, cheerleading or science), tutoring, extended baseball/ softball/soccer seasons and, of course, the all inclusive, tropical destination, family vacation. We can only hope that our little angels will create unique ways to create their own childhood memories of Sizzling Summers.

22 A Trip to the Moon
The Ultimate Summer Vacation

July is the month when a lot of families take their summer vacations. Economics aside, most American's set aside enough disposable income to allow mom, dad and the 2.5 children (this is a national average and not meant to imply that a majority of American families consist of a least one height impaired little person) will travel vast distances to a pre-destined destination for the traditional summer vacation. With July 20th being the 40th anniversary of the Apollo 11 Lunar Mission and man's first steps on the moon, it was inevitable that I would consider the moon as a summer vacation option for my family. Imaging that interplanetary travel is a possibility (if you have crazy mad cash), the moon seems like the perfect place to spend a couple of weeks this summer. During our annual "summer vacation family caucus" this past March, I desperately tried to rally the support of my family. The competition was Wally World. My campaign slogan was "The Moon: an out of this world vacation experience." I should be in advertising instead of commercial real estate. Although I lost the popular vote, 3-1, I possessed an extra three (sympathy) votes because I spent a week at my in-laws' house in Michigan last summer. Consequently, I ended up pulling out an upset victory, 4-3. With just T- minus four months until lift off, I would need to act fast to get everything ready for our big trip.

The moon is approximately 234,608 miles from earth. If we chose to travel by traditional Apollo space capsule, the trip would take approximately 75 hours (3.3 days) each way. That's like driving to Dallas, Texas or Vancouver, Canada. If there was a galactic highway allowing families to drive to the moon using a minivan, SUV or pop-up camper, the trip would take about 3,351.54 hours (assuming you were traveling at approximately 70 miles per hour). Assuming my math is correct, that would be 139 days just to get there. That's 278 days round trip before we even factor in time for an occasional potty stop. If we're going to spend that much time in the car, we're going to want the stay on the moon at least two weeks. Now we're looking at being gone almost a year. That's crazy—we'd miss Mustang soccer season. Needless to say, rocketship would be the way to go.

The first thing the family is going to do is sign-up for some type of astronaut training. I initially wondered if it might be offered as an enrichment program at the kid's school. It wasn't, but we did enjoy the Irish River Dancing classes. Disappointingly, it also wasn't offered at any of the local community colleges, which really surprised me because I remember junior colleges offering every slacker course imaginable to boost my GPA. Don't judge me, it got me into a four year university. Fortunately, Google helped me finally find a beginning space travel course on-line at *www.lunacy.com.* Coincidently, the website also offered discount prices on space suits, Tang, catheters and space food sticks. The meat salad paste is actually quite delicious.

Once we are "astronaut ready," we'll have to book a flight on the next space shuttle heading to the moon. I'll check Priceline and Travel Zoo, but I'm guessing round trip passage to the moon will run me about $800,000 per person or $3,200,000 for the four of us. Maybe I can get it down if we bring our own food and skip buying the shuttle headsets. Of course, we will have to get everyone to Cape Canaveral, so add an additional $1,800. Wow, this is getting pricey. If the Government really wanted to balance the budget and rid the country of its national debt, President Obama would get NASA's space travel program up and running soon. There's been talk for years about allowing the average civilian (with enough crazy mad cash) a chance to buy a ride on the space shuttle for an orbit or two around earth. Once the economy picks up, (think second dot-com boom or another real estate run-up), that will be a money making goldmine.

There's no doubt that a mission to the moon would be incredibly exciting. Just the take-off alone would be cooler than hanging out with the Kardashian family. The space shuttle is launched from a vertical position with thrust provided by two solid rocket boosters and three main engines. At liftoff, both thrusters and all three main engines are working. The total thrust at launch is almost 7.8 million pounds. To achieve orbit, the shuttle must accelerate from zero to a speed of almost 28,968 kilometers per hour. After about two minutes, when the shuttle is approximately 28 miles high, the propellant in the two main boosters is exhausted and the booster casings are jettisoned. The closest you can get to that kind of rush is being strapped naked to the top of a motor home doing 80 mph down Interstate 5 during a thunderstorm. So I've heard.

Assuming we get off the ground without any of those pesky weather delays, which space missions always seem to encounter, we should be traveling about 17,500 miles per hour while in orbit. Knowing that our view of the earth will be spectacular, eventually that novelty will wear off, probably after about 10 minutes, knowing my kids. We could always watch a movie, but I probably wouldn't recommend *Apollo 13* (starring Tom Hanks) or *Armageddon* (starring Bruce Willis). The subject matter might be questionable. If only we could make a stop at the Space Station or the Hubble Telescope. I'm not entirely certain there isn't a Starbucks in our galaxy somewhere. Think about it, STARBUCKs. We all get what the "buck$" part is referencing. Regardless how families travel (covered wagon, train, car or space ship) or where they are headed (mountains, beach, Disneyland or the Milky Way Galaxy), the same cliché phrases will inevitably be heard coming from the back seat. "How much longer?", "Are we there yet?", "I'm bored," "Tell him/her to stop touching me," "I have to go to the bathroom," and my favorite, "Daddy stop using naughty words." After any type of family vacation, I'm usually ready to use the Abu Ghraib waterboard form of punishment to get my kids back into compliance.

Once we arrive and touch down on the moon's surface, I hope the kids aren't disappointed. If memory serves me correctly, there isn't a whole lot to do up there other than that whole "anti-gravity, jump-around" thing. I recall seeing Alan Shepard playing golf on the moon during Apollo 14's 1971 mission, but my daughters hate golf and there's no way the wife will let me get a round in on my own. Maybe we could rent the moon buggy that the Apollo 17 crew left behind in 1972 and do some sightseeing. A moon buggy is very similar to a dune buggy, but come to think of it, if they have dune buggy rentals in the deserts of So Cal, do we really need to go to the moon just for a buggy ride? Truth be told, being on the moon would be similar to staying at a crappy, pool-less resort in the middle of Nevada, Arizona or Utah during the dead of winter. It's essentially desolate, cold and boring, but the view of Earth would be cool (for about 10 minutes). The more I think about this planetary excursion, the more reasons I'm finding not to go. Maybe Wally World wouldn't be so bad after all.

As I weigh the expense, preparation, travel time, accommodations, lack of amenities and potential explosion at reentry to Earth's atmosphere, I think it's time to abort the mission. I have the utmost respect and admiration for the dedicated men and women that have shaped our country's space program. Neil Armstrong's famous quote, "One small step for man, one giant leap for mankind," is almost poetic in its magnitude. As Major General Charles Bolden takes over the NASA space agency, he has a lot of work to do for America to remain a leader in science and technology through space exploration. Hopefully, we'll get to see the successful accomplishment of President Obama's goal of returning a man to the moon by 2020. Who knows, maybe it will be one of my daughters. If so, I hope she'll send me a post-card that reads: Dear Dad, Wish you were here!

23 June Swoon

I have always loved the month of June. The sun is out and the temperatures are consistently warm in this region. The daylight hours are peaking as we near the summer solstice (June 15th-26th) and summer officially begins June 21st. People tend to spend more time outside gardening, going to ballgames or just taking in a leisurely stroll. Around the neighborhood, families are BBQing, washing cars and the kids are playing in their yards or at the pool. There is somewhat of a buzz of excitement in the air as the school year ends and summer vacations begin. I associate so many good memories from my youth with the month of June that it may in fact be my favorite month of the year.

Baseball's June Swoon: The term June Swoon typically refers to a professional baseball team that starts the season off extremely hot and then cools down come the start of summer. For almost my entire life, I watched the San Francisco Giants experience some type of swoon, not always in June, but at various stages of the season. There were even a few years when they were out of the division race by June. That was until last year, baby! El Gigantes stayed just close enough in the hunt during the regular season to peak at the right time and run the table in the National League playoffs and World Series. To experience the excitement of my home town team becoming World Champions was a boyhood dream come true. I only regret that my dad wasn't alive to see it as a shared love for the Giants was a strong, common bond between us.

June Weddings: Historically, June has always been the most popular month for weddings. That is where the term "June Bride" comes from. The month of June derives its name from Juno, the

Roman goddess of marriage. It was anciently thought that couples who married in June would be blessed with prosperity and happiness. Yea, right! There haven't been any studies done that I'm aware of, but my guess is just as many couples end up in divorce court who were married in June as any other month of the year. However, I do love June weddings. Where else can a suburban man take his wife to an elegant show, dinner and dancing, all for the cost of a crock pot or wok? I truly don't mind getting all gussied-up, sitting through a ceremony that would cure a bad case of insomnia, just to get to the open bar. What wedding is complete with unrealistic nuptials, bad music and an odd assortment of boorish friends and dysfunctional family members? It's all good, as long as the bride's family didn't cut-costs on the food. Eating a wedding cake made by Buddy "The Cake Boss" is on my bucket list. Granted, there are usually a few self-indulgent toasts throughout the festivities, but once I get my dance floor groove on, it's "Party-Time." My wife loves it when I break out *The Running Man*, *Mr. Roboto* or the *Cabbage Patch* dance moves. MC Hammer's got nothing on me.

School gets Out in June: As the master showman, Alice Cooper once sang, "Schools Out for Summer!" Although in 1972, when that song was number one on Billboard's chart, Alice was an androgynous, make-up wearing, boa constrictor toting, certifiable creepy guy that scared the snot out of me. Growing up, the last day of school ranked right up there with Christmas and my birthday as far as day's I loved the most. Our last day was always June 8th, which meant three uninterrupted months of blissful chillaxing. The last day of school was often celebrated with water balloon fights, milkshakes, doorbell ditch and an over-night sleep out in the backyard with my bestest buddies. Granted, we had things to do throughout the summer, but nothing like the overloaded schedules our kids now keep. No wonder why every nine year old in Danville has an iPhone. They need to text their peeps to coordinate carpools and manage their swim/cheer/baseball/soccer/lacrosse and camp schedules.

Father's Day is in June: Granted Father's Day is not as grand a celebration as Mother's Day, but I'm not complaining. While Mother's day is really an entire weekend of pomp and circumstance filled with expensive dinners, formal brunches, elegant flower arrangements, Hallmark greeting cards, elaborate gifts (preferably jewelry), a lot of pampering, compliments and several hours of alone time, dads do typically get to pick the dinner menu on our special day (assuming it's approved by our wives). I, myself, am a big fan of the homemade cards, paper-mache office supplies and burnt toast served in bed with a soggy newspaper. All kidding aside, as a child I looked forward to Father's Day as a way of putting my dad up on a pedestal and letting him know how much I appreciated everything he did for us as a family. Now, as a father, I enjoy this annual day of heartfelt adulation. Being a dad is hard work, and as gratifying as it is, Father's Day is always very enjoyable.

Summer Vacations: It didn't matter if we were driving cross country (an agonizing form of incarceration and torture as a child) or just heading to the Santa Cruz beach for a few days, summer vacations were the best. Back when driving was an economical alternative to flying, the family vacation road trip was how virtually every family started their summer vacation. Now, when most SUVs get three gallons per mile and there's a chance we could be paying $6.00 per gallon, air travel seems darn right affordable. As a kid, summer vacations often meant visiting family or friends. My parents apparently enjoyed the Bed and Breakfast ambiance of someone else's house, even if we only went across town. Unfortunately, living in an affluent community often dictates that you vacation in the Hawaiian Islands, the mountains of Jackson Hole, Wyoming or the theme parks of Orlando, Florida. Sadly, given the economy, my children may have to settle for the Osage Theme Park of Danville, with the exclusive five star camping accommodations of our very own backyard. I hope my HOA allows campfires.

On a side note, *National Lampoon's Family Vacation* is a must have for any serious movie collector. Released in June of 1983, this brilliant madcap misadventure chronicles the Griswold family's cross-country road trip to the Wally World theme park. Suffice it to say, the cross country car trip proves to be much more arduous than the Griswold's ever anticipated, not unlike my highly anticipated drive-in movie date with the lovely, Sandy Besthorn, to see the movie when it was first released. Let's just say that Miss Besthorn was much more interested in the Academy Award worthy acting of Chevy Chase, than she was the smooth moves of one, Mike Copeland. Sadly, the virtually obsolete drive-in theaters were functionally terrible, but socially (and romantically) a wonderful summer time diversion.

As we enter June, the coolest month of the year (cool like awesome, not cool like put a jacket on), it's time to kick-back in our hammocks and soak up the good vibrations (A song released by the Beach Boys in June of 1966). June Swoons are something to be embraced (think camping), not dreaded (potential air condition breakdown). June is the start of all of the summertime rituals; baseball, weddings, and family vacations, to name just a few. Just don't forget Father's Day (June 19th), because if Dad's not happy, it could be a long summer... starting in June.

24 The Last Days of Summer
Creative ways to Wrap-up the Kids' Summer Vacation

The last days of summer can have a dramatically different meaning to kids and their parents. For kids, each remaining day appears to be racing by at the speed of sound, seemingly over before they start. Just about the time they roll out of bed it's time to say goodnight again. For us parents, the day just never seems to end. It's not unusual to hear our little ones say, "I'm bored" at the breakfast table and, "What are we doing tomorrow?" at bedtime. Each day can feel like an eternity as we try and fill-up their last days of vacation with fun and memorable activities.

Needless to say, the last days of summer are a bittersweet time for both kids and parents. Giving up freedom for structure can be both good and bad. I know my girls don't want to give up the lazy days of summer, but they are getting anxious to reacquaint with their friends, find out what teachers they have and see what everyone is wearing with the latest back-to-school fashions. At the same time, my wife and I will miss the relaxed schedule-free atmosphere around the house. There's a big difference between letting them gradually roll out of bed mid-morning and my 6:15 am wake up call, more commonly known as me screaming, "Get' Up Now!" Bedtimes, in early August, aren't as rigidly enforced as they are in late August. During the school year we can be heard, repeatedly saying, "Go to bed, now!" "Turn off that TV, right now!" and, "Your homework better be done." The transition also includes sayings such as, "No, you can't have a sleepover tonight," "Hurry up, soccer practice starts in five minutes," "Do you think we like yelling?" and of course, "Quit whining, you're giving mommy a headache."

So, knowing that the last days of summer are supposed to be a fun and joyous time, let's all relax and enjoy it. There's still time for a few sleepovers, some relaxing pool time, catching an A's or Giants game or perhaps organizing a neighborhood BBQ. Freaking out at the end of summer is natural for kids, but maybe the following ideas can lessen the stress for us parents.

THE DAY TRIP Leave in the morning and be home by dinner. By the last days of summer a lot of parents are plumb out of ways to entertain their kids. For the most part, the family vacation is over, the kids have grown gills from 10 weeks of swimming and the thought of the little devils entertaining themselves for more than an hour conjures up visions of a trip to the emergency room or a visit from the police department. Local points of interest that are within a relatively short drive can be a day full-o-fun. The Santa Cruz Beach Boardwalk, Six Flags Discovery Kingdom, Jelly Belly Factory, Mt. Diablo, the U.S.S. Hornet, Roaring Camp, Winchester Mystery House or Alcatraz are all wonderful local day trip destinations. "What if the kids misbehave? you ask. Threaten to leave them on "The Rock," or tell them they'll be having a sleep over with Sarah Winchester...at her house. That should snap them back into line real fast and allow you to enjoy the day.

BACK TO SCHOOL SHOPPING It doesn't have to be as unpleasant as a root canal. Granted, back-to-school clothes shopping can be demanding, fatiguing and downright hostile because when you get right down to it, what kid past the age of eight wants to spend the day with mom roaming the isles of Liberty House, looking for the trendy yet practical outfits? Kids either don't care or care too much about what they're wearing or what other kids will be wearing. Parents just want them to wear what we've bought more than once. My advice is to team up with another family and break the day up into 1-2 hour bop and shop sessions. There's the shoes session, the clothes session, the supplies session and the attitude session (award them for good behavior by ending the day with a movie or iTunes gift card). Toss in lunch at McDonald's and you will feel both McHappy and McProductive.

BACKYARD CAMPING All the comforts of home because it is home. If you can't get to Yosemite, Big Basin or Lake Del Valle, the next best place to camp is in the backyard. Set-up the tent, lay out the sleeping bags and spray on the bug repellent. Just check your Homeowners Association bylaws because there may be something against building a "Burning Man" bonfire. The good news is, at Camp Backyard-O-Fun you won't very often see hungry bears, rabid raccoons or naked and intoxicated Dead Heads. The campgrounds are fully equipped with running water (backyard hose), cooking access (Weber Propane BBQ) and latrines with showers (assuming Dad lets the kids come in the house). Just be careful as it relates to foul weather because it can start raining at any time if someone accidently trips the sprinkler controller.

TV AND ELECTRONICS REHAB The first step is admitting there's a problem. In this electronic age where anything you want or need is just a click away, our kids are programmed from a very young age to rely on television and electronic gadgetry for entertainment and education. Before we had the internet, we used a dictionary or encyclopedia to look things up. Sometimes, if we were, desperate we even resorted to asking Grandpa. Today's kids get impatient when their connection is too slow or if they only have 168 channels to choose from. It's addicting when you have such easy access to Wii, PS2, Gameboys, iPads, iPods, iTouch, Kindals, On Demand, Pay-Per-View and a DVR. Is it any wonder our children become hooked on this stuff? Attend the meetings, find a sponsor and keep coming back. One day at a time, it works.

> *"Sleeping in and just being lazy are my favorite things to do the last couple days of summer vacation."*
> —Kat K. Age 12

CELL PHONE AND TEXTING REHAB The first step is admitting there's a problem. First it was emailing, then IM, and now every kid past the age of 10 has their own cell phone with texting capability. Besides the obvious gossip, bullying and inappropriateness that is sent out, I think we'll all agree that this heavy reliance on electronic communication is stunting the development of our childrens' social communication skills. Terms like 2 hot! SUP? STBY, OMG, RU Kidn? and What Ev aren't encouraged when giving an oral report in school. Fortunately, my daughters are too young to have their own cell phone (not that they don't ask daily) but I've heard many parents complain about their child's inability to disconnect from friends while on vacation, at church or going to the bathroom. Unfortunately, cell phones have become a necessary evil in today's society. Once kids get to middle school they inherently want to be around Mom and Dad less, which in turn requires Mom and Dad to enforce the "never out of touch" rule to ensure their safety and our sanity. Before texting became the norm, at least kids were expected to actually talk to the person on the other end of the line, but not anymore. Maybe gorilla parents aren't so envious of the whole opposable thumbs anymore knowing the headaches associated with texting. The last few days of summer can be a great time to wean our kids off their trance-like reliance to phones and texts.

During my research for this article, I talked with a lot of parents (Dana K., David C., Kent McC., Julie C., Darcy VS, Krista K., Mike M., Susan O., Tony M., Zack H., Laura K. and Ken L.)

who said the last days of summer can be a little sad. They all referenced feeling closer to their kids as the result of hanging out together for 10 weeks, the fun experiences and adventures they shared, not to mention the candid conversations that took place. Everyone agreed that the summer flew by and the kids are growing up way too fast. For the kids interviewed, the anticipation that's building is counteracted by the realization that summer is almost over again. It's safe to say we all can't wait until next summer.

I like reading the books that I like before going back to school. Once school starts you only have time to read school stuff.
—Rachel S. Age 9

I try and cram as much fun as I can into the last remaining days of summer.
—Andrew H Age 10

I get a familiar pit in my stomach during the last days of summer. A feeling similar to the one I got as a kid leading up to the first day back at school.
—Kim K. Age 34

V

IDEAS ON THE FLY

Some of my articles are carefully planned out, but most are done on the fly with an idea provided by my editor, my wife or my daughters. Rain, Wind, Pizza, Spring Cleaning, Writing, Pets, Celebrities, Facebook and Cars were all rough concepts that I crafted and tweaked while sitting in front of my computer, usually late at night. I'm the first to admit I get wordy, I ramble and I jump around a bit, but I try to have fun with the topics. What makes me smile, smirk or chuckle may have an adverse effect on readers making them shirk, grimace or retch. However, I do my best to keep the articles light and entertaining trying never to take myself or my subject matter too seriously.

25 The Vroom Principle
Guy's and Our Fascination with Fast Cars

Women have never understood guys' fascination with fast cars. From the time we're crawling around the floor in *Pampers* until we're shuffling around the house in *Depends* when we see and hear a fast car on the road, it immediately grabs our attention. In some psychology circles it's called the Vroom Principal. We as men are infatuated, intoxicated, and at times, inebriated by the combination of power and speed that these cars possess. Is it the revving of the engine, the tight lines, the lifted rear end, the aloof attitude (sounds like most of the girls I dated in college) or a combination of all these things that is so undeniably alluring that we are drawn to it like a defensive lineman to a Raider QB? We long to run our hand along the polished quarter panels; we need to look under the hood; we desire to feel the leather interior and ultimately we would give our left nut to drive it. If driving equates to a form of freedom to most men, then the appeal of a souped-up, tricked-out muscle car must be the equivalent of prison break. A guy's guy longs to slide behind the wheel of a Camero or Mustang and put the responsibilities of suburbia behind him. I want to put the pedal to the metal and "punch it," tearing off down some long, lonely, deserted road with the song *Radar Love,* blaring out of the car stereo speakers.

I, and I think I speak for most men, admit this obsession began when I was very young. I can remember pushing a *Tonka* or *Matchbox* toy car along the kitchen floor, imitating the various sounds I instinctively knew a car made. There was the peel out, the shifting of the gears as it picks up speed and the familiar sound of slamming on the brakes as it comes to a screeching halt. I can't say for sure but my first word may have been "Vroom." My favorite birthday gift in 1970 was a new set of *Hot Wheels* (miniature muscle cars), the wheel shaped garage/carrying case and the much desired, HW Fast Tract, with full loop-d-loop. In the early "olden days," long before there were video games, *Hot Wheels* were the rage for boys my age. Every guy in the cul-de-sac thought they had the coolest, fastest car and we wagered our hand printed pink slips to determine who was King of the Court. As we got older, Hot Wheels transcended into hand held remote controlled track cars which were replaced by radio controlled street cars. There was always an emphasis on bigger, faster, stronger. The highlight of my first trip to Disneyland was getting to drive the Autopia Cars in Tomorrowland. This was followed by years of banging around in bumper cars at every carnival, fair and amusement park on the West Coast. I wasn't a bumper car banger, instead I chose to pick up speed by circling the perimeter or the sheet metal track. It was all about getting behind the wheel to test the limits of mind and machine. Vroom Wannabe.

By the time I turned 16, I was ready for the real deal. My first car was a used 1966 Chevy Malibu. Being of a gold color I nicknamed it "the flame." Somehow I talked my parents into what was perceived as a sensible car, primarily because they didn't realize this bad boy was packing a 420 horsepower engine. I don't want to give anyone the impression that I was reckless or irresponsible youth, but on occasion I may have been known to exceed the posted speed limit late at night while driving down a quiet street in the commercial section of my home town. Needless to say, my high school peers were a little jealous. Vroom envy, if you get my drift.

The growing appeal of NASCAR just substantiates my Vroom hypothesis. If 32 fast cars are placed in one place, at one time, and driven around a large oval track at a high rate of speed, over and over, upwards of 100,000 men (and a few women) will pay good money while enduring the blazing sun, deafening loud engine noise, dangerously toxic exhaust fumes and poor nutritional options (beer and fried foods) to sit for hours in a semi comatose euphoric state of bliss. The fact that most of the cars are painted fancy colors and have stickers all over them explains the petrified smile observed on most of the men in attendance. Vroom orgasm. During a recent trip to Las Vegas, my friends and I visited the Las Vegas Motor Speedway to participate in the Jeff Gordon Racing Experience. For those of you unfamiliar with the ultimate adult thrill ride, it's the opportunity to take four laps with a professional driver around the famed Sin City race track, while strapped into the passenger seat of a certified NASCAR going approximately 160 miles per hour. Of course that's after signing away your life in their 40-page, no liability, full indemnity, waiver. Our hearts were pumping as we slapped high fives and suppressed the urge to puke. It was the thrill of a lifetime—Vroom Heaven.

It's not improbable to think that our forefathers had similar feelings, but before there were cars their passion was satisfied by horses. Wait, that didn't come out right. If men are empowered by speed and strength, then I'm certain the bigger and faster the horse, the more men at the turn of the century took notice, in a manly way. Henry Ford came out with the Model T in approximately 1930 so prior to that there was inevitably some guy who jumped on a monstrous wild stallion, sped through town kicking up dust and then riding off into the sunset while other men stood around and uttered the immortal phrase, "dude, check that out." Before an engine oriented word like, "Vroom," entered our vocabulary the men of yesterday probably expressed themselves with a term like, "Clippity Clop," or just, "Clippity." Maybe this love affair goes back to the Romans and Chariots or all the way back to the prehistoric days of cavemen and dinosaurs. Darwinism Vroom.

Today, the muscle cars of our youth have been replaced by sensible cars of suburbia. Almost every house in San Ramon/Danville/Alamo has the obligatory European sedan

(Mercedes, BMW, Audi or Volvo) along with the regulatory SUV or Minivan. It's not that we still don't have that need for speed, it's just been replaced by our desire for comfort and safety. It's still rare that I won't turn my head when I hear the rumble of a hemi engine with modified tail pipes, because that's what guys do. Just the way men will never understand a woman's attraction to shoe shopping, we don't expect women to understand or appreciate our fascination with fast cars. Regardless of age, race, religion, politics or education, man's genetic evolution stops one chromosome sort of being able to avoid the *Vroom Factor*.

26 The Spring Cleaning Triathlon
A House, Yard and Garage
Beautification Competition

Spring is in the air. Birds are chirping, flowers are blooming, and the President's stimulus package is stimulating. Now that we've all given up on our New Year's resolutions, or at least postponed them until after Easter, it's time to think about Spring Cleaning. Or, as I like to call it at our house, the Spring Cleaning Triathlon; the traditional time of year when we plan a major clean up of our house, yard and the garage. This is no easy chore (or collection of chores). It takes preparation, conditioning and training. Back when I was a kid, my parents took great pleasure in participating in our annual springtime neighborhood beautification project. I can still remember my mother's Spring Cleaning slogan of 1973, "Clean it and I mean it," or her 1979 catch phrase, "If it don't fit, it ain't legit," and my all-time favorite, 1985's "My louse of a spouse better clean this damn house." I think mom was mad at my dad that year. In most household's, spring cleaning still remains a necessary evil, and the month of April is when most families tackle this ritual. Everyone loves a nicely detailed automobile. Isn't spring cleaning a great opportunity to "detail" our homes? For most of us, our home is our single largest investment and considering that, given this struggling economy, we'll be spending more time around the house than ever before, so a little curb appeal wouldn't hurt.

The House: In this day and age, where everyone needs the newest, fastest and coolest of everything; where nothing is built to last, but everything is recyclable, a lot of us accumulate an excessive amount of junk around the house. Growing up, my parents insisted that during SC week, we pack up our home like we were moving across country. This fun little task allowed us to clean-out, throw-out and organize the contents of our 1,800 square foot house after 11 months of hoarding, storing and ignoring the place. It was amazing what we would find around the house as we emptied closets, rearranged furniture and unloaded cabinets and cupboards. Sadly, anything from a Santa suit to old Halloween candy to a petrified missing pet could potentially be uncovered. Discoveries like these would inevitably bring up a few interesting questions, such as...Why did Santa leave his suit at our house? Who's the chocoholic hoarding Kit Kat bars? and, What made Mr. Wiggles committ suicide? Room by room, the Copeland Clan would ascend on our targeted living space assignment with one goal—to beautificate the premises.

As parents, the term clean-up may be too simplistic a term when it comes to the thought of tackling the hard-hat excavation of our kid's bedrooms and closets. With the amount of crap kids of today can accumulate, I like to think of Spring Cleaning at our house as the great discard of accumulated worthless junk, a purging of broken and needless toys and school supplies and finally, the general discarding of out-of-style/non-fitting/butt-ugly clothes and sports apparel. If memory serves me correctly, I didn't have one tenth of the stuff my kids have lying around the house. I never had a Play Station, Wii or Nintendo DS (or even an Atari console for that matter). I didn't even know what an ipod, laptop or cell phone was. I owned one pair of sneakers, not several pairs of Heelies, flip flops and Uggs. Of course it was the 70's which might explain not having some of these things, but is it any wonder that my daughters' rooms resemble a stinky second-hand thrift store?

The Yard: Sadly, my yard isn't any better than the house. With all of the rain we've had this year I have weeds in my lawn, weeds in my shrubs, weeds in my rock beds and weeds in the cracks of my concrete/driveway. My koi pond has weeds, my horseshoe pit has weeds and my sport court has weeds. Even my beautifully manicured weed garden has weeds. Not to mention, every plant-like green thing outside of my house is overgrown to the point that my backyard looks like the Amazon rainforest or Rainforest Café. Back in the day, my Dad would rally his pre-pubescent children around him on a Saturday morning and begin by having us spray the strongest pre-emergent chemicals sold over the counter, throughout the yard. After that, he would give us access to the sharpest gardening tools in the shed for a hardy day of pruning, trimming and weeding. Finally, after a 10 minute break for lunch, he would point us in the direction of the power mower. But hey, except for an occasional tick or tremor, I turned out OK. Now those pesky OSHA restrictions and child labor laws limit our kids to raking leaves and using the hose. I can't even get the little buggers to clean up the dog poop. Is it too much to want a little curb appeal? If it wasn't against the HOA CC&Rs, this would be the perfect time of year to shape my out of control, Red Tip Photinia shrubs, into the shape of various zoo animals. Truth be told, my yard just needs a backhoe and some flowers to keep my neighbors from shaking their heads in disgust as they drive by the house and don't wave. What do I look like, an environmental horticulturalist (aka gardener)?

The Garage: The garage is the biggest and most difficult of the three Spring Cleaning Triathlon events. It takes strength, endurance and steroids (if you've got them) to get the wife's car back into its rightful spot. It is not uncommon to fill every square inch of my garage each year, much like a Public Storage unit in Richmond. Last spring, I found my next door neighbor's ping pong table, kegerator and his mother-in-law in my garage. I have no idea how any of those things got there, but I returned his mother-in-law.

A proper garage Spring Cleaning can consume an entire weekend. First thing Saturday morning, I start by removing every last item out from the garage and placing it in alphabetical order on the front lawn and driveway. I'm kidding of course. I just throw junk anywhere. Next, I like to slip into a pair of cut-off jeans, my Leonard Skynard, 1978 World Tour, muscle-T and my wife's neon green flip flops and strut around the front yard yelling out to the neighbors, "Welcome to the trailer park, my name is Earl." Once the garage is swept, power washed and deloused there's the job of returning everything to its rightful place, less the 30-50% that gets tossed, hauled, donated or sold at the big Copeland Family (Price Slashing, Inventory Reduction) Garage Sale, taking place bright and early Sunday morning. If all goes we'll, I can usually slip the little woman's oversized SUV into the garage for about a week before we start accumulating new junk and the garage becomes overrun again like a hoarder's mini storage unit.

It appears as though we'll all be forced to spend more time around the house this year (the old "staycation"), given our ever-reducing amount of disposable income. Don't you think it's time to put forth a little effort into making our homes as clean and orderly as possible? There's no denying that a triathlon is a lot of work, but the results will be rewarding and assuredly worth the effort. You don't need to win, you just need to finish. If you get the kids creatively involved, (think sport-camp theme), you'll kill two birds with one stone. I actually found two dead birds in my hall closet last year. Granted, I've already trademarked the term, The Spring Clean Triathlon, but for a small licensing fee I would be happy to send you a kit on how to get started, along with an order of SC 2009 Triathlon t-shirts in assorted colors and sizes. Think of the slogan possibilities, "Our House Will Shine in '09," "Rad Dad and The #1 Clean Team," or more to the point, "Damn Right I'm Mean—Now Quit Whining and Clean." My mom would be so proud.

27 I've Met Famous People
Chronicling My Celebrity Encounters

When I did my interview with the now very famous Captain Chesley "Sully" Sullenberger and his wife Lorrie for *Alive Magazine,* they shared with me that one of the perks of their new-found celebrity status was the opportunity to meet other Famous people such as; The President and First Lady, Barack and Michele Obama, Governor Arnold Schwarzenegger and Maria Shriver, Academy Award winning actors Michael Douglas and Sidney Poitier and famed journalist, me. If I recall correctly, the Sullenberger's found most of the famous people they came in contact with to be pretty nice and enjoyable.

In my travels as a man about town, I've met more than my share of celebrities at both the local and national level. While there is an undeniable thrill for the average suburban dweller to meet a bon-a-fide celebrity, not all celebrities are all that anxious to meet the American public. While some celebs are welcoming and appreciative, others act like they are in the midst of a prostate exam. When encountering someone famous, the experience can depend on several factors; timing (celebrities tend to be nicer in the evenings), setting (most celebrities hate being approached at the gas station, dry cleaners or in the gym), your opening line (never say, "I thought you were dead") and their receptiveness to being recognized at that moment in time (if they scream, threaten bodily harm or start dropping "F" bombs simply turn and walk away... slowly).

Famous people come in every shape, color, sex and size. We're talking about actors, musicians, athletes, newscasters, authors and politicians. I've met celebrities at fundraising galas, sporting events, concerts and a few in clubs/restaurants. I have even met a few at the grocery store. Meeting celebrities is all a matter of luck, timing, awareness and not being intimidated to say hello.

The response one gets when presented with the opportunity to meet a celebrity can vary. A celebrity can be anything from friendly and gracious to obnoxious and condescending (or rude). I have had one ask for my autograph. More on that later. A lot of the interaction comes down to how you approach Mr. or Ms. Celebrity. Depending on their celebrity status, there's a good chance that the subject has been hounded, pounded and surrounded by fans or paparazzi. Don't be offended if they come-off a little guarded and reserved. Never rush up to someone famous, but approach if/when the opportunity presents itself. An opening like, "Excuse me," "Pardon me," or "I don't mean to bother you," work so much better than, "You look so much older in person."

My daughters know that I once lived next door to Paula Abdul. They love sharing that tidbit with all of their friends. The Paula Abdul I knew was the effervescent Lakers Girls choreographer, not Paula Abdul the self-medicating, babbling nut-job on *American Idol*. Paula and I both lived with roommates in a lively apartment complex near the California State University Northridge campus. Paula was sweet, warm and vivacious. Once we got to know each other, we would get together to watch *Hill Street Blues* at her place every Thursday night. She baked cookies for my roommates and me and often gave us tickets to the Lakers games. I seriously doubt Paula would even remember me today. Her life has become tabloid fodder due to her recording and AI success. It would be interesting to run into her again, but I don't kid myself thinking she's followed my career. In all likelihood, her bodyguards would likely pound me to unconsciousness before I ever got close enough to her to shout, "Remember me?"

While living in Southern California from 1982-1985, and working for a valet car parking company at private parties, I met such celebrities as Henry "The Fonz" Winker (very cool), musician Rick James (very super freaky), LA Dodger Steve Garvey (very LA arrogant) and Heather Locklear (very Dynasty/TJ

Hooker hot). I also had a meteorology class with Genie "General Hospital" Francis. I'm pretty sure she got a better grade than I did due to our professor's unhealthy obsession with soap stars. I met Jamie Lee Curtis at the Fitness Connection, dealt cards to Dick (life of the party) Butkus and Vidal (walking dead) Sassoon at a fundraising Blackjack tournament and talked to Football legend Merlin Olson on the phone.

Athletes, by and large, are pretty cool. Sure, some of them can have egos as big as their steroid-enhanced muscles (I met former Oakland Athletic Mark McGuire at The Saddle Rack), but most are totally down to earth (I met former Oakland Raider Tim Brown at P.F. Chang's). I was introduced to former 49er and member of the Pro Football Hall of Fame, Ronnie Lott, at his first All Stars Helping Kids fundraising dinner. Ronnie comes across as pre-occupied, but that's just because he's always in networking mode. Similarly, there's Chris Mullin (High Tech Burrito) who is cordial, albeit brief and intense. I met John Elway at a Nob Hill Supermarket in Los Altos while we were in the same checkout line. John simply didn't want to be bothered, but he was polite and talkative when his dad and I struck up a conversation. Similarly, Steve Young was very cold and aloof when I met him at a CD release party for a mutual musician friend. Maybe it's a quarterback thing.

On the flip side, there's former San Francisco 49er tight end, Brent Jones who is always gregarious when anyone approaches him around Danville. Brent has a constant smile, is engaging, likeable and incredibly accommodating. The same could be said for East Bay Olympic swimmer Natalie Coughlin. She is sweet and charming.

Musicians can be the toughest to engage because they often keep vampire hours, so if you meet them during the day their body clocks can be totally out of whack. It's hard to believe that I first met Metallica front man, James Hatfield, at a Disney,

Princess on Ice show, at the Oracle Arena. When I approached him, he laughed at being recognized at such an unusual venue. Several months later, I ran into James again at a showing of Mama Mia in San Francisco. I accused him of stalking me.

James was nowhere near as cordial as Steve Perry, formerly lead singer of Journey. I met Steve at Scoma's Restaurant in Sausalito. I approached Mr. Don't Stop Believing, once his salad plate was cleared away. Perry was funny, talkative and generous with his time. I've seen new Blackhawk resident, Vince Neil of Mötley Crüe, entering the downtown Starbucks and leaving the Shell gas station, but I haven't yet had a chance to meet him yet. Hopefully I'll run into Dr. Feelgood when he returns from his Crüe Fest 2 Tour. It's just a guess, but I bet he prefers being on tour to life in the suburbs.

I played softball against MC Hammer at the Twin Creeks Softball Complex in Sunnyvale. Although I didn't get to actually meet him (bad ass bodyguards/teammates = You Can't Touch This), he was the funniest guy on the field, constantly jabbering from his short-stop position, at the plate or from the dugout. Mr. Hammertime was a good athlete and a lot of fun.

Actors are, in most cases, incredibly egotistical. It must come with reaching such a large number of people every time their work hits the screen. Rob (St. Elmo's Fire) Lowe showed up at a Sigma Chi fraternity party in 1985 and acted like he was playing the part of Jesus. It worked on the sorority girls. The part of God was eventually played by Kiefer (24) Sutherland, who I met in the VIP tent while working as a volunteer for the World Cup during a soccer match at Stanford Stadium in 1994. What a tool. Equally impressed with himself was actor, writer/director Jon (Elf, Clerks, Wedding Crashers) Favreau who I met in line for soft pretzels at Disneyland. He cut in front of me. Lucky for him, he and his family were with a Disney staff personal escort or it could've gotten ugly. I love soft pretzels.

Since living in the Tri-Valley, I've met news anchors Dennis Richmond (grocery store) and Diane Dwyer (holiday party) who are both as smooth and professional in person as they are on air. Danville must be the Mecca for sports broadcasters, because I've run into Larry Biel, Fred English, Greg Papa, Duane Kuiper and Joe Fonzie at various places around town.

All of these sportscasters are very cordial guys, but when it comes to truly great guys, it's hard to beat Mark Ibanez. Mark and I met at a fundraiser and he has been a friend ever since. Mark was the subject of one my very first personality profiles for ALIVE. Unfortunately, there were several erroneous errors in my article. Mark should have been angry, but instead he passed along valuable advice. I will always appreciate his forgiving and helpful manner, as opposed to the verbal beat down I was rightfully due.

Perhaps the best celebrity experience I've ever had is the Tri-Valley's own, John Madden. John's accomplishments as a Super Bowl winning football coach with the Oakland Raiders, commercial spokesman, author, actor, radio personality, member of the National Football League's Hall of Fame and undeniably the most popular football commentator in the history of television, has made Mr. Madden a celebrity of icon status across the country. You know you're famous when there are people earning a living impersonating you. I have had the pleasure of doing real estate business with John and his son, Mike. John is easily recognized everywhere he goes and this type of attention undoubtedly gets old, but John seems to accept it and is gracious to everyone who approaches him. It's funny how excited people get to meet him, as I was the first time, thanks in large part to John's larger than life personality and his immense "everyman" likeability factor.

With the recent passing of such celebrities as Michael Jackson, Farrah Fawcett, Ed McMahon, David Carradine and Steve

McNair, there is a tendency to pile on a certain amount of hero worship on anyone who is the least bit famous. Celebrities shouldn't be considered, or confused for, a hero. They have been graced with a talent to entertain, which allows them to be recognizable.

A hero is someone who makes sacrifices in his or her personal life for the purpose of aiding or protecting others. Heroes are our military personnel, public safety officers (police, fire and rescue workers), teachers and volunteer coaches, fundraisers, mentors and people like Captain Sullenberger, to name just a few. The only sacrifice most entertainers are prepared to make is not parking in the handicap stall when they stop to get their nails done, although most probably do.

The next time you're in position to meet a celebrity, put the star-struck adulation aside. Simply be as relaxed and respectful as you would be when meeting anyone else. As my dear old dad used to say, celebrities put their pants on just like us, one leg at a time.

Trivia question: Which celebrity asked for my autograph? That would be tennis great Brad Gilbert. We attended community college together and he was the cockiest person I had ever met in my life. His request for my autograph was his was of assuring me he would eventually become a recognized celebrity and I would live in obscurity. Thankfully Alive Magazine has proved him wrong, but his comments cut me deep at the time and still hurt today. I hate that guy.

28 I Don't Like Wind, It's too Blustery

The month of March has a reputation for being windy. I believe there's an old saying that goes, "Spring comes in like a lion and goes out like a lamb." Translation: March is usually pretty blustery and I don't much like the "blust." Wind makes me cold. It messes up my hair and it causes a massive amount of leaves to be distributed throughout my yard, giving the appearance that my landscape is not well maintained.

Considering all of the forces of nature, wind has quite a mystique and following. Wind has been the subject, or at the very least a word used in the title, for countless movies, songs and books. There must be something to this infatuation with the wind and all of its actual or perceived power.

When it comes to movies, *Gone with the Wind,* staring Clark Gable and Vivien Leigh, is by far the most recognizable film with the word "wind" in the title. However, this movie isn't about wind at all. It's a timeless classic love story centered around the time of the Civil War, but people, women mostly, think it's still cool (no pun intended) to watch these cheesy old movies on a rainy Sunday afternoon. Other "wind" titled movies include *Inherit the Wind*, based on a real-life case in 1925, two great lawyers argue the case for and against a science teacher accused of the crime of teaching Evolution and, *Blowin' in the Wind*, a documentary film examining the secret treaty that is allowing the U.S. Military to train and test its weaponry in Australia. *Windwalker* is a little gem of a film and rates as a 'must see' for anybody interested in an authentic portrayal of Native American life in the winter of 1797 and finally, *Wind,* a story set around the 1987 America's Cup yachting competition in Perth, Australia, starring Matthew Modine and, if I'm not mistaken, a post nose-job Jennifer Grey.

Songs with the word "wind" in the title include, *Ride like the Wind,* by Christopher Cross, with backing vocals by Michael McDonald; "Gonna ride like the wind/ until I'm free/ gonna ride like the wind/ blah, blah, blah." What a cool (no pun intended) easy listening tune from early 80's. Back then, I would jump on my Stingray bike, pop on my Astro Tunes portable cassette player and, well…ride like the wind around the neighborhood. Other "wind" songs you might recognize include, *Blowin' in the Wind* by Bob Dylan; "How many roads must a man walk down/ before you can call him a man/ the answer my friend is blowin' in the Wind/ the answer is blowin' the wind." *Candle in the Wind* by Sir Elton John; "Goodbye Norma Jean/ though I never knew you at all/ you had the grace to hold yourself/ while those around you fall/ like a candle in the wind," *Dust in the Wind* by 80's rockers Kansas; "I close my eyes/ only for a moment and the moment's gone/ pass before my eyes of curiosity/ all we are is Dust in the Wind." My all time favorite "wind" titled song is, *Wind Beneath My Wings* by Miss Bette Midler; "Did you ever know that you're my hero/and everything I'd like to be/ I can fly higher than an eagle/for you are the wind beneath my wings." Don't judge me.

Books with the word "wind" in the title include *The Shadow of the Wind,* by Carlos Ruiz Zafon, a coming-of-age tale of a young boy who, through the magic of a single book, finds a purpose greater than himself and a hero in a man he's never met; *Grasping the Wind,* by Andrew Ellis, provides students a unique opportunity to study an application of Chinese medical language in a clear and culturally valid context; *Wind Flowers* by Oscar Wilde, a collection of Wilde's shorter poems which include; Impression du Matin, Magdalen Walks, Athanasia, Serenade for Music, Endymion, La Bella Donna Della Mia Mente; and, *The Name of the Wind,* by Patrick Rothfuss, the tale of the magically gifted young man who grows to be the most notorious wizard his world has ever seen and his life as a fugitive after being accused of murdering a king. This last book, *The Name of the Wind*, sounds like the only "wind" titled book that won't cure insomnia. It appears to be a "Harry Potter on Steroids" type read.

I suppose if wind was an integral part of your job/vocation or hobby, you might feel differently about it than I do. If you are an accomplished yachtsman, like Dennis Conner, or a professional windsurfer, like Phil Horrocks, then wind is essential to your livelihood. Kite flyers like the wind, but I was never much of a kite runner, despite many a March day in my youth spent trying to get a kite airborne. Back in the day, my friends and I would purchase an intricate kite kit at the local drug store for a quarter. It was a light-weight, paper kite with a balsa wood cross frame. It also required the addition of a perfectly engineered knotted tail, made from an old dress shirt, to increase the lift-versus-thrust ratio.

Assuming we didn't manage to destroy the kite fabric during the assembly process, which happened way too often, our adolescent kite gang would all head out to our elementary school with a bag lunch and a ball of string to spend the day running around like lunatics in our attempt to master aeronautic acrobatics with a precision instrument that cost a quarter. When we did occasionally catch the wind just right and get our kite into a suburban jet stream, we would spend hours maneuvering our kites in the perfect wind currents as a metaphor of our youth. More times than not, our kites ended up in a tree, tangled up in the overhead power lines or smashed beyond recognition after an ill advised nose dive, reminiscent of a Kamikaze pilot.

We could've used the services of Chris Maxa, General Manager of the Kite Loft in Ocean City, Maryland. Chris is the most recognized professional kite flyer and instructor in the world. Yes, there is a Professional Kite Flyers Association (PKFA).

Whenever someone talks of "going green," energy is part of the conversation. Wind energy is not just the next big thing, but perhaps the biggest thing ever. Confronting the peril of greenhouse gases and climate change happens to be a multi-trillion-dollar business opportunity. The solar and wind energy markets, which totaled about $80 billion in 2008, are projected to nearly triple in size in 10 years, employing 2.6 million people worldwide, according to Clean Edge, a "Cleantech" research group. The payoff is a low-carbon economy and tens of thousands of new jobs. That's called "research," my friends.

Virtually everyone in the greater Bay Area is familiar with the Altamont Pass Wind Farm. The turbines form lines scattered about the hilltops, around an area of about 15 kilometers in diameter. Hundreds are visible from the highway. According to online info, there are approximately 4,900 of them, being the world's largest wind farm in terms of number of turbines. Although you can hear the whooshing from the blades from a fair distance, it is hard to get anywhere close to these high-tech windmills since there is no paved road leading to them, there are specially trained guard cows scattered throughout the hillside and the wind, not surprisingly, is very strong in that area.

Collectively, they have a capacity of 576 megawatts (MW), producing about 125 MW on average, and 1.1 terawatt-hours (TWh) yearly. I truly don't know if that's enough juice to illuminate a single nightlight for a week or all the houses in the Tri-Valley for a year. That's called "lack of research." I do, however, think these high-tech windmills look cool, positioned along the hillsides of the Altamont Pass, giving travelers something to gawk at as they head toward the popular destination spot of Manteca.

In retrospect, perhaps I've been too hard on the wind. I do like wind chimes and I suppose knowing the wind-chill factor (the temperature of windless air that would have the same effect on exposed human skin as a given combination of wind speed and air temperature) is helpful at times. Chicago is known as the

Windy City and I think Chicago is a very cool (no pun intended) place—even cooler than Manteca. However, when that wind whips off Lake Michigan, it cuts through you like a knife—a freezing cold knife.

I believe there's another saying that goes, "Women are known to change their mind like the wind changes direction," or something like that. Well if that is in fact true, then after further analysis, I, as a man, will change my mind and proclaim that wind is Cool (no pun intended). Given its unbelievable strength and power of destruction (one word: tornado) there's no reason to give *Aeolus,* the God of Wind, any reason to get all blustery on me.

29 I Wish I Was a Dog

Our family recently got a puppy. She's a very cute little Cocker Spaniel/Chihuahua mix. Her name is Ivy. She has a white fur base with maple colored spots. At 16 weeks, she weighs 3.5 lbs and is about the size of a Guinea Pig. Truth be told, she may very well be a Guinea Pig, but for the sake of my kids and this article, let's assume she is a dog: A carnivorous domesticated mammal, also known as a canine, a pooch, a hound, or mutt.

Ivy's charming disposition has blended well with our other dog (Trudy) and our two cats (Annie and Smokey). My daughters love her and even my wife and I have grown attached to the adorable little fur ball. Ivy spends her days barking at dust, wind, undetectable sounds or the subtle shift of the earth's axis. She eats everything she encounters (i.e.; dried animal poop, dead birds and discarded bathroom tissues, in addition to the gross stuff).

Our little Pit Bull wannabe loves tormenting the aforementioned household animals, in addition to pooping/peeing (wherever she pleases) and sleeping approximately 20 hours a day. That is "the life!" The closest resemblance to a dog's life that we humans can relate to is probably that of a rock star. I bet, when they're not in the studio or on tour, John Meyer, Beyonce, Bono, Eminem and Lady Gaga spend their days much the same way Ivy does. Next time someone bumps into Blackhawk resident and Motley Crue front man, Vince Neil, ask him how he spends his down time. I bet it's similar to that of a dog and if it is, I wish I was a dog (or a rock star).

After months and months of tenacious/relentless/crazed persistence, my two daughters finally wore us down (we caved in). Technically, when we made the promise that at some point in their young lives we would get them a puppy, we were secretly hoping that their other interests and activities, such as sports, school, friends, fashion, music, theater, scouting, boys, money, television and the lifelong study and practice of origami would keep them distracted until we were ready to ship them off to college.

Alas, the desire to have a furry, barking machine proved to be stronger than we anticipated and we finally acquiesced to their non-stop begging, pleading and cries of lonely desperation. When I live my next life, as a dog, I'm hopeful that my highly developed hearing will completely block out the excruciating whine of a "tween" girl begging for an iPhone, Facebook account, boy friend, extended text time or worst of all, a puppy.

Searching the local area animal shelters in hopes of finding a dog is actually quite enjoyable. We found our first dog, a terrier mix, at the SPCA in Dublin. The SPCA has a beautiful facility, qualified staff, educational classes and a very nice collection of mature adult dogs. Our area also supports other organizations such as ARF and East Bay Animal Shelter. Adopted dogs are wonderful, in large part due to their appreciative attitude being given a second chance at life. I suppose knowing that if you aren't adopted you may be chasing Frisbees in Heaven makes rescue dogs inherently grateful.

As terrific as above-referenced local agencies are, when searching for a puppy, we elected to work with the folks at the Tri-Valley Animal Rescue. Our friend, Nikki Steffens, whose family fosters dogs for the TVAR, was very helpful throughout the process. She worked with us to define what type of puppy would be best for our family, given the petting zoo atmosphere we are nurturing in our suburban home. Did I mention we've also had hamsters, rats and fish? I'm currently looking for an anaconda, a giraffe and a Ligor (a lion bred with a tiger) to qualify as Dr. Doolittle of Danville.

Once we finally identified the most appropriate dog for our family, that being a curious, rambunctious, bright, loving dwarf dog with attitude, Ivy seemed to find us. Pleasanton's weekly Farmer's Market often hosts animal adoption days so that's where we headed and that's where we found Ivy.

If I was a dog, I would like to be a German Shepherd. Not because I'm of German decent. If human heritage was the determining factor in breed, I would be an Irish Setter/English Bulldog half-blood. German Shepherd's are, by nature, protective, strong, brave and intelligent. All of those qualities are admirable if you're describing a dog or human.

Growing up, my family had a pure white German Shepherd named Snowy. I have many good memories of times spent with that dog. Summer sleep outs in the back yard, long runs getting ready for the start of football season and insightful talks about politics, religion and girls. Snowy was deep. Snowy assessed everything he came into contact with as Friend, Foe or Food. It's simplistic, but not a bad way to go about making impressions and assessments.

In Doggyland, I could scratch myself, lick myself, pee and poop wherever I wanted, drink from the gutter, pool or toilet, sniff human crotches, sniff my friend's behinds (it's like shaking hands), bark, howl or growl until my throat hurt and sleep, sleep, sleep. Did I also mention that dogs don't get married? That's right, they "hook-up." I don't judge them. In fact, I appreciate their animalistic approach to relationships. They take care of their primal instinct/physical urges and yet don't feel the need to comply with the institution of marriage.

That's not to say that if I were a dog I would forgo my fatherly duties. I would undoubtedly want to be there for the delivery of my litter and would stick around to help raise my pups, but that whole marriage thing just isn't part of dog life.

In this fantsy world, I would have a neighborhood full of female "dog friends with privileges." That is until my owners took the responsible action of having me neutered. Oh, the shame. Come to think of it, once that happened, I might settle down with a nice Collie.

History is filled with famous dogs in every form of art, athletics and literature. The painting of dogs playing poker is a masterpiece. While dog fighting makes me sick, dog racing has been around since early Egyptian times. Racing the incredibly fast and agile Greyhounds is immensely popular while watching dachshunds (aka wiener dogs) run is just delightfully amusing.

Dog actors, such as Lassie, Old Yeller, Rin Tin Tin, Toto, Benji, Air Bud and the Shaggy D.A. haven't won any Academy Awards (yet), but they have made significant contributions to some wonderful movies. There have been dogs on television going back 50 years, starting with Pete, Spanky's Pit Bull on the *Little Rascals*, Tiger, a sheep dog who lived with the *Brady Bunch*, Buck, also a sheep dog who housed with the Bundy's on *Married with Children* and finally Eddie, the cute little Jack Russell terrier on *Frasier*.

Many of us can all recall commercial pitch dogs like Loren Green's dog, Duke, chasing sticks for *Alpo* dog food. Then there was the *Taco Bell Chihuahua* and *Budweiser's Spuds Mackenzie*. There are also the always-entertaining, comic strip and cartoon dogs including *Marmaduke, Scooby Doo, Under Dog, Lady and the Tramp, Clifford the Big Red Dog, Bolt* and, of course, *Snoopy*. Snoopy was just too cool for school!

Finally, in literature, who could forget *Shiloh, White Fang* or *Cujo*? However, to truly understand dogs, take the time to read the beautifully crafted book, *The Art of Racing in the Rain*, by Garth Stein. The entire story is told in the words/thoughts of Enzo, a Golden Retriever. If you've ever wondered what a dog thinks, this book provides you with an enlightening notion.

I'm not saying everything about a dog's life is ideal. Dogs can't get a job, pay bills, drive carpool, follow politics, look for a job, invest in a 401K, Tweet on Twitter, shop, mow the lawn or dance. Who am I kidding? I don't even like to do any of those things. Dogs don't need materialistic possessions or stressful responsibilities. A dog's life is awfully darn appealing right now, especially given today's economy.

As I do believe there is a possibility of reincarnation, maybe I will be a dog in my next life. Fifty or seventy-five years from now I might be a German Shepherd guide dog, who greets people at the library or grocery store with my sight impaired human partner. My name will be Thor or Rock and I'll shake my tail and extend my paw because life is good.

30 Pizza: An American Staple

By and large, and by that I mean a large sausage, black olives and mushroom on thin crust, American's love pizza. Pizza has become an American staple, similar to bottled water, mobile phones, coffee drinks, and GPS devices. Americans spend approximately $39.8 billion on fresh and frozen pizza each year. From the chain pizza parlors such as Round Table, Pizza Hut, Straw Hat, Little Caesars, Garlex, New York, Godfather's, Domino's, Z Pizza and Papa John's, to the higher-end, local pizza establishments such as Amici's, Ascona's, Skipolini's, Gay 90's, Zachary's and California Pizza Kitchen, pizza is everywhere. Costco even sells pizza for gosh sakes. Every supermarket in the country carries a full line of frozen pizza including Totino's, Red Baron, DiGiorno, Freschetta's, Healthy Choice and Stouffer's. Pizza is big business and I, for one, contribute to the great pizza economy every chance I get.

Based on rough calculations, I have determined that in my lifetime I have consumed approximately 3. 2 tons of pizza. If you lined up every pizza I've eaten side-by-side, you could create a walking bridge from Danville to Australia. If you balled up the equivalent of just the dough and cheese base from these subject pizzas, scientists and engineers might have a reasonable cap for the BP oil leak in the Gulf of Mexico. Needless to say, I, like a majority of the American public, love pizza. My mouth waters just thinking about a piping hot pie made of a rich tomato sauce, melted mozzarella cheese, a perfectly baked crust, the right combination of garlic and herbs and a collection of delectable toppings. Whether you like a traditional cheese or pepperoni or a unique combination, such as Canadian bacon and pineapple, thick or thin crust, cheese in the dough or one that's glutton-free, the beauty of pizza is that you can get it made-to-order. If the government really wanted to reduce our country's growing deficit they would get into the pizza business. The tips alone could fund our national parks system.

Thanks to my friends at Wikipedia, I learned that pizza dates back to the 16th century, where in Naples, Italy, it was flatbread covered in a white sauce. Pizza was considered a dish for poor people and not thought of as a kitchen recipe. It was kept warm in copper cylindrical drums with false bottoms packed with charcoal from the ovens and sold on the street. Pizza made its appearance in the United States with the arrival of Italian immigrants in the late 1800's where it was sold at neighborhood cafés and grocery stores in Italian-American communities. The location of the first U.S. pizzeria is disputable, but it was believed to be in the Little Italy section of Manhattan. An entire pizza sold for five cents. The modern pizza industry was born when troops who had fought in Italy during World War II returned home with a new appreciation of the delicious treasure they had discovered. Pizzeria Uno, in Chicago, opened in late 1943.

Personally, my relationship with pizza dates back to my toddler years. I was often served Gerber's Creamed Pizza baby food from a jar. I just couldn't get enough strained pepperoni and pureed bell peppers, but I never did acquire a taste for the beer flavored formula. As a child growing up in rural Mountain View, Round Table was one of the first local pizza parlors in our area and a trip to that wonderfully edible paradise was better than any meal my mother slaved hours over. Sorry mom. To watch the pizza cooks work their craft of spinning a wad of dough in the air was magical. Occassionally, I would drop a quarter in the jukebox and play the song, *Dream Weaver*, by Gary Wright and fantasize about one day being a pizza man myself. When we didn't eat in we would bring our pizza home on a square piece of brown cardboard, covered with tin foil—that was long before the elaborate pizza boxes of today. Monday nights during the fall were a special "pizza time" at our house. My family would all sit around the huge 17-inch black and white television screen to watch an important football game between powerhouses like the Los Angeles Rams, Baltimore Colts, Houston Oilers and St. Louis Cardinals. Howard Cosell, Frank Gifford and Dandy Don Meredith would broadcast the action while we ate our triangular slices of heaven off a stand-up TV tray while guzzling RC Cola. Those were good times.

By the time I got to high school, and then on through college, pizza became as much a social networking medium as it was a meal. Pizza was our Facebook. Back in the olden days, people actually met face-to-face to talk and find out about each other. Pizza was an affordable, delectable, plentiful food source, used to nutritionally enhance a group gathering or an inaugural romantic interlude (aka, first date). You don't have to be a rocket scientist to know that if you locate a pizza joint anywhere close to a high school or college, you'll probably be printing money, (assuming the pizza you cook up doesn't taste awful). Come to think of it, we even frequented the awful tasting pizza places too, if they had a large screen television programmed to a sporting event and cold, cheap beer.

Today, as a mature adult and responsible father, I still consume pizza approximately 2.5—15.75 times during any given month. Pizza is an easy dinner decision after a long week of work. Pizza is a logical meal choice to serve at a birthday parties or when the kids have friends over to the house. Pizza is too convenient to not pick-up following a mid-week school function and how many times do we grab a pizza on the way home during a typical suburban weekend day spent racing around the greater Tri-Valley attending a variety of sporting events such as little league baseball, softball, soccer, football, lacrosse, swim or track. It's not documented anywhere, but my rough guess is that my family has celebrated 132 youth sports season ending parties at one local pizza parlor or another around the Town of Danville. If a simple slice equaled a share of restaurant stock, I would be the controlling partner of both Garlex Pizza and Primo's by now.

It's funny how we have come to rely upon something like pizza. Sadly, I can admit that I've eaten cold pizza for breakfast, heated up pizza for lunch and gone out for pizza for dinner...all in one day. Added to the traditional pizza options, there is a plethora of pizza-type products like pizza pockets, pizza rolls, pizza bagels, pizza flavored Doritos and Jamba Juice's new pizza flavored smoothie. Okay, I'm kidding about the smoothie, but obviously the pizza industry continues to thrive, and for good reason. Pizza has become an American staple.

31 Anyone Can Be a Writer

People ask me all the time (once) how I became a writer. After almost 80 magazine and newspaper articles, a book of children's bedtime stories and a screenplay, I suppose I do technically qualify to call myself a writer; however it's difficult for me to consider myself a "real" writer. When I think of "real" contemporary writers, names such as J. K. Rowling, Suzanne Collins, Stephanie Meyer, John Grisham, Buzz Bissinger and Tony Hicks come to mind. I don't kiddingly group my name with that group of illustrious Pulitzer hopefulls. I write because I enjoy it, not to pay my bills. Truth-be-told, only the elite of the writing profession make any real money. Most writers write to satisfy their creative side and since everyone has a creative side, I truly believe anyone can be a writer. Also, having a narcissistic ego doesn't hurt. Whether it's a journal, diary, poem, lyric, sonnet, story, article or a great American novel, provided one has inspiration, there's a writer inside everyone.

Inspiration can come to a writer in a variety of ways. When people occasionally (once) ask me what inspired me to start writing, I give credit where credit is due—Tony Subia. Tony sat next to me in Mrs. Krause's third grade class at Edith Landels Elementary School. One rainy winter day, Mrs. Krause read a hysterical action packed tale, that Tony had scribed, about a band of dress-wearing ninja aliens who visit earth in search of Bubblicious bubble gum to sustain their race. Cut me some slack, it was 1972 and I was nine years old. I, along with my academic peers, roared with laughter hearing this brilliantly crafted short story. If memory serves me correctly, Mark Belyan (or me) laughed so hard he wet his pants. Experiencing, firsthand, the type of reaction a brilliantly crafted story, ripe with interesting characters, plot development and subtext, can have on a group of people was intoxicating, dare I say, inspirational.

Not surprisingly, I spent the next week crafting an equally brilliant yarn of polka dancing cowboys who rescue a herd of kittens in the Wild West. My story wasn't received with the same enthusiastic vigor as Tony's eventual best seller (that boy was truly gifted), but from that point forward I have strived to pen the perfect 1,200-1,500 word masterpiece.

Writing can be therapeutic and cathartic. It's certainly cheaper than therapy. All of us living a suburban slow death tend to be bingers when it comes to our lives. We are so busy inhaling every aspect of our lives, including work, kids, travel, sports, art, electronics, entertainment, food and wine that we forget to purge. If a person were to channel their passion for a hobby or interest into a series of written words, they would be, by definition, a writer.

During high school, I eagerly signed up to be part of the MVHS *Eagle Gazette* staff. In my early attempts to be liked and accepted by everyone, I pitched an idea for a piece called *Around the Quad*. The monthly column described the various cliques on our military base feeder campus. However, I cleverly twisted the stereotypes of our richly diverse multi-cultural student body. My school chums loved it and I loved the accolades. When I moved on to Foothill Community College, and later Cal State Northridge, my literary focus was based on what I knew best—sports. My first attempt at interviewing people was for a column called *In the Locker Room*, a behind the scenes glimpse of my football teammates and other colligate athletes at CSUN. Not surprisingly, I found it to be much more creatively rewarding to humorously pick on my contemporaries' insecurities.

Upon starting my career in commercial real estate, writing proved to be a distinctive way for me to get some name recognition in an industry filled with much smarter and more talented brokers than I. Again, my sophomoric, juvenile, self-deprecating humor rang through. While my efforts weren't *Wall Street Journal* worthy, it did get me the exposure I was seeking in my market territory. As I grew older and more open-minded, my interests and articles expanded to include history, politics, human rights and religion. I'm only kidding. I kept writing ridiculously silly humor lifestyle and personality profile pieces for a variety of local papers, newsletters and magazines. Once you build-up a body of work, people take you much more seriously when you submit an article for consideration.

The coolest thing about writing was getting my rambling rants published and read. Oddly enough, it still is (see narcissistic ego comment above). A typical article takes on average about ten hours to draft, tweak, proof-read, modify and eventually final. It's not that hard if you write about what you know, if you like doing it and if you believe someone out there might share your thoughts or gain from your insights. If you've ever written a family holiday newsletters, maintained a blog or twitter excessively, you are a potential magazine writer.

ALIVE Magazine is always looking for contributions from local area residents on virtually any subject. We encourage anyone to submit a positive, fact or fiction based article for consideration to Editor-in-Chief, Eric Johnson. Who knows, you could be the next Paul Hirsch.

32 To Friend or Not to Friend
Facebooking with Childhood Friends
(with Mindy Joshua-Matthews)

Would it be overstating the obvious to say that Facebook is a modern day phenomenon? While most of us were doing "who knows what" in our college dorm rooms, Mark Zuckerberg and his buddies at Harvard developed a social networking internet sensation that would forever change the world. Facebook, simply put, is a mash-up of all things communication. From smoke signals and the telegraph to letter writing, email and instant messaging, Facebook is a revolutionary tool to connect people. The question is, do we want to connect with everyone? "Friending" someone is such a friendly thing to do, yet haven't we all occasionally regretted "friending" someone who perhaps over utilizes this medium? Childhood friends are especially susceptible to this type of temptation.

To "friend" or accept a friend invitation from…well, friends, family, neighbors, the parents of your kids' friends, fraternity/sorority brothers/sisters and attractive work associates is easy; but is it always wise to accept a friend invitation from a second grade tether-ball partner we haven't seen in thirty years? I'm all for reaching out through cyberspace, but how far does that reach need to extend? This question may best be answered by the open line banter between two childhood friends now located on opposite ends of the state. Please allow me to introduce you to my new Facebook fiend, Mindy Joshua.

Mindy: I can't believe Mike Copeland is a writer for a magazine. In school, I wasn't ever truly convinced you could read or spell.

Mike: Nice! Mindy and I have known each other for roughly 44 years, ever since we sat in little chairs around a very small table on the first day of school in Mrs. Vanderveer's kindergarten class at Edith Landels Elementary School in Mountain View. The year was 1967, when during an interactive lecture on the texture and contrast intricacies of finger painting, Mindy had an accident. Unless I'm mistaken, Mindy was still sweaty from a recess Double Dutch exhibition and I was coming off a paste high after sneaking a taste at the urging of known paste dealer, Jimmy H. (Who knew that paste was considered a gateway drug?)

Mindy: It's true. We have known each other that long. Can't the number be abbreviated using creative license or something? Mike's overactive imagination may have some of the details wrong. Mike's place in my life was mostly right next to his best friend, Jeff M., the unrequited love of my childhood. I loved Jeff's beautiful brown eyes, his thick jet black hair, his perfect jaw line and his stoic manliness. Even at six years old. I loved him, even if he never loved me. I loved him for never saying a word to me when I tinkled in my pants in Kindergarten. Come to think of it, Jeff never said anything to me, ever, but Mike did. Mike seemed so willing to be verbally smacked down. I honed the sharp knives of my wit on his naïve and totally unprepared-for-the-likes-of-me spirit, and that was the start of our friendship.

Mike: Mindy was the smartest girl in our class—in every class K through 12. Mindy's schoolyard hobby was to mentally terrorize the boys in class for their academic incompetence, yet, her verbal approval of my contributions to a class could pump up my confidence like a five time Jeopardy champion. However, whenever I displayed laziness in a subject, her cutting sarcastic wit would leave me feeling like a disgraced U.S. Congressman prone to inappropriate texting. Thank you for caring, Mindy.

Mindy: Mike was always there—in virtually every class—and naturally, I took him for granted, like only a child can do. My recollection was that we were constantly sparing. Mike and I would verbally jab and punch while the object of my affection (Jeff M.) stood by, lifeless. Now, as an adult, I don't take the dynamics of either relationship personally, but my connection with Mike was definitely more real. Jeff, however, still seems devoid of human emotion, much like a dull garden tool.

Mike: Let's fast forward. I had a great time seeing and getting reacquainted with Mindy at our 20th high school reunion, so when she didn't make (blew off) our 30 year reunion last fall, I was disappointed. When I heard that Mindy had run into our mutual friend Derek S. last September at the Mountain View Art and Wine Festival, a hometown cultural event we have all been attending for almost 40 years, I accessed Derek's FB friend list and reached out to Mindy with a "friend invitation" hoping to reconnect with a LOG (Landels Original Gangster).

Mindy: Wrong! When I found myself missing the reunion and asking myself why, I started connecting to all the friends I could find on Facebook. I got Mike's Facebook link through another mutual friend (Sharon D.) and it was I who reached out to him for a little on-line messaging banter. Apparently, he was so incredibly busy that day he apparently missed my FB friend request (or rejected it?). Yes, sadly I admit that I did also extended a friend invitation to Jeff, who accepted but rarely (never) engaged. To no one's surprise, least of all mine, he has since disbanded his Facebook profile

Mike: Still with the Jeff, Jeff, Jeff! Get over him already. Regardless who started our Facebook interaction, Mindy is a cool FB buddy. After I perused her profile, checked out a few of her family photos we began communicating. If there's a question I have about the past, I ping her and when she has time she pings me back. If we both happen to be free at the same time, we send condescending and sarcastic zingers back and forth, usually with some reference to our ancient history or old friends.

Over the last two years, I have gotten numerous friend invitations from childhood acquaintances and have accepted all of them. They are my FB friend until they do something that deems then "unfriend" worthy. If someone (Franz N. and Cheryl W.)

161

documents where they are every second of the day with an annoying FB posting, "I'm at the proctologist's office,"...unfriend. Newsflash: I don't care where you are! I also get worked up over rambling, extremist rants on politics, religion and parenting (Mark P., Terri W. and Steve C., respectively). Share something interesting or relevant, otherwise don't post. I assume that if someone does come to the realization that they have become "unfriended" by me then they can also figure out that it's because of the nauseating or boorish nonsense they've been posting.

I've never stopped to consider that people can now check to see who's been viewing their pages, not that my viewing could ever be considered stalker-ish (unless you're Jennifer Lopez in which case my attorney says I must make a public apology).

Mindy: I checked out Mike's life a little on FB and it all looked pretty normal and decent, but then Mike always was pretty normal and decent. Not terribly fancy, just solid and reliable. Mike and I traded a few friend leads and he was right about Mark's page. He is politically "out there." I'm pretty sure he didn't see me come and go from his page—he's obviously too busy as working on the Ron Paul 2012 Presidential campaign committee. Like Mike, I deplore the Facebook friend that reports on every less-than-riveting event that is going on in her life and the lives of her attractive and polite children. I know they are attractive and polite because Stacy (real name not disclosed) posts every second of their adolescent development on her Facebook page. However, now that I've "friended" her and she knows I'm paying attention, I'm confident she'll notice and be offended if I "unfriend" her. I've always liked her, but do I need her constant commentary clogging up my newsfeed? Is "unfriending" considered rude and well, unfriendly? What to do?

Mike: Facebook has opened the door for virtually anyone to track people down and reunions are a logical time to connect with childhood friends. I suppose, if you didn't want to be found, you wouldn't have a FB page. I'm relatively certain Ted Kaczynski never had one. It is scary to think that at our next high school reunion we'll be nearing 60 years old and we'll likely remember fewer and fewer of the people we went to school with thanks to old age and failing memories.

Mindy: Mike makes a good point—that is, if you don't want to be found, then don't have a FB page. Then again, you give up the ability to see if the prom queen got fat and shaves, or the varsity quarterback has a multiple personality disorder. I prefer to know these things. I decided, while tossing over the friend versus unfriend dilemma, that neither is personal. FB is not meant to be; it's just another way of communicating, something like "communication lite." If you really want to connect, then do it the old-fashioned way, via email, phone or (gasp!) in person.

Both Mindy and I agree that Facebook is likely here to stay. While I have heard about "Facebook Addiction" and "FB Burnout", most people we know appear to use the social network in moderation. Parents have an inherent responsibility to monitor their children's usage of the site. We all want to ensure that the kiddies aren't practicing some form of FB dark arts (a shameless Harry Potter reference). A recently released movie entitled *Trust,* soon to be available on Pay Per View or DVD rental, is a wake-up call to all parents on the harmful aspects of our children utilizing the internet as an often times anonymous form of communication. As for adults and friends from our childhood, I wonder how many elementary school friends have tried to friend Mark Zuckerberg, Eduardo Saverin, Dustin Moskovitz, Chris Hughes or the Winklevoss twins? Good luck with that!

33 Rain, Rain, Go(ne) Away

Just the other day, I was listing to my favorite song, *It Will Rain* by Bruno Mars (from my favorite movie, Breaking Dawn) when I realized that we are in need of some rain. It has been said that I have a keen sense of the obvious. You don't need to be a meteorologist, although I would make a totally awesome meteorologist, to know that winter = rain and we haven't had much precipitation in these here parts. If I'm not mistaken, at the time I penned this article, it had rained but once since Thanksgiving and only twice since the Fourth of July, or something like that. We desperately need that water like substance that falls from the sky to make our grass green, to fill our lakes and streams, to hydrate our crops (especially the medicinal crops that are so popular and profitable) and to wash my car. Yea, I don't pay for car washes during the rainy season and my ride is filthy right now.

For the Al Gore Global Warming conspiracy theorists, I will admit that this winter in the Bay Area it has felt more like a dry summer in Texas, except that the temperatures have certainly been winter cold during the nights and mornings. The San Francisco Forty-Niner footsy flannel pajamas I received at Hanukah have been getting a real work out this season, while I haven't even opened the "Mitt for President" umbrella I got for Christmas. As kids, my mom taught us songs such as *Raindrops Keep Falling on My Head,* by BJ Thomas, *Rainy Days and Mondays* by the Carpenters and *Kentucky Rain* by Elvis Presley. Singers and songwriters have always had a love affair with rain so wouldn't it be nice if one of the contestants on American Idol or The Voice would bust-out a soggy song to woo Zeus the Lord of the Sky and the God of Rain?

Many Native American cultures have been known for their rain dances. A rain dance is one of the most famous ceremonial dances out of a long line of choreographed movements that once held the responsibility of appealing to the various Native American Gods. The rain dance, in particular, was a way to gain favor and summon rain to come down and nourish the crops that would serve as sustenance for a specific tribe. It has been documented that tribes such as the Osage and Quapaw actually tracked the weather patterns and then performed the dances as a form of trade when their was a higher likelihood that it would bring the desired results. The term, "Rain Dance," today refers to any ceremonial action taken to correct a hardware problem with the expectation that nothing will be accomplished.

Please allow me to share with you a wonderful poem by Shel Silverstein, a very talented man and poet, entitled appropriately, *Rain.*

I opened my eyes
And looked up at the rain,
And it dripped in my head
And flowed into my brain,
And all that I hear as I lie in my bed
Is the slishity-slosh of the rain in my head.

I step very softly,
I walk very slow,
I can't do a handstand
I might overflow,
So pardon the wild crazy thing I just said
I'm just not the same since there's rain in my head.

When you think of rain, one can't help but think of Gene Kelly, a very talented song and dance man of the 40s and 50s, who starred in the popular movie, *Singing in the Rain,* along with Donald O'Connor and Debbie Reynolds. More recently, the cast of Glee did a musical mash up of *Singing in the Rain* and *Umbrella,* by Rihanna. In typical Glee fashion, it was an amazing production, featuring water raining down on the cast in the McKinley High School theatre. If not for the unrealistic water works extravaganza, given the budget public schools have for the arts in the year 2012, I loved it. Conversely, I found the movie, *Purple Rain* written by, directed by and starring Prince, didn't actually feature a purple colored rain. There was a lot of cool singing and dancing by a freaky little guy who wore a lot of purple outfits, but alas, no precipitation. Dustin Hoffman turned in an incredible performance as an autistic-savant in *Rain Man.* He was a wiz with numbers and a fan of Judge Wopner, but again—no rain.

At the risk of insulting any of my seven or eight loyal readers, most of you probably know that rain also makes snow. Am I assuming too much? As bad as the people of Northern California need the sky to open up and water droplets to pour down on us, the folks living in the Sierra Nevada Mountains need snow for their livelihood. Everyone connected to the ski industry, from the ski resort operators to the beloved snow chain installation technicians, are undoubtedly praying for the fluffy white powdery stuff to cover their mountain home. No snow = no money. Sadly there aren't as many cool songs about snow as there are about rain. Did I mention, *Set Fire to the Rain* by Adele? One word... Brilliant! Snow Patrol is one of my favorite new bands and yet I can't recall a single song they sing related to snow. Now if Snow Patrol (or Cold Play) recorded an alternative rock version of the holiday tune, *Let it Snow,* they would totally rule the Winter Olympics in 2014.

Although I may have strayed a little from my original theme, I would hate to think of the negative repercussions a rain-less winter would have on our region. Drought is a dirty word around here. I want to "make it rain" like an insurance conventioneer with a fist full of $20.00 bills at a Vegas strip club. With any luck, by the time this article appears in type, we'll be wearing raincoats and galoshes amidst a couple of months of consistently strong rain. I'm not talking Noah's Ark—forty days and forty nights of torrential flood-like rain or anything, but enough of the wet stuff to sustain us for the balance of the year. An "April Showers Bring May Flowers," type of rain would be just fine.

34 I Play Words with Friends (by myself)

Words with Friends ("WORDS", "WwF" or "Palabras con Amigos") the mobile device app, has become insanely popular—so addictively popular—that people of every race, religion and species are playing "words" everywhere; at home, while driving, in the gym, at their kids' sporting events, even at church (I picked up 18 points for the word "heathen" last Sunday). The popularity of WwF was never more evident than when acclaimed thespian, Alec Baldwin, was thrown off an American Airlines flight for failing to turn off his game when asked to do so by a flight attendant. As popular as Words with Friends has become, we all do realize it's just the game Scrabble played alone, right? It's Scrabble played on your phone, iPad or laptop, but it's still Scrabble. The biggest difference between Words and Scrabble is that Words is played in cyberspace with supposed acquaintances, while Scrabble is a board game played with actual friends who gather together to engage in communication, camaraderie and the consumption of Doritos or M&M's.

While apps and online games have replaced the need to actually interact with real live people, once you're engaged in a desolate and lonely game of WwF, it's hard not to be competitive. Let's say someone, who will remain nameless, plays the word "conquistador" for a triple letter, double word, quadruple back flip for a total of 324 points, I, because of my poor draw of letters, can only play the word "dot" off her "o" for a whopping three points. See, it's Scrabble, but now I play, as the popular 70's singer Eric Carmen sang, "All By Myself." For the purpose of this article, I am currently engaged in a game of Words with Friends with my wife/friend, Julie, who is obviously not so nameless anymore. While most people might think my twenty-year career as a brilliant, word-crafting writer would give me an unfair advantage, those same people might also be surprised to learn I have never beaten the woman at this game of chance. However, as I organize my thoughts for this article, I will also be utilizing the thesaurus of my brain to, once and for all, annihilate my competition in this Scrabble-like game.

Words with Friends, while highly entertaining, is just another example of our lone wolf society. When you have your phone or iPad, who needs actual friends? Our children have been playing computer games by themselves since they emerged from the womb. Nintendo DS was a favorite of our girls when we embarked on a road trip, when they tired of television, when they went to the bathroom or when they simply desired some down time. While the games do greatly enhance their hand/eye dexterity, it left them with thumbs the size of a corn dogs. Nintendo transcended into Play Station and Play Station eventually found its way to the bottom of a dresser drawer with the emergence of Wii. Fortunately, Wii did encourage some social interaction with family and friends, however once it was determined that Wii could also be played alone, my wife became a Wii widow. Speaking of my wife, she just played *Quoz* for 589 points. In what language is *Quoz,* a word? bequoz, I think she's cheating.

Back in the day, the neighborhood kids (Clifford, Terry, Felicia and Angela) and I would gather together on a rainy day in Cliff's sunroom to play board games for hours on end. When you're a "gamer" or "board playa" in kindergarten, the games we rocked included Chutes and Ladders, Candy Land and Hungry Hungry Hippos. Granted, we did live a little fast in those early days. Games become much more interesting when you've got something riding on them. Not money of course, because a six-year old can't really get his hands on cash. No, instead we would stake a game with Oreo, Chips Ahoy! or Nutter Butter cookies. Playing board games was a chance to develop our social skills, which was crucial to our adolescent development. I recently read about an eight-year old child in Florida who proclaimed her best friend was her Droid cell phone.

As my underground game gang matured into our tweens, our board games of choice naturally evolved along with us. Me and the boys (Jeff, Derek, Troy, Luis and Mark) moved our high stakes games into the backyard fort at Jeff's house. It was really his older brother's fort, but he allowed us to rent it for $2.00 an hour because he had taken up heat lamp gardening. Chris became quite the businessman selling his extremely popular and odiferous plants to the neighborhood teenagers. Games such as Clue, Masterpiece, Life and Yahtzee were now our thrill of choice. Of course the stakes also matured and the grift became items such as firecrackers, cassette tapes and *Playboy* magazines (for the articles). Our conversations also moved away from topics such as cartoons to sports, girls and girl sports. Julie just played "dominatrix."Let's see, with her three double boggy letter and four triple word squares, she just scored 713 points. Fortunately for me, I was able to follow that weak play with the word "dirt" capitalizing on her "t" for a nifty 11 points.

Perhaps the Godfather of all board games is Monopoly. Monopoly, a game of high stakes real estate, requires a player to exhibit guts, strategy, negotiation and a knack for getting out of jail free. Monopoly marathons in college were commonplace. Often following a wicked fun night of partying, we would commence a rousing game of Monopoly at the FRAT house around 2:00 a.m. and go until dawn. Assuming we could convince a few Sigma Chi little sisters to join us, the stakes became clothes, and it was mandatory to down a shot of Jäger every time someone passed GO and collected $200. Oddly, I remember losing my pants when I landed on Park Place one too many times, but I was usually the last one to lose my dignity. Of course, there was more to the game than alcohol consumption and naughty voyeurism. There was deep, meaningful dialog on topics such as Reaganism, the Magic Johnson versus Larry Bird rivalry and of course, MTV's hair band rotation. Julie played on my word, "dirt," and her word, "dominatrix," and scored 666.5 points in two different directions with the seldom-used word, "ambidextrous." I strategically countered with the word, "farter," using six letters for a total of five points. How did that happen? Score: Julie, 1,594 points and Mike, 26 points.

I'm not saying that there aren't positive aspects of a game such as Words with Friends (or Mobile Scrabble as I like to call it) which does require that the participants utilize their brains far more than say, Brick Breaker or Bejeweled, but my question is where does it stop? Will our children's children eventually engage in youth sports online instead of actually going to a park or field to participate in a game of soccer, softball or lacrosse? Will virtual swimming take the place of swim team? My fear is that our society will become a bastion of overweight, socially inept computer hackers that's can't communicate in the real world. We've got to force ourselves to promote meaningful interpersonal interaction and it might start with a hard copy board game. Darn it, Julie just played the word "gortex" for 214 points and I'm left with five "U" letters, a "Q" and a "Y." I quit this stupid game and am going straight to the closet to find a healthier game, such as Apples to Apples, Balderdash or Sequence. Hey kids, "Daddy's done working and it has just become Family Game Night. Tell mom to put down her iPad and join the fun."

VI

SCHOOL DAZE

My articles on school enabled me to flash back to a time in my life that brought back laughter and night sweats. None of us realize it at the time, but school provides us with a framework and training for life. Time management, conflict resolution, schedules, deadlines, product roll-out, presentations, employee management and leadership all begin as early as kindergarten. Thoughts of teachers, classrooms, classmates, homework, lunch time, recess, tests and the changing of the seasons allow us to flash "Back to School" and flash forward to that hyper happy time known as "School's Out" for summer.

35 Back to School
Sentenced to Another Year

With just two weeks officially left of their 2007 summer vacation, I recently asked my daughters, Hannah and Claire, if they were looking forward to going back to school. "Who's got a yearning for some learning?" is how I think I put it. To no one's surprise, least of all mine, they both replied negatively. Claire, my eight year old going into third grade, politely responded with a, "not me," and went back to feeding her Webkinz addiction on the computer. Hannah, who is almost 10 and going into fourth grade, was watching *High School Musical 2* for the seventeenth time, and despite the zombie like expression on her face managed to belt out, "I want to be famous!" like that replaces the need for an education. But given the state of today's Hollywood youth, maybe it does. Considering the amount of money she (and her mother) spent adding to her fall "back to school" wardrobe, I might have at least expected some type of Vogue elementary school fashion curiosity, but alas nothing but pained despair. Truth be told when I was a kid we tracked the days leading up to the first day of school much like a convicted man tracks his last few days of freedom in the outside world before turning himself over to authorities to begin doing his time. To me, school was like serving a series of nine-month prison sentences, but fortunately we were paroled for the summer.

Granted there are elements of a typical school day that may, in fact, resemble a prison schedule. As great as school is (compared to work), I imagine most kids will resist giving up the independence summer allows. The thought of waking up early (can you say, "alarm clock?"), rushing so you're not late for carpool, putting in a full day of classes to then juggle extra curricular activities such as sports, band, scouts, church or cheerleading. To top it all off you spend the evening doing homework (completing assignments and preparing for tests) before calling it a night with a set bedtime. That's daunting to say the least. Come to think of it, prison might actually be an easier way of life.

Back when I was growing up, my mom, bless her heart, would try to make my sisters and I believe that going back to school was an exciting time to be cherished. She resembled a lawyer using a clichés such as, "structure is good for you," which translated meant, *now I can finally get back to my own routine*, or she might try, "you'll be with your friends," again code for, *now I don't have to entertain you all day.* I especially liked, "think of everything you'll be learning that you'll use in the future," which of course meant, *you better get an education because your father and I don't plan on supporting you for the rest of our lives.* My Dad (aka the judge) talked about how lucky (and pampered) we were because he had to walk 15 miles to get to school and back, uphill both ways. He also says he had to drop out in the 8th grade to help support the family. Of course he lived in the flatlands of Texas where they don't have hills and Grandma told me he joined the Navy after graduating from high school because he was wanted a more worldly learning experience.

Back-to-school also means school picture day (mug shots). Before the days of digital photography, the photographer took one shot. Good or bad. Now parents have always gotten their kid's hair cut or bought a new outfit prior to school picture day, but I've heard tell that some parents had their kids practice posing/smiling in front of the mirror, just to ensure that the traditional school picture is nice enough to share and display. Could you blame them? Considering the money spent on picture packages, who wants to mail family and friends a school photo of their nine year old looking like an extra from a Marilyn Manson music video? Back in our day, the boys begrudgingly behaved for the individual head shot (at the risk of being punished), but anything went when we were all assembled in the multi-purpose

175

room for the class photo. That's when we could really mess up a group shot with some inappropriate pose or strategically engineered oddity. In my fourth grade class photo I appear to have three arms and my best friend Derek Sousa looks like he has a tail.

Back to School Night is something else we parents all look forward to because it's our first chance to find out what our work load will be like this upcoming school year. As much as I like meeting the teacher (the prison guard) assigned to my child's cell block, it's painful to learn that my wife and I will be assisting with more homework now than we probably did during our senior year of college. Back to school night is actually easier than Open House night during the spring. That's when a lock down of 30 hyperactive kids (aka, inmates), their exhausted parents, a broken teacher, a stale smelling class room with no air conditioning and a visit by the warden (I mean principal) usually results in anarchy and chaos? Add in a lethal dose of cookies and fruit juice and it's no wonder riots get started.

Although kids may say they aren't looking forward to going back to school, there is undoubtedly some form of excitement and anticipation in all of them. What teacher did they get? Who's in their class? Has the lunch menu changed? How many days until the Halloween party? Each grade holds new adventures and new challenges. Moving up to middle or high school is like being transfered from Santa Rita Jail to Folsom Prison. You go from being a big fish in a small pond to a small fish in a shark infested metaphorical ocean. We, as parents instinctively adjust to the new routines—it may take us a little trial and error to restructure our schedules but it inevitably falls into place (usually right around Spring Break). We share in their growth, accomplishments and their life lessons of sadness and joy. Being sentenced to another year of school may feel like incarceration but it has its perks too. Who's ready for family BINGO night?

36 The Back to School Experience
As Viewed by a Parent and Child

Another summer has passed and the dawn of a new school year is upon us. A fresh start awaits each and every student with a variety of encounters, challenges and awakenings ahead of them. Back to school means new teachers, different classrooms, blossoming friendships and sometimes even a change of schools if a student is transitioning from elementary school to middle school or middle school to high school. As both students and parents embark on this journey of educational exploration, social expansion, fashionable extravagance and backpack excessiveness, it can be very enlightening to learn how differently a parent and child will perceive the BTS experience that awaits them. To provide a diverse viewpoint, I've engaged the assistance of my soon to be eleven year old daughter, a 5th grader at one of Danville's fine elementary schools.

Hannah initially responded by saying, "Is this a test, I'm not taking a test at home." Once I assured her that this exercise was to help dad with his "magazine homework" she quickly took interest and assumed the role of teacher. We were each assigned the same list of Back to School topics to comment on, and at that point I was told to quit talking. "Social time is over," is how she put it. I was instructed to sit at my desk and raise my hand if I had to go to the bathroom. She presented me with a number two pencil and informed me that she would be watching me. Somehow I was transported back to the fall of 1972, feeling that pit in my stomach as I headed back-to-school.

Back to School

Hannah: Summer went by way too fast. I don't want to be back in school. I guess I do want to see friends that I wasn't able to hang out with during the summer, but I don't like going to bed early, I don't like getting up early and I really don't like homework. Mom says we still need to do more back to school clothes shopping, but trust me, I have enough stuff. During the first few weeks of school the weather is still hot and I can't concentrate. I would rather be at a pool than in a classroom. Also, it's hard getting used to eating lunch in the cafeteria, to having projects due and getting your brain to work again.

Dad: I know as kids we all dreaded going back to school, but I've got to tell you, as an adult I look forward to it. Maybe part of it is all the mother-daughter confrontations that seem to be constantly occurring after 10 weeks of togetherness, but really there's more to it than just the screaming. It truly amazes me when I hear about what they'll be tackling during the school year at Back to School Night and I'm genuinely blown away at the Open House in June when I see how much they've learned during the school year. It's also impressive to see how much the kids have grown in both height and maturity.

Schedules/Routines

Hannah: Every morning we have to wake up early, get dressed, eat breakfast and then rush out of the house for carpool. Once we get to school we unpack our backpacks and wait for the teacher to get class started. Mom makes us start our homework the second we get home from school. Then there's all the other stuff like practicing for sports, projects, showers and a bedtime. We hardly get to watch TV at all. It's boring and every day is the same. During the summer, life is so much more relaxed. When I'm an adult I want a job that is flexible.

Dad: Welcome to my world. I get up five days a week at 6:15. Back to school means I'll have someone to talk to at the breakfast table again, even if she is Miss Grumpy Pants. Little do my girls know it, but we had them on a routine during the summer, too. It was just less regimented. They still had to get up at a certain time so they weren't late for swim practice. They had scheduled soccer/softball practices, play dates and library time. Everyone enjoys relaxed free time but there's nothing wrong with a subtle structure. There was a study done some time ago that said college athletes performed better in the classroom while their sport was in season because they learned how to manage their time. It's a lot easier to say yes to that raging kegger party during the off season.

The Classroom and Curriculum

Hannah: The new classroom always smell funny the first few weeks. I liked my classroom last year better. You have to get used to the new class layout because every teacher has a different way of organizing their stuff. It's good if your classroom is located right smack in the middle of the multi use room/cafeteria, the playground and the library. Maybe close to the nurse's office too, just in case. My favorite subject is reading and writing and I really like going to the library. My least favorite class is science because it's too dull and sometimes it's gross. Like when we dissect things. I like switching classes for math and writing. It's cool having a different teacher and classroom for different subjects. I think that will be interesting once I get to middle school next year.

Dad: I think their classrooms smelled funny by the end of the year. It was an odorous blend of sweat, exhaustion and science project funk. I always liked it when my classroom had a window view of the playground or athletic field. I would look out and plan my escape. It was like being incarcerated at Alcatraz back in the 30's and staring at the San Francisco skyline. Back in the day, female teachers would over-decorate the room with Thomas Kincade watercolors, stimulating window treatments and scented potpourri, while male teachers slapped up the alphabet chart, a "Spices of the World" calendar from their dry cleaner and called it quits. As a kid I had my favorite subjects of course but as parents, my wife and I find every subject interesting. We take an active interest in the class curriculum because it's also a chance for us to learn along with the girls. It's amazing how much we forgot or didn't know. Mostly didn't know.

Homework

Hannah: I think homework is pointless. I hate starting my homework as soon as I get home from school. Why can't I do it when I want to, like at night time or in the morning? I would like it if I had enough time to finish my homework at school so I didn't have to bring it home and waste my time. Homework can also make you late for the other stuff you have to do, like soccer and horseback riding, which are so much better than homework. Parents get frustrated when kids don't get all their homework done or have trouble with it. No kid I know likes homework but we all know it has to be done or there are consequences. There are teacher consequences and parent consequences.

Dad: I have homework. Homework from the office, paying bills homework (which really bites), ESPN homework and then there's helping with the kids homework. I studied just as hard as Hannah for those darn 4th grade science tests and I would've totally nailed Claire's 3rd grade 60 second multiplication sweep. When a young couple thinks of starting a family, it's probably a safe bet that they never consider the rigors of elementary school homework. Growing up, homework was just a way of life in my house (see consequences above) but now I tell my kids homework is the foundation of a strong work ethic. I sound like just like my dad.

Teachers

Hannah: I really liked my old teacher. Not that she was old I mean last year's teacher. Why can't we keep a teacher we like and are comfortable with for more than one year? Some teachers are nice, some are funny, some mean, some strict, some calm, some crazy. I like nice, funny, calm ones. I've been pretty lucky when it comes to teachers.

Dad: I like nice, funny, calm teachers too. Growing up I had good teachers (Mrs. Marquett), great teachers (Ms. Slater) and terrible teachers (too many to name...Mr. Boudreau). Teachers have an unbelievably difficult job and aren't compensated near what they are worth. I have the utmost respect and admiration for teachers. Virtually all of the parents at our elementary school feel very fortunate that this area has such high teaching standards and because of it we're blessed with wonderful teachers.

Friends

Hannah: It's fun to see old friends and meet new friends. It can be sad if someone you were looking forward to seeing has moved and you didn't know it. Sometimes I hang out with friends in groups. I guess at every school there's the cool group, the good athlete group and the nerd group. I'm kind of in the middle, but I'm not sure there's a group of middle kids. Sometimes I feel like I'm the only one in that group.

Dad: Elementary school friendships can be the most long lasting, especially if you continue on to middle school and high school with a core group. Unfortunately, because of the creative district mapping, kids get split up around here when they move on to middle school. Thinking back, I too felt like I was the only person in my middle group, but then again, that wasn't a bad place to be because the middle group kid can be friends with all of the other groups of kids.

Extracurricular Activities

Hannah: What? Do mean like band and stuff? I didn't like band because it was in the morning before school on Monday's and Thursday's and I had to get up even earlier than normal. Enrichment Classes are like extra classes but on cool stuff like dance, Spanish, tennis or pets and animals. Some of those were pretty neat. 4H was fun last year and I think every kid in Danville plays Mustang Soccer.

Dad: Kids have so many more things to choose from than we had when we were young. I wish I could take some of the enrichment classes they offer at my daughter's school. Technically I guess I could enroll at Las Positas Community Collage and take courses on subjects that interest me, such as Comic Book Illustration or Ultimate Fighting, but who's got the time? I give it up to all the moms out there that can coordinate the logistical challenges of getting their kids to a multitude of extra curricular activities. It's probably safe to say that if moms and dads all of a sudden switched places tomorrow, there would be a lot of kids not making it to their extra curricular activities.

Review and Conclusion

Strangely there's a slight contrast in our responses to the above topics. Not quiet as copasetic as I would have imagined. We have always had a saying at our house, "We can agree to disagree." This has never been more evident than how we perceive The Back to School experience. For Hannah school appears to be a necessary evil, while I view it as a wonderful adventure with endless opportunities. To conclude, we both were asked to finish the following statement; School is _____.
One of us wrote the word "Torture," while the other wrote, "an educational journey and microcosm of society." We will let you decide who wrote what, as you prepare for, or reminisce about, going Back to School.

VII

DOUBLE THE FUN

I have written several two-part pieces over the last five years. Having a chance to expand on an idea or theme gave the topic more depth and finality or in some cases probably bored the pants off readers twice. Sequels usually never are as strong as the original, but in my case, the original wasn't all that strong. Maybe I'll do an Alive and Kickin' Part II?

37 I See Dead People
The East Bay's Most Notable Ghost Haunts

When it comes to ghosts, spirits, spooks, phantoms or wraiths I have three distinctly different frames of references, all a product of Hollywood and what I saw on television or in a movie growing up. The first is *Casper,* the friendly ghost. Casper was a sweet and gentle ghost who, along with his nice witch friend, Wendy, would go around making friends while helping people understand that ghosts were nothing to be frightened of, as long as you kept an open mind. When I was six years old, I talked my mom into buying me a Casper costume for Halloween. Unfortunately, being somewhat husky, I more closely resembled the Michelin Tire guy's illegitimate son. In my teens I was introduced to the wildly silly, paranormal activity in the movie, *Ghostbusters.* Who could forget Bill Murray's character, Dr. Peter Venkman, getting slimed while chasing an especially nasty green-tinted apparition from the afterlife, while the catchy "GHOSTBUSTERS" theme song played in the background? More recently, M. Night Shyamalan brought us his impression of what I've always imagined real ghosts to more closely resemble— Bruce Willis in a bad hairpiece. In his celluloid masterpiece, *The Sixth Sense,* the audience is blown away by the plot twist at the end of the movie. Finding out that Willis' character had been dead for most of the flick and only the innocent Haley Joel Osment could see and communicate with his ghost freaked out the entire theatre.

In the greater East Bay Area, we don't hear about many ghost sightings on the Channel 7 evening news or in the *Contra Costa Times.* Oh sure, we've all had that feeling from time to time of a spirit-like presence in our vicinity at Broadway Plaza, and who hasn't heard a melodic voice wafting through the trees while walking alone on the Iron Horse Trail? I can't be the only one who has had their furniture inexplicably moved around the room while they've slept in peaceful Danville? But ghosts? Come on. In a phone interview with Loyd Auerbach, a Director at the Office for Paranormal Investigations in Martinez and an instructor of Parapsychology Studies at the HCH Institute in Lafayette, I learned that while older East Coast cities, such as Boston, New York or Philadelphia, where the age of a structure and the history of the area contribute to the chances of paranormal activity there are places of unusual phenomena sprinkled throughout our local suburban landscape. The fact that Mt. Diablo (translated means Devil Mountain) sits in our back yard has some relevance. Apparently many of this area's most active spirit hangouts are within eyesight of Mt. Diablo. Mt. Diablo can be said to have either an unusually dynamic soul of supernatural activity or it's the geomagnetic fields in the surrounding earth that can explain the incomprehensible metallurgy which get misreported as spirit sightings. Mr. Auerbach says that while there is significantly more commotion reported in East Bay homes, there are a few relatively well know public locations that have had people talking for years. The Banta Hotel in Tracy, the Rosehill Cemetery in Antioch, the former Quail Court Restaurant in Walnut Creek (currently vacant), the Black Diamond Mines of Concord and apparently the City of Clayton (at the northeastern base of Mt. Diablo) which has been routinely recognized for its abundance of paranormal activity ever since the infamous Poltergeist of 1957. Now I don't know if the '57 Poltergeist was anything like the film, but just to be safe, I'm never moving there. In fact, just to be safe, I don't plan to ever play golf at the Oakhurst Country Club again.

Perhaps the best known East Bay spectral destination is the famed aircraft carrier, the USS Hornet, which is now a museum and event center berthed at the decommissioned Alameda Navel Air Station. The Hornet has long been recognized for having a reputation as a haunted ground. While the trustee's that run this

National Historic Landmark and popular tourist attraction downplay any actual ghost sightings or unusual occurrences, Mr. Auerbach says that the treasured history of this storied vessel could explain its reputed spirit visitations. The Hornet is the eighth ship of the United States Navy to bear the name dating back to 1775. Its wartime legacy is impressive. The vessel currently housed in the East Bay, CV-12, is one of the most decorated combat ships in the U.S. Naval fleet and holds the record for the number of enemy ships and aircrafts destroyed during World War II. The USS Hornet also had the honor of retrieving Apollo capsules 11 and 12 from the Indian Ocean upon their splash down following trips to the moon. After being decommissioned and languishing at the Bremerton Shipyards in the state of Washington, the Hornet lay in disposal status until in 1997 when a determined volunteer effort was successful and the proud ship was converted into a floating museum and relocated to Alameda. Since the ship's renovation began, the number of phantom sighting is rumored to be in the hundreds. Due to the Hornet's popular, Youth Liveaboard Program, they do not sensationalize this aspect of the ships appeal but Mr. Auerbach has consulted for several TV specials on this very subject.

Whether or not ghosts actually exist is up to each person's own beliefs. In an informal poll of roughly 20 people, it was split evenly between the believers and non believers. Loyd Auerback says that while most occurrences he investigates are easily explained, he adds the possibility of a spirit's presence or the sighting of an apparition, especially if the historical circumstance of the location would dictate a reasonable explanation, does exist. Visit any library, bookstore or Amazon.com and you'll find thousands of books and documentaries on the subject of ghosts, paranormal activity, supernatural occurrences, etc. Logic usually prevails when it comes to things we can't explain, but if you keep an open mind it's not impossible to accept the possibility of a ghostlike existence in our living world. In the immortal words of Ray Parker Jr., "I ain't fraid a no ghosts."

SIDE BAR:

Loyd Auerbach, M.S., is a respected parapsychologist. He is a Director at the Office of Paranormal Investigations in Martinez and a teaching member of the staff at the HCH Institute in Lafayette. Newsweek proclaimed his book ESP, Hauntings and Poltergeists as "Sacred Text" on the subject of ghosts. Mr. Auerbach has appeared on over 100 local and national television shows on the subject of ghosts and paranormal activity and has consulted on countless movies, television shows and books. He is typically contacted through referral sources such as the Rhine Research Center but he is also listed in the yellow pages under "Parapsychologist."

Once Auerbach has been contacted about an unusual occurrence he first tries to explain away the event in a phone interview. He says, "often times a person mistakes what they saw, the sighting occurred too far in the past, or they're just plain nuts." He adds ,"if it is a current phenomenon and there is some type of history connected to the person or place, and an investigation is warranted, I will make it a point of doing my investigation immediately." The investigation itself consists of Auerbach visiting the area, talking with those involved and getting a sense of the psychic energy. The Moss Beach Distillery, a popular restaurant in Half Moon Bay, is Auerbach's favorite haunted spot and the site of his most vivid experiences with a spirit coined, "The Blue Lady."

You can read learn more about Mr. Auerbach, his services and adventures at www.mindreader.com, or contact him at esper@california.com.

38 I See Dead People
Part Deux

Ghosts, spooks, spirits, phantoms or wraiths have a definite appeal to the general public. Apparitions have ingratiated themselves into our pop culture. Look at the success of movies such as *Ghost, Ghost Busters, The Sixth Sense, Beetlejuice* and the soon to be released *Ghost Town.* The novel, *Lovely Bones,* sold over one million copies and was on the *New York Times* Bestseller list for more than a year. A movie version of the book is currently in production and is being directed by Peter Jackson. Television currently broadcasts a variety of popular spirit themed shows including *Medium, Ghost Whisperer* and *Ghost Hunters.* Even the immensely popular band, The Police, had a hit song entitled *Ghosts in the Material World.* There's a certain mystery (obviously), intrigue, curiosity, even a joie de vivre about a soul that just can't make the transition to their eternal resting place and in turn spends his or her afterlife days roaming familiar structures, and in some cases, communicating with the living.

After my article entitled *I See Dead People* appeared in the October 2007 edition of *Alive East Bay I* was repeatedly stopped by people anxious to share their "ghost experiences." There were also folks anxious to identify a local real estate destination that they believed was haunted. A good buddy, recently shared his story of a camping trip to Lake Del Valle, where he and several others in his party thought they heard a whispering voice, wafting through the trees, repeating the words, "Don't Fear." Granted, the reveler of this tale admitted that his group of outdoorsmen had been drinking a lot that evening and, "Don't Fear," does sound an awful lot like, "Get Beer," but I didn't want to come across like I worked for the office of Paranormal Investigations in Martinez. A co-worker and his wife swore me to secrecy as they delivered a spellbinding tale of a spirit known as Bubba, that supposedly inhabited their new home and could clearly be seen by their young children (anyone seen the movie *Poltergeist* recently?). Of course, we had enjoyed several glasses of red wine on that particular evening and the wife did crack up every time I sang the phrase, "When there's something strange in your neighborhood..." Finally, while volunteering as an adult driver/chaperone for my daughter's school field trip last spring, one of the other adults pulled me aside to point out the colorful history of our destination which included a reported spook or phantom whose presence had apparently been seen/felt in the vicinity. Fortunately, to the best of my knowledge, the person in question had not been drinking but thinking back, there was a strong scent of Altoids on her breath.

Among the local haunt spots, when it come to reports of paranormal activity that I failed to mention in last year's article, is the One Room School House, off Finley Road in Danville, the Pleasanton Hotel in downtown Pleasanton, the Historic Green's Store, a one time Pony Express stop on Dublin Blvd. in Dublin, and the David Glass House, which is visible from Interstate 680 in San Ramon. My wife and I even had our own paranormal experience while staying one weekend at a Rutherford House, situated on the grounds of the Beaulieu Vineyards ("BV") in Napa. Late that Saturday afternoon, as I attempted to nap off my wine tour buzz, the door of our guest room unexplainably opened and closed several times. I admittedly thought it odd as there wasn't a cross breeze, the door appeared to be securely shut and no one else was upstairs at the time. Throughout our weekend together, the four couples we were with commented on the odd door play and flickering of lights throughout the house. It wasn't until we were preparing to leave on Sunday morning that a caretaker for the property told us the story of the house's original occupants and their precocious daughter who died young (around 9 or 10 years old) and apparently chose never to leave her family home, originally built in the early 1900's. People have reported seeing the little girl's spirit and experiencing her sense of humor for over 100 years. Upon hearing this enchanting yarn of the supernatural, it was a race to the cars for our group of scared Sh*!@% less wine snobs.

If you access the internet site *legendsofamerican.com/GH-celebrityghosts2*, you'll find a plethora of famous ghost sightings. The list includes such deceased celebrities as magician Harry Houdini (Las Vegas), writer Mark Twain, entertainer Liberace (Las Vegas), Presidents Abraham Lincoln and Andrew Jackson (the White House), actress Jean Harlow, outlaw Jesse James, Confederate General Robert E. Lee, actor George (Superman) Reeves, mobster Bugsy Siegel (Las Vegas), director Orson Wells and musician John Lennon (The Dakota Hotel). The most famous and frequently spotted spirit appears to be that of Marilyn Monroe. Her ghost has reportedly been seen numerous times at the Roosevelt Hotel, where she frequently stayed, her Hollywood hills home, where she died of an overdose of sleeping pills, and the Westwood Memorial Cemetery, where she was laid to rest. According to psychics, Marilyn has relayed to them that her death was an accident not a suicide.

As the annual holiday of Halloween draws near, ghosts will once again become part of our culture. However, a lot of folks don't know how the whole costume connection to the date of October 31st began. There are numerous reports as to the origin of Halloween but they all date back to the ancient Celtic festival of *Samhain*, over 2000 years ago. It wasn't until the seventh century when Pope Boniface IV designated November first as *All Saints Day* (also known as *All Hollow*) to honor deceased saints and martyrs. Hallow meant sanctify. The night before November first became known as *All Hallows Eve*. In 1000 A.D. the church would mark November second as *All Souls Day* to remember the dead. Eventually all three days of celebration became known as

Hallowmas which transcended into *Halloween*. It was customary to celebrate this joyful time with bonfires, parades and costumes. A costume honoring a dead spirit or soul has always been the most popular. The whole Trick or Treating for candy thing is just a wonderful byproduct of this festive season, undoubtedly concocted by the people who make M&Ms and KIT KAT bars.

As we get ready for our suburbia night of terror festivities which include costume parties, office themed dress-up contests and neighborhood Trick or Treaters, civilized people everywhere will once again eagerly disguise themselves as a ghostly presence. Most of us remember the animated television holiday classic, *It's the Great Pumpkin Charlie Brown*. This time honored masterpiece features wonderful acting, a catchy soundtrack and an intense plot line. While numerous Trick or Treating children (minor characters) don the white sheet as a favorite costume selection, our hero, the socially awkward Charlie Brown, not surprisingly cuts far too many holes in his sheet. He unwittingly resembles either a homeless person wrapped in discarded linen from the Salvation Army or a drunken college freshman draped in a soiled bed sheet after a fraternity toga party. As you'll recall, poor Charlie Brown never got any good treats, such as Milky Way or Snickers; instead he got a bag full of tricks from his neighbors. If that Charlie Brown ghost-boy had lived on my block growing up, the families that gave him rocks and coal would have felt the wrath of about two dozen raw eggs raining down on their cars, garage doors and front porches.

When it comes to ghosts, I'm still not certain that I'm a true believer. I would definitely say I'm more open to the possibility than I was last year. As long at there is the slimmest, slightest, remotest of chances that a paranormal otherworld might exist in our otherwise ordinary mortal lives, I'm willing to keep an open mind. Maybe the next time I'm getting my freak on and can't explain what feels like a dead person's presence or energy nearby I'm going to hang on to it for awhile and question my surroundings. If I think I've heard an indeterminate, nebulous voice in the breeze maybe I won't just assume it's my imagination. I might even talk back (in a whisper of course). I'm no longer going to be so quick to ignore, shrug off or discount the frequent paranormal occurrences I can't explain. From now on I'm going to embrace these ghosts or spirits as part of the "in crowd" because who doesn't want to hang with the cool and popular people...even if they are dead?

39 I am a Disney Channel Dad

I'm glad the kids are back in school. I loved having them home for the summer, but I started to notice certain changes in my lifestyle; sleeping through my alarm clock, an unhealthy obsession with the video game, *Call of Duty*, a diet that consisted of chocolate milk and *Oreo Snacksters* and watching way too much TV. Not the typical guy television, like sports (baseball, golf and UFC), cable series programming (*Rescue Me* and *Entourage*) or On Demand horror movies (*The Unborn*)—no, I was hooked on Disney Channel shows. It dawned on me that I might have a problem when one night during dinner with our friends, Kurt and Amy, I mentioned how much I was looking forward to the upcoming Disney Channel music video by a collaboration of the network's stars including; Miley Cyrus, Selena Gomez, Demi Lovato and the Jonas Brothers. My dinner guests looked either impressed, or horrified, when I added that I was disappointed other DC celebs like the Cheetah Girls, Mitchel Musso and Kyle Massey weren't included.

I never imagined that as an adult male my TV viewing would consist of programs with slang titles such as *Suite Life, Joe Bros* and *Wizards,* not to mention wonderful movies such as *Hatching Pete, Camp Rock* and *Princess Protection Program*. I'm relatively certain that while the Nielsen ratings system does appreciate my viewership, there's a strong chance that I don't fit the Disney Channel's target market demographic. I know this because I don't purchase Clearasil, Kidz Bop CD's or the snack food Gushers. These companies regularly advertise their products during the frequent programming breaks. Although, come to think of it, I recently caught a screening of the new movie, *Band Slam* and now, oddly, I can't wait to see who gets slimed at this year's Kids' Choice Awards, so maybe the subliminal advertising *is* working.

Growing up, I loved watching TV. Unlike the kids of today, we had fewer entertainment options. Heck, when it comes to TV, we had way fewer network options. In addition to the big three, NBC, CBS and ABC, we had a few local stations (KTVU) that played mostly weird offbeat programming—anyone remember Creature Features? Technical advancements such as DVR/TIVO, On Demand and Pay-Per-View didn't exist. Heck, most of us didn't have remote controls. I was the remote control at my house, constantly getting up to change the channel for anyone older than me in the room. This was pre-cable too. We used rabbit ears on the back of our TV set until we were able to secure an antenna to the chimney. Broadcasting began to mature in the mid-1980s with the addition of the Fox Broadcasting Company, but the industry really exploded with the emergence of cable stations such as ESPN, Nickelodeon and the Disney Channel.

My connection to the Disney Channel began when my oldest daughter began watching the marvelously written and acted show, *That's So Raven*. The premise revolved around the madcap misadventures of a psychic teenager, Raven, her zany friends Chelsea, Eddy and her mischievous little brother, Corey. Unlike Patricia Arquette's psychic gift in Medium, which allows her to communicate with murdered dead people, Raven's ability only lets her see glimpses into the future which always gets her into "I Love Lucy" type of trouble. For those grandparents, childless couples, or singles out there still watching adult television, let me fill you in on what you've been missing as the Disney Channel has expanded its line-up of top rated shows.

The Suite Life On Deck - A zany comedy about the madcap misadventures of polar opposite twin brothers attending school aboard a luxury cruise ship owned by Billionaire hotel magnet Mr. Tipton. Originally titled *The Suite Life of Zack & Cody*, the boy's initially lived with their divorced mother (a cougar lounge singer) at the swanky Tipton Hotel. Mr. Tipton's empty-headed, materialistic daughter, London, also calls the hotel home and is now also attending a semester at sea with the boys. Additionally, the highly-strung, anal-retentive hotel manager, Mr. Mosby, has been transferred to the ship. Unfortunately, Maddy, the hotel sundry store clerk has skipped the cruise, apparently to accept a promotion to housekeeping. I miss her. Think, *The Courtship of Eddie's Father* (in this case, the mother) meets teen Love Boat, with a permanent guest appearance by Paris Hilton.

> *Zack and Cody are so funny and they are always getting into trouble.*
> —Mason C., age 10

Hannah Montana - A zany comedy about the madcap misadventures of a schizophrenic teenager who splits her time between typical American suburban teenager (Miley Stewart) and international pop star (Hannah Montana). Miley lives with her brother, Jackson, and their widowed father Robby Ray Stewart (brilliantly played by Miley's real life father Billy Ray Cyrus) at their Malibu Barbie Beach House. By day, Miley deals with typical high school stress with friends Lilly, Oliver and Rico, but at night she cavorts with LA's "in crowd," as Hannah, dealing with publicist, concerts, celebrity appearances and the paparazzi. Think *The Partridge Family* (if Laurie was a solo act) meets *Family Affair* with a little adolescent *Laverne & Shirley* mixed in.

> *Hannah Montana is a great show and my favorite person is Lily. She is hilarious and really good at comedy.*
> —Maddy T., age 9

Sonny With a Chance - A zany comedy about the madcap misadventures of a teen girl from Wisconsin who gets selected to be on the hottest teen sketch comedy show in L.A. Sonny, moves across country to the fast paced Hollywood lifestyle and right away begins a tumultuous relationship with the show's diva,

Tawny. It's a classic city girl versus farm girl clash of values. Added to the mix is the devilish Chad Dylan Cooper, the hunky heartthrob of *McKenzie Falls*, a *Beverly Hills 90210* knockoff show. He's flirtatiously competing with the girls for viewers and ratings. Think a teen version of *30 Rock* meets *The Mickey Mouse Club.*

> *Sonny is a good show, but Tawny is my favorite character because she's so girlie. Tawny likes to pick on Sonny, but they're really friends.*
> —Gianna G., age 10

Jonas - A zany comedy about the madcap misadventures of three fictional pop star brothers (Joe, Nick and Kevin). When not on tour (groupies), they attend a high school for the performing arts. The high jinks ensue at school and the boys' converted firehouse loft, with the help of their costume designer, Stella, and her best friend Macy, their #1 fan/stalker. Music is also a big part of the show, which won't hurt record sales or concert attendance. Think *The Monkees* meet *The Partridge Family* if The Partridge Family only consisted of Keith, Danny and Chris. Maybe there's a hint of *The Brady Bunch* too, if Mr. Brady had never married Mrs. Brady and Greg, Peter and Bobby were pop star orphans crashing in an abandoned firehouse.

> *I like Jonas except its weird that they live in a firehouse, because why wouldn't big stars live in a mansion? Nick is my favorite because he's always trying to do things to cheer people up.*
> —Megan W., age 9

Wizards of Waverly Place - A zany comedy about the madcap misadventures of three sibling wizards whose parents own a big city sandwich shop. Their dad was a wizard at one time but lost his powers when he married a mortal. What was he thinking? Justin, the oldest brother is a cuter/cooler version of Harry

Potter. He's a whiz kid wizard being groomed for the big time. Max, the youngest brother, doesn't take his wizard powers seriously and is basically a slacker. The real star of the show is Alex, the precocious sister, who misuses her powers like any teenage girl would and that gets her in all kinds of trouble. The only person who knows the family secret is Parker, Alex's nut job best friend, who brings the crazy up a notch. Think, *Bewitched* meets *I Dream of Jeannie,* if Jeannie and Samantha were teenage girls (with brothers).

> *I like Wizards because Alex always gets into funny trouble using her magic and big brother Justin has to save her because they're family.*
> —Taylor H., age 10

The people behind the Disney Channel shows are brilliant. They have brilliant writers, brilliant casting agents and brilliant directors. There is no doubt in my mind that they know parents will be on the periphery, casually absorbing the story lines behind their hit shows, so the geniuses at the network craft a product that will appeal to the entire family. From its early programming successes, which included *Lizzie McGuire, Even Stevens* and *That's So Raven,* the network has found a concept that works (zany comedy about the madcap misadventures of...). Disney has always had an eye for talent and their early series have launched the careers of teen stars Hilary Duff, Shia LaBeouf and Raven-Symoné, who have managed to keep their audience loyal as they've transitioned into more mature roles. It's a pretty shrewd and diabolical plan because, as a confirmed Disney Channel Dad, I'm the first to admit it works. Don't even get me started on the *High School Musical* trilogy, because I've seen each of those movies like 15 times and know the words to every song. I'm so embarrassed. What would my fraternity brothers say?

40 I Was a Disney Channel Dad
Now I'm into the TLC Reality Shows

Last month, I confessed to this magazine's readership that I was, in-fact… A Disney Channel Dad. The symptoms connected to this type of TV Viewership self diagnosis includes a morbid obsession with the story lines connected with the network's various situation comedies, an unhealthy awareness of the teen actors playing the charming and charismatic characters and an unquenchable thirst for Juicy Juice. It is important to keep in mind that the Disney Channel's network is geared toward a demographic of tweens and young teens (10-15 year olds), the incarcerated and agoraphobics still living with their parents. As a 47 year old husband, father and businessman, I never expected to become consumed with juvenile television programming. Fortunately, kids TV tastes change as frequently as their tastes in music, clothes, friends, etc. so before my dependency on the mouse-eared station required an intervention, I found our family experimenting with new shows on a new network.

Gone were the characters I considered friends, such as Selena, Joe, Nick, Kevin, Demi, Mitchell, Emily, Dylan, Cole, Brenda and Miley and now I'm getting to know Buddy, Clinton, Stacy, Randy, Nicole, Joe Bob and Michelle, Matt and Amy. While I have now been weaned off shows like *Hannah Montana, Wizards of Waverly Place* and *The Suite Life on Deck*, I am now engaging with TLC's reality line-up. TLC is an acronym for *The Learning Channel.* Unfortunately the only thing I'm learning is that it's not a good idea to work with family, have too many children, go shopping for a wedding dress or marry a woman who wants her child to enter and win a beauty pageant. I wonder what I might discover on the Discovery Channel?

What began as idol curiosity about some couple named Jon and Kate Gosling and the day to day shenanigans of their eight adorable kids (Maddy, Kara, Aiden, Hannah, Joel, Alexis, Colin and Leah) has now morphed into televised voyeurism. Why do I care so much about how bad some people dress or the kooky family dynamics at a famous New Jersey bakery? Why would I be captivated by the stressed-out employees of a fancy wedding gown store and the bizarre home life of some family with enough kids to field two baseball teams? Slowly, my daughters and I (mom is too strong and independent) were becoming fascinated by the lives of this alternative network's real life personalities. My viewing allegiance may have shifted from Disney to TLC, but is reality based programming any better for me than situation comedies? Here is my overview on several of the more popular shows on TLC.

What Not To Wear - Style gurus, Clinton Kelly and Stacy London, are recruited to transform frumpy, trashy or mismatched fashion ugly ducklings into swans by giving them a life changing fashion makeover. Usually, they hit a home run, but occasionally they do strike out. Case study #1 is an unsuspecting 30ish female attorney from Cincinnati, Ohio who is blindsided by her co-workers because her misguided fashion sense has her wearing a man's suit to court, complete with tie, boxer shorts and wingtips. Once Clinton and Stacy teach her how dress for success on a $5,000 budget, provide her with a $500 haircut/highlights and a $1,000 make-up consultation, she is transformed into a smoking-hot barrister, brimming with confidence and renewed self esteem. Case study #2 is an unreceptive biker chick from Reno, Nevada in her late 20's who wears Daisy Duke shorts, a tube top and UGH boots when collecting rents as the resident manager of her trailer park. Even the camera guy knows that no matter how much money Clinton and Stacy spend on clothes, hair and make-up, the minute the production team leaves town, this chick is going right back to the thick mascara, spandex leggings, a shredded Kid Rock t-shirt, rhinestone flip flops and aviator sunglasses.

Clinton and Stacy are like Batman and Robin (if Batman was gay and Robin was a woman). This fashionista dynamic-duo strives to rid the county of women dressed like the Joker, Riddler and the Penguin.

Cake Boss - Buddy Valestro is one of the most renowned cake artists in the country. Master Baker of Carlo's (named after Buddy's late father) City Hall Bake Shop in Hoboken, New Jersey, Buddy, along with his mother, four older sisters and three brothers-in-law, create some of the most outrageous, creative and visually astounding cakes imaginable, for virtually any occasion. People come into the bakery with an idea or notion and Buddy and his team of dessert artists (Mauro, Frankie, Danny) transform a sheet cake, fondant and frosting into a masterpiece worthy of display at a Manhattan art gallery. Buddy's inspiration and execution takes place while he deals with the craziness of a big, loud Italian family made up of characters straight out of the Sopranos.

Buddy is like Tony Soprano except instead of hanging out at the Bada Bing and whacking guys, he spends his days baking cakes. Buddy is the mob boss of an organized crumb family. Forgetaboutit.

18 Kids and Counting - Michelle (43) and Joe Bob (44) Duggar are just your normal everyday average American family raising their eighteen children. Hasn't this couple ever heard of prophylactics, abstinence or vasectomies? As if 6, 10, 14, heck 18 kids weren't enough, now the Duggars are expecting their 19th, but not before their oldest son (Josh) and his wife (Anna) have their first child. It looks like Michelle and Joe Bob's grandchild will be older than his/her uncle or aunt. What a surprise, they live in Arkansas.

What if Jon and Kate had 19 kids? What is Steve Martin's movie was called *Cheaper by the Dozen and a half + one.*

Say Yes To the Dress - In search of a wedding dress? Its pandemonium when visiting Kleinfeld's in Manhattan. Every staff member (Mara, Dianne, Nitsa, Joan, Randy, etc.) tries to make each bride completely satisfied on the most important purchase for the most important day of their lives. Most men know that trying to satisfy a woman is next to impossible, but add stress, anxiety, budgets and her mother to the equation and it's a recipe for emotional meltdowns, financial let downs and all out psychotic brake-downs. Occasionally, the unexpected happens and a woman finds the dress of her dreams that meets her budget and fits her figure. That's called a sale (and a miracle).

When two women want the same dress its Queen Kong meets Bridezilla. Unfortunately, not every marriage in America lasts forever and couples don't always live happily ever after. I wonder if Kleinfeld's takes trade-ins.

Toddlers and Tierra's - The over-the-top nut job parents (mostly moms) of little girl beauty pageant contestants pushing, prodding and cajoling their children to act/behave/perform like trained seals or monkeys. These whack jobs spend thousands of dollars and countless hours traveling across the country, all in an attempt to get their pre-pubescent daughters (and sometimes sons) to win some lame beauty pageant. The kids fluctuate between adorable and talented, to obnoxious and annoying, as they parade around a cheesy hotel ballroom stage in make-up, spray tans and fake hair to be judged on their beauty, personality, costumes and talent. Preparation leading up to the competitions is intense and often involves private coaches, extensive rehearsals and costume fittings. These activities will eventually be replaced with therapy sessions, psychoanalysis and medication/rehab when the tots become resentful teenagers.

This is what happens when the crazy chick from high school, whose only goal was to be Homecoming Queen, becomes a mom.

Little People Big World - Matt and Amy Roloff are a vertically challenged couple (dwarfs) raising four kids (one little person child and three of average size). They live on a 34 acre farm outside of Portland, Oregon. Matt sells software and Amy raises and family and runs a charitable foundation. I think the Roloff's seem like a very pleasant, hard working couple. They appear to be good parents and social advocates for the Dwarf Athletic Association of America. Surprisingly, I really don't have anything disparaging to say this nice family and their heartwarming show.

Unfortunately I have to wait for the kids to go to bed to watch the racier TLC shows such as, *L.A. Ink, American Chopper* and *Police Women of Broward County*. It's gotten to the point that I almost have to watch *Kate Plus 8* (as of November 2nd the show will have a new name) after they're asleep too. Jon has become an absolute dick, Kate is always agitated (although she loves the camera) and it chokes me up to see sadness on the kid's faces. Excuse me while I take a minute....Thank you, I'm better now.

The people behind TLC are almost as smart as the folks over at Disney. They have produced inexpensive shows chronicling the good and bad experiences of normal, albeit uniquely compelling, peoples lives. Their target market is much broader than the Disney "tween" crowd as evidenced by the advertisers such as AT&T, American Express and Jack Daniels, etc...I meant Jack in the Box. I'm not even sure there are 12-step meetings for TVaholics, but it would certainly help if I could just watch TV in moderation and not get so consumed with the programming. Maybe next month I'll get out of the house and try hiking, biking or go door to door talking with people about the President's health care plan. Now there's a reality show TLC might want to consider.

41 Things I Just Don't Get

Despite my age (48) and relatively uneventful suburban lifestyle, I like to think I'm cool. I have a youthful taste in music (Timbaland and Timberlake, Katy Perry, and Ke$ha), my television viewing preferences are cutting edge (*Friday Night Lights, Glee* and *Modern Family*), and while I did enjoy *Despicable Me* slightly more than *Inception*, I thought *Eclipse* was better than both. Did I mention that I Facebook? I Facebook like crazy. I post, comment and game. However, whether it's demographic, geographic or telegraphic (I needed a third graphic reference), there are a lot of things in this world that I just don't get. There are a lot of fads, whims and trends that strike me as silly, dopey or lame. A lot of traditions seem dated, out of touch or ridiculous. Does that make me un-cool? I don't think so! In my opinion it makes me relevant. The following is a list of pop culture things I just don't get.

I don't get every periodical having a BEST OF issue. It would seem that every magazine, newspaper and family blog has an annual BEST OF issue. The best sea food restaurant, the best drycleaners, the best free WIFI location within a book store or chain coffee shop or the best antibacterial suppository. If everything is voted The BEST, is anything actually the best? Do loyal patrons of the establishments stuff the online ballot boxes? Does a retailer's advertising contribution to the periodical have anything to do with their BEST OF rating? At last check, eleven different nail salons in the Tri-Valley have framed BEST OF awards hanging in their entrances. Being somewhat new to the pleasures of nail maintenance, how am I supposed to know the best place to get a mani/pedi if every place proclaims to be the best? My vote for the Best magazine that doesn't have an annual BEST OF issue is... Alive.

I don't get the fascination with vampires. Those bloodsucking, non-dead, twenty-something runway models in the *Twilight* saga, *True Blood*, the *Vampire Chronicles* or in the band Vampire Weekend all seem so dark and creepy. Not that I have anything against dead people, we preach acceptance at our house, it's just that I find living people to be much more fun and spontaneous. The problem is, dead people are cold, pale and they only want to hang out at night. I'm a warm blooded sun worshiper who tends to get tired around midnight. While I can't really say that I'm a Team Jacob dad, those darn Vampires are everywhere. You can bet you're O+ virgin neckline I won't be vacationing in Forks, Washington anytime soon.

I don't get Tweeting. Why do I want to know someone's every mundane action or thought? I don't. I truly have no interest in knowing that you're having coffee on the veranda, enjoying a book while at the dog park or that you're in the process of inserting the best antibacterial suppository. I know that I'm interesting and entertaining, but I don't have some inflated self worth that leads me to believe anyone else will find me interesting or entertaining. Actually, I do, that's why I write these magazine articles. Tweeting is a way to say everything you wouldn't otherwise say, because secretly we truly know—NO ONE CARES! And yet, when people Tweet, they have the illusion that their 140 character bites are insightful, motivating or newsworthy. LOL. Granted, this text based social networking and microblogging service may be the future of communication, but I'm going Tweetless for now.

I don't get Justin Bieber. This marginally talented kid appears to be either part troll or part Muppet. I get that he was discovered by posting You Tube videos of himself singing and dancing, but come on, he's all of 4'11," he wears hip hop outfits from Old Navy and all three Jonas brothers can sing circles around him. For all you parents reading this, isn't Justin just the modern day Keith Partridge? Except David Cassidy (aka Keith Partridge) could act and play guitar. Maybe Justin is the modern day Danny Partridge. Years from now, I could see Justin hosting some sad radio call-in show, making personal appearances at grocery store grand openings and appearing as a B-list celebrity on *The Surreal Life* or *Celebrity Boot Camp*.

I don't get Back to School Shopping. Why shop for school clothes before school starts? Wouldn't it make more sense to show up in last year's clothes to see what's hot and fly (that's right, I used the word Fly) before you spend thousands of dollars on your academic wardrobe. Every school has a Fashionista clique who will set the tone for the next nine months, so why let your kids make their own decisions when you know it will end with them saying something like, "I need to buy all new clothes," by the middle of September.

I don't get campaign spending. Why would you spend a gazillion dollars just to get elected to a crumby government job that pays maybe forty grand a year? Does the title of Senator, Governor of Congressman carry that much prestige and power? How good does it feel to spend all that money and not win the election? Here's a thought, if you really want to make a difference in the community why not contribute some of that "throw away" money to a few of the local deserving charities. Chances are, if the check is big enough, organizations such as Children's Hospital or Camp Arroyo might be willing to designate a title for you. "The Earl of Donationville," or, "Lord Big Donator," sounds pretty important and swanky.

I don't get Jamarcus Russell. He was the number one draft pick by the Oakland Raiders in the NFL a few years ago and now he's chugging cough syrup in the basement of his mom's house. Where is your pride man? If the statistic I heard is correct, only about 1% of the college football players are drafted into the NFL each year and this guy has the audacity to hold out as a rookie, finally taking millions of dollars from the hapless Raiders, and when it does come time to show up and play he's overweight, out of shape and can't learn the plays. Who did the advance scouting and personality profile on this prospect, Al Davis? Back in the day, I would've paid the NFL to let me play for any team in their league.

I also don't get gouging fans on food prices and parking at professional sporting events. I really don't get bi-partisans voting in the House and Senate. Does anyone get Mel Gibson, veganism, Polka music or Ultimate Frisbee? It would appear that there are a lot of things I just don't get or understand. Maybe I am getting old and crotchety. What's the old saying, "If the music's too loud, you're too old" or something like that? Come to think of it, I don't get why kids play the music so loud in their cars. If the bass is pounding so violently that the fillings in your teeth are coming loose, you might want to turn down the volume. That's not un-cool, that's just good common sense.

42 Things That Scare Me

With Halloween on the October calendar, it conjures up the image of cute little kids dressed as scary ghouls, ghosts and goblins. I'm not easily scared. I have, in fact, even been considered brave when it comes to killing big nasty spiders or climbing on the roof of my house to retrieve a Frisbee. So while no one has ever dared refer to me as a "fraidycat," I am unnerved by a few things in our world that likely put a little fear in most everyone.

The Devil Scares Me. When I was young, I almost never wet my bed thinking the Boogeyman was in my room, yet when I saw the Exorcist I couldn't sleep for weeks. I'm no more or less religious than the next guy, but the idea of the Devil existing amongst us mortals here on earth makes me quiver. In theology, the Devil is described as the personal supreme spirit of evil and unrighteousness. Whether referred to as Lucifer, Satan or Beelzebub, the Devil seems to have a stronger presence around Halloween than say, Groundhog's Day. Preferring good over evil, I'm all for boycotting the Devil this spooky season as he undoubtedly has something to do with the bad economy.

Scary Movies Scare Me. Beginning with the afore mentioned *Exorcist*, my history of weeping and shaking hysterically while curled up in the fetal position under my theatre seat is long and slightly embarrassing. Why did I subject myself to *Nightmare on Elm Street, Friday the 13th, Carrie, The Omen, The Sixth Sense, Scream, The Blair Witch Project, The Ring, Halloween* and the *Devil Wears Prada*? Only my therapist knows for sure.

Movie studios have made hundreds of millions of dollars off people like me. More recently, the movie trailers for *The Last Exorcism* and *Devil* make my head spin 360 degrees and cause me to vomit something resembling Progresso's split pea soup all over the couch. I need to stick to movies made by Disney or Pixar.

Big Snakes Scare Me. While I'm fascinated by the Animal Planet's specials on Anacondas, Boa Constrictors and Pythons, the thought of wrestling one of those constricting slithering reptiles is enough to make me lose my breath. We all remember how Kaa, the snake, tried to manipulate Mowgli for Shere Khan in the Disney animated adaptation of *The Jungle Book*. (Note to self: strike Disney movies.) It's really no surprise that snakes also have a connection to the Devil. Raise your hand if you knew the serpent in the Garden of Eden became a willing conspirator with Satan in deceiving Eve? Need I say more? I didn't think so.

Biker Gangs Scare Me. However, I'm totally into the FX series, *Sons of Anarchy*, about a fictitious biker gang based in a fictitious Northern California town. The biker characters are tough and mean and do things that could be perceived as slightly illegal (gun running, extortion and arson) however, the father and stepson running "SAMCRO", appear to have heart, compassion and a moral compass, albeit slightly off course. Real bikers might not be as remorseful after they pummel a potential witness with a tire iron or drag a rival down a gravel path tied to the back of their hog. Biker gangs are especially scary if they have evil names such as Devil Dogs or Satan's Warriors. However, if I was in prison or facing off against some other angry social networking group from the streets, I'm relatively certain I would be grateful to have the assistance of a biker gang. But, for now, I'm just going to keep my distance from the Danville chapter of the Hell's Angels.

Sixteen Year Old Kids Driving Scares Me. Sure I couldn't wait to get my license at the age of sixteen, but if 50 is the new 40 then 16 is the new six, and no six year old should be operating a moving vehicle. I think I showed up at the DMV at 12:01 am on July 29th in 1978, but the thought of my daughters maneuvering a 3,000 pound SUV through the city streets of the Tri Valley terrifies me. Sixteen seems too darn young for that type of joyriding responsibility. I question whether or not teenagers should be allowed to operate Vespa scooters, motorized Razors or riding lawnmowers. A visit to the DMV has been described as a trip to hell, which is reason enough to suggest they delay the license age to eighteen.

The Economy Scares Me. When are we going to see local and national companies see a pick-up in business and begin hiring again? I have several out of work friends who are educated, motivated and right now, aggravated. If you didn't believe in former President Regan's trickle down theory before, I bet you do now. Corporate revenues are so low that companies are either not hiring or have asked employees to take pay cuts. If your disposable income has been reduced, you aren't going out to lunch or dinner as often as you once did. Restaurants are forced to reduce staff or close on slow days. Sadly, waitresses end up doing their own mani/pedis and waxing. Conversely, spa employees are now forced to cut out their leisure and entertainment expenditures, such as tickets to the Ozzy Osbourne and Black Sabbath concert at Sleep Train Pavilion. Poor ticket sales forced The Blizzard of Oz to cancel his entire North American tour. Wait one "Prince of Darkness" minute, wasn't Mr. Osbourne accused of Devil worship in the 1970's? All of a sudden, everything is becoming very clear to me.

If you add Raider fans, middle school dances and a call to my computer company help desk as other things that scare me it would appear that the Devil has his fingers in a cornucopia of activities. It doesn't help matters much that we live at the base of Mt. Diablo (Devil Mountain). While it might be difficult to prohibit kids from dressing up as a New Jersey Devils hockey player or discourage local area cougars from adorning a naughty demon outfit at Menar's annual Exotic/Erotic Ball, lets all pledge to admonish the Temptor, the Evil One or Apollyon from future neighborhood activities. Truth be told, the Devil is what scares me the most.

VIII

LIGHTEN UP!

Issues facing most of suburban America such as parenting, elections, aging, money, friends, the economy, ecology, youth sports and marriage can be pretty heavy, but I have always tried to find the lighter side of these topics in my articles. My style has tended to be more sarcastic and self deprecating. That type of humor appealed to me whenever I read articles by writers I admired. It's how I honed my craft, if you call it a craft. I call it a gift. It's a lot like when a Super Hero finally realizes their secret power. My power is writing something the reader can identify with and be amused by—that is if the reader is a mere mortal!

43 Taking One For The Team

I believe it was Dr. Phil, or maybe Tony LaRussa, who said a good marriage is all about teamwork. Being a former college athlete, teamwork was something I could both understand and appreciate. The best teams I played on consisted of one or two stars and a lot of hard working role players committed to achieving a common goal. As it relates to a family, the woman (wife and mother) is usually the home run hitting, five tool player and future Hall of Famer. We men (husbands/fathers) are just journeyman utility infielders, there to provide backup and support with an occasional spot start or pinch-hit appearance. In many homes, the wife forgoes a career to tend to the house and kids while we, as men, do our best to provide financially and be actively involved dads. Together we share the common goal of establishing a loving and nurturing home for our children.

Last year, when our youngest daughter turned five, the subject of sacrifice came up as it related to family planning. Knowing that in our early forties we weren't planning to have any more children, I, using baseball vernacular, stepped up to the plate and volunteered to "take one for the team" and get a vasectomy. To many men, this is the baseball equivalent of being beaned in the crotch by a 97-mile per hour C.C. Sabathia fastball so Buster Posey gets a chance to hit with men in scoring position. In our early twenties, my buddies and I talked about graduating from college, entering the workforce and building a solid financial foundation. By our thirties, it was meeting the right girl, traveling, and starting a family. Now in our forties, it's very common to hear "Have you been snipped yet?" at the gym, in the office break room, or in the dad cliques while attending your children's elementary school functions. If vasectomy doctors ever wanted to market to their forty to forty-five year-old male target audience, they should take out billboard ads in the outfield of the Little League parks, print ads in the school newsletters, or sponsor a booth at one of the local art and wine festivals.

I Googled "vasectomies," and found that between 300,000 and 500,000 surgeries are performed annually. While getting a vasectomy may be a relatively common medical procedure, the average man will admit to having difficulty with the concept of sterilization. More specifically, men as a sex (doctors included), aren't too crazy about the idea of someone cleaning out their dugout while wielding a sharp instrument. I envisioned a machete although the actual scalpel is about the size of a butter knife. While the thought of an actual surgical procedure in that delicate region was daunting, it seemed like the noble thing to do, given what my wife went through during childbirth. It's not like I didn't know where babies came from before becoming a father, it's that I never had a seat behind home plate when a little one came sliding in (or out, in this case).

Women, as a sex, are incredibly tough. When we learned my wife was pregnant, I wanted to be there during every inning of the game. As she went through the monthly prenatal gynecological exams, we were amazed by the ultrasound. I held her hand when she had an amniocentesis. When it came time to delivering the baby, however, I could only stand around like a third base coach holding a cup full of ice chips and giving signs. I did yell, "breathe, baby, breathe," as she positioned her legs in the stirrups and baring her private parts to half the hospital staff (orderlies included). Ultimately, she delivered an enormous blob of baby in a way only "miraculous" can accurately describe. There was a lot of pushing, screaming and sweating going on, and I'm certain my wife wasn't very comfortable either. Since men have no physical participation in the medical delivery of life—unless you consider the distribution of ice chips physical—it seemed only fair that it should be the man that handles the post-game wrap-up.

Once I had made the decision to get a vasectomy, it was up to me to take the first step and schedule the pre-op appointment. Little did I know that this meant attending an informative class on vasectomies with a room full of other men made of steel or, in a few cases, Jell-O. The consultation consisted of a nurse initially passing out illustrated pamphlets on "The Big V" that most of the men would probably never read. She talked about the nobleness of our choice, as it's far less complicated and invasive than a hysterectomy or tubal ligation for women. The introduction alone prompted two guys to walk out, claiming they were in the wrong room.

A grey-haired doctor came in a few minutes later, quickly going into the fact that a vasectomy is a relatively simple procedure that caused minor discomfort and, typically, a quick recovery. He began the discussion with an explanation about the need to shave our genital area the morning of the procedure. Not surprisingly, this caused one gentleman, weighing in at around 360 pounds, to fake illness as he ran from the room hyperventilating. Finally, Dr. FunGalore described the procedure itself and the recovery. He concluded by saying that if our marital situation changed and we wanted another child later in life, a vasectomy was reversible. The thought of preparing the field for an old-timers game wasn't of immediate interest, but it was nice to know I had that option, should I be traded or my playing status changed down the road. Knowing what my wife had to go through to give birth to our two beautiful and healthy daughters, my upcoming "grip it, snip it and rip it" adventure didn't seem like it was going to be such a big deal.

I reminded myself that my father, cousin, brother-in-law and several close friends had gone through it at one time or another, and they all seemed to be living normal and productive lives. One neighbor even boasted that it improved his virility and stamina (but he was always known around the block for talking a big game).

The Friday morning of the big game, I groomed and shaved myself as if I was going to be on the cover of the Speedo swimsuit calendar. The shaving part wasn't too awful, and I truly felt more aerodynamic. Arriving on time at the hospital, I had my temperature and blood pressure taken to confirm I wasn't ill and quicker than you could say "Hey batter batter," I was escorted into a sterile operating room by a female nurse who barely looked to be twenty years old.

I changed behind a curtain into an open back hospital uniform, which seemed misdirected considering the game was being playing in the front yard. Trusting that my coed nurse knew what she was doing, I complied. As I lay down on the operating room table I was greeted by the same grey-haired doctor from the pre-op consultation. I was comforted thinking that if they let this guy teach a class, I must be in good hands (figuratively and literally). The doctor informed me that this was his first of five scheduled vasectomies that day. I instinctively wondered if it was best to go first, last or somewhere in the middle; it probably didn't matter, but I liked the idea of leading off.

He politely asked if I had read all the literature, to which I assured him l had, after which he stated, "Then let's Play Ball." He talked me through the procedure again and then promptly threw out the first pitch. Approximately 30 minutes later, with very minimal discomfort or anxiety, I was told everything went fine and I could head for home whenever I felt ready.

The young nurse, whom as my anesthesia wore off now bore a striking resemblance our teenage babysitter, returned once I was dressed, handed me a couple of ice packs and some ibuprofen, and told me to come back in two weeks so the doctor could check-up on the incisions. I would also be required to leave a semen sample for the lab to confirm everything had healed properly. The nurse informed me that my wife was welcome to attend that appointment if it would be "helpful."

I drove myself home that day to a hero's welcome. My wife treated me like an All-Star and the kids were told Daddy had been to see the team doctor after being beaned in the "lower tummy" area. They understood that I was on the injured reserve list and wouldn't be taking batting practice or fielding grounders for a few days. With my ice packs strategically placed, I sat on the couch all weekend, watching baseball games and milking the attention. I was back on the team bus ready for work by Monday.

One morning a few days later, It was comforting to know — thanks to a vividly arousing adult dream — that all my affected parts were in good working order. The post-op appointment and lab work were just a formality and it wasn't long thereafter that my wife and I resumed the season. Now we can play as many games as we want without the fear of bringing up a player from the minor league farm system.

I would imagine that virtually 55-79% of the men who have had a vasectomy had a similar experience to mine. Never once did I have any regrets or experience any physical or psychological damage. A vasectomy doesn't cause impotency or make you feel like less of a man — by getting a vasectomy, we are not doing anything extraordinary or brave, just being a good teammate. We are simply, "taking one for the team," when our teammates have done so much for us.

Being accountable and responsible is also not a bad example to set for the rookies on our team, although I'm certain it will never come up during a pre-game meal.

44 Freedom & Independence In The Suburbs

With one out in the bottom of the sixth inning and runners on first and third, the eight and under girls All Star softball team I was coaching was feeling the pressure. This being the second game of a two game tournament, intensity was high. Little Jillian, the heart and soul of our team, dug in at the plate and with one swing of the bat her single to left drove in Madeline for the winning run. The dug out erupted with the shrieking sound of little girls, as they poured out onto the field to celebrate the victory. They were as genuinely excited as if they had just won a nationally televised Olympic game against a heavily favored team from Cuba. As I looked around the field at the sight of proud parents, engaged coaches, euphoric and disappointed players, meandering siblings and relieved league officials, I thought to myself, could we be any luckier? Could freedom and independence in the suburbs be any more clearly defined than by a competitive softball game for little girls on a beautiful Sunday morning?

With another Fourth of July (Independence Day) just around the corner, I am so thankful and appreciative for the liberty we enjoy in our charmed Tri Valley lives. We drive our impractically large SUVs three blocks to purchase an overpriced Grande Mocha Al Pacino at Starbucks; we watch meaningless reality shows on our massive plasma TVs and we have cell phones that are also computers, music players, cameras, video cameras and God knows what else, when the alert is switched to vibrate. Common sense tells us we have too many extravagances in our lives and we should make more of an effort to conserve for our country, ourselves and our kids' future. Maybe it's idealistic to think that most of us would be willing to do something—anything—to ensure that our children grow up happy, healthy and safe, pursuing their childhood dreams, whether they are on a field, auditorium, classroom or stage. Freedom and independence does have a price and just to be grateful doesn't seem like enough.

It's not a revolutionary statement to say life isn't so free in other parts of the world. Not just in Iraq or Afghanistan, but in hundreds of countries around the globe, organized youth sports is not part of the daily routine. Sure, kids will always find a place to play, but children in those countries live with poverty, fear, and atrocities, the likes of which we'll never know. Yet on any given day of the week you can drive the city streets of suburban neighborhoods around the United States and see kids of every age participating in soccer, softball, baseball, basketball and even lacrosse (which I don't yet get). This is where the spirit of competition is first experienced. To score a goal, to catch a fly ball, to finish a race, is a beautiful production. Is there anything more pure than a child's smile when he or she accomplishes an athletic feat for the first time? As parents, it is our responsibility to nurture this opportunity by ensuring that our kids appreciate these activities or by volunteering our time to be involved as a coach, umpire or league official as an expression of our appreciation.

Granted, it's hard to keep the kids uncorrupted with the attention the media gives professional athletes in this country. If an athlete does something good we hear about it (Tiger Woods, Oscar De La Hoya, Natalie Coughlin) if it's bad we hear about it (Barry Bonds, Michael Vick, Pac Man Jones) and if it's entertaining you hear about it (Dale Earnhardt Jr., Venus Williams, the Golden State Warriors). Pressure to achieve is everywhere. Even in youth sports there's over-the-top coaches, parents and peers constantly looming. I admire organizations like the Positive Coaching Alliance ("PCA") for their ongoing commitment to assist organization such as the San Ramon Valley Girls Athletic League ("SRVGAL") and Mustang Soccer in their never ending quest to remind parents and coaches that it's just a game. Kids participating in sports can have either a positive or negative experience, and it ultimately comes down to the philosophy and culture instilled by those in charge. Unfortunately, too often it's the coaches and parents who truly need to embrace PCA values that are in the back of the room talking, outside on their cell phone or don't bother attending the meetings at all. But like any organization with a large membership, you can only hope the fundamentals are in place and a majority of the members participate for the right reasons.

Getting back to our All Star game, after a close first game against the other U8 North team, we squared off against a team from the South division in the consolation game. "Consolation" means we "lost" the first game. At our two week day practices prior to Sunday's tournament, my coaches (Traci and Kathy) and I tried to instill a sense of pride, teamwork and sportsmanship in our recently selected All Stars. All Star players, at this age, are chosen by their coaches and teammates to represent their respective team. We told the girls everyone will play and we would be rotating positions so that every player could contribute equally. While competition is healthy and winning/losing is a byproduct of talent and preparation, we as coaches know there will be plenty of "must win" games in their future, so it was more important to us that the girls had a wonderfully fun experience. Did I mention that most of the girls are seven years old? Needless to say, it's more fun to win than lose and in the second game we pulled out one humm-baby of a victory. All tied up, going into the top of the sixth inning, the other team loaded the bases before our girls recorded three straight outs highlighted by a running catch in center field by Kelsey to end the inning. Fortunately when we scored in the bottom half of the inning our players got an opportunity to experience the sweet taste of victory.

When recently asked what comes to mind when I think of the term Freedom and Independence, I thought of our pitcher

Amanda, with a 100 watt smile on her dirt-smudged face, looking up to be at one point during the game and saying, "Coach Mike, this is really exciting." Freedom and independence for me is living in a place that allows our kids this endearing freedom to just be kids and the independence to participate in sports for the love of the game.

45 I Hate Shopping
With My Wife

I hate shopping. Let me be more specific—I hate shopping with my wife. There's a distinct difference. Shopping, by and for myself, is easy and I love my wife, but put the two together and it's a lethal combination. Shopping for me begins when I identify that I have a need for something. Once I determine which store has what I need, I visit the store, find the item and I buy it. How simple and efficient is that? My wife, on the other hand, views shopping as relaxation, recreation, socialization, participation, execution and a contribution to the local economy. Maybe it's me, but that's way too many "tions" to roll into any one activity.

When it comes to shopping, I will typically only visit a department store, outlet center, power center, neighborhood center or strip center when there is something I need/want or can't live without. My wife on the other hand will visit one of these retail friendly locations more often than she'll visit her relatives. When stopping at any given retail oasis, my wife A) doesn't need to buy anything to enjoy the shopping experience, B) if she does need something she will typically visit a minimum of 17 stores to compare price, style, size and color options before she makes her purchase, and C) if she does actually purchase an item there's a very good chance she'll return it to the store after she brings it home and decides she doesn't like it as much away from the store's flattering lighting.

To be honest, I can't figure out why my wife drags me along on these shopping expeditions. I complain, I sulk, I schlep and I grumble while tagging along behind her. Misery aside, I know I serve a purpose if she feels the need to take the kids shopping with her. I am either the babysitter or the walking ATM machine. My primary job is to watch the little kids so they don't: 1) Knock over a priceless item at some overpriced store that we have no business visiting or intention of buying anything at; 2) Keep them corralled like wild stallions so they don't run out into the parking lot or drown in a project's water feature, or more than likely; 3) Buy them something—a DVD, hair ribbons or $400 Gucci slippers—it really doesn't matter because like their mother, my daughter's are genetically predetermined to possess the biological gene that makes them shopaholics. One day they'll likely be in the basement of some church attending a 12 step program for people that can't say no to a shopping spree. Ever since they could stand and take steps, they would walk their little diaper wearing butts into the nearest store and started grabbing any item they could get their fishy cracker stained fingers on. To this day, someone has to run interference and that someone is me. Now if we happen to be somewhere without kids, and my wife were to suggest shopping as a way to spend quality time together I laugh. She's kidding right? Quality time would be a walk in the park, a conversation over coffee or watching a sunset. I'm relatively certain that tagging along after my wife as she dashes in and out of a variety of women's stores isn't really "quality time." Me, glumly leaning against a wall, catalog rack or checkout counter commiserating with other husbands, probably isn't in Dr. Phil's book, *Relationship Rescue.*

Now I'm the first to admit that I'm partially to blame for my wife insisting that I still go shopping with her because, at one time, I faked shopping enjoyment. But that was back when we were dating and I had ulterior motives. Often I was either hoping that this special time together would somehow translate to "special" adult time spent together later that evening or by accompanying her on her retail acquisition excursion, I in turn, expected her to then accompany me to some activity that I drew pleasure from, like attending one of my 15 weekly softball games, visiting my mother or attending a monster truck rally. On occasion visiting mom and the monster truck rally were actually one and the same, as mom often traveled with the Western U.S. Monster Truck Rally Tour. It was worth an afternoon of shopping to see that old lady drive a Ford F150 on steroids, appropriately named Momzilla. Can you blame a guy for trying to work an angle?

Now after many years of marriage, my wife reads me like a book. She knows that I would rather pull out my fingernails than power walk around the 600 acre spread, more commonly known as an Outlet Center, in an exhausting attempt to visit each and every one of the 1,749 shops. Does anyone else think an outlet store doesn't actually offer any better prices/ value than the standard mall stores? As we drive from our Danville home to some weekend getaway destination, my wife knows for me to even consider stopping at an outlet center I must be promised some type of treat. As much as I despise the thought of power shopping our way through the Gap, Ann Taylor and Nine West, I also resent the mind numbing effect the word "outlet" has on people. Sure everyone is looking for a deal but slap "outlet" on a retail center and people will plan vacations around a quick diversion to pick up a belt or off-brand perfume. I've seen the buses full of tourists piling out for a 1-2 hour break. But alas, I digress because ultimately I'm like a little kid that must be bribed with a cookie to behave at church, except now my incentive to make a detour from our ultimate destination is something from one of the sporting goods chains. I'll grumble and moan, but the reality is I'll let the little woman drag me around stores for hours if I know there's a new Under Armor shirt or pair of Nike sneakers in it for me.

Grocery shopping is really no different. Alone I'm fine. In fact, I take a visit to the neighborhood grocery store as a quasi military task. Once I get my orders from the general (my wife) I land my amphibious all terrain SUV in the parking lot and commandeer a shopping cart. Next, utilizing night vision goggles, I search out the insurgent items, secure my assigned targets, and maneuver an assault on the nearest check stand before we load up and transport the cargo back to base. If I should encounter a hostile (someone I know), communication is minimal. "Hey, how ya doing, unfortunately no time to talk. I'm on a mission. We'll catch up soon. Give your family my best." The only time I draw attention to myself is when I wear the Adidas camouflage sweat suit my kids got me for Christmas last year. Now my wife, on the other hand, can be at our local grocery store for 2-3 hours when we only need a head of lettuce and a bag of Cheese Puffs. Even grocery shopping as a couple becomes a half day time commitment and I am forced to miss valuable sports TV time. Don't even get me started on the big box wholesale outlets. We lost my sister at a Costco back in '98 and I haven't seen her since.

There is no doubt that years from now after the kids have grown up and moved away and we're enjoying the twilight of our retirement, shopping will take on a new meaning in life. It might be a chance to get some exercise, a way to connect with friends or just a reason to get out of the house. Whatever the motivation, I'm sure I'll still be tagging along after the little woman. But in the big picture, knowing there will likely be bigger issues that will undoubtedly arise such as IBS, ED or some sleeping disorder, I may not hate shopping (with my wife) so much. There could be worse things than hanging out with your best friend for the day. That said, she better be prepared to buy me something cool or I will undoubtedly sulk and complain.

46 What Ever Happened to Customer Service?

Have you ever been given attitude by the counter person of a fast food chain while trying to make a simple chicken nugget purchase? What about being ignored by a sales clerk while looking for assistance at a major department store, or rudely spoken to on the phone by a customer service representative for a financial institution, phone company, insurance carrier or utilities provider? Is it just me or can we all agree that there is a complete lack of customer service in the customer service industry these days? Maybe the motto "the customer is always right" has become obsolete. Let's face it, there are a lot of jerk customers and grifters out there, but if I'm spending my hard earned money at a store or restaurant or dealing with a help desk/customer service representative for some company/service provider, then I, like the legendary Aretha Franklin, expect a little R-E-S-P-E-C-T.

When did it become tolerable for an employee to treat customers with indifference, arrogance and disdain? Are employers so hard up to hire anybody that they fail to train their new hires in the art of customer service? Shouldn't the first sentence in the employee handbook read, *Be nice and helpful to our customers or your employment is terminated*? Case in point, over the holidays I stopped at a store in the mall to purchase a gift card. Now I don't want to name names, but it rhymes with Babacrombie and Twitch. Granted, I'm not in their 12-18 waif target market, but for a brief moment in time, I actually thought I had taken on powers of invisibility as I stood , with gift card in hand, in front of three teenage staffers involved in a conversation about manicures and pedicures. Finally, I had to politely interrupt them and ask if they would mind accepting my money. Next example, last summer I was at a high end electronics store, sounds like Circuit Town, looking for a new flat screen TV and the college age sales clerk behind the counter is yelling at his apparent roommate for some bathroom infraction. Not once, as I impatiently stared laser beams into him from across the counter, did he ever acknowledge my existence, nor in any way let me know that he would be with me shortly or did he attempt to flag down someone else to assist me. After about 10 minutes, I found my way to the store manager's office, where after relaying my experience I walked out the door headed for a competitor's store. Final case study; recently I had an issue with a major credit card company located geographically south of where Canadian Express has their headquarters. Understandably, now that most everything is online, many companies have downsized their call center support operations, but it took me seventeen prompts to even get to a live person and that person belittled me for not using the online applications to resolve the incorrect billing issue. Needless to say, I no longer use that card for any transactions other than to remove bird poop from my car windshield. It would be interesting to know how many sales transactions and customers are lost each year because of poor customer service.

The Avis Rent-a-Car corporate motto used to be "We're #2, so we try harder." Knowing that Hertz was the industry leader Avis built their reputation on customer service. They hired quality applicants that exhibited friendliness and personality, trained them with an emphasis on providing the custom with excellent service and rewarded them with bonus incentives based on positive customer feedback. Avis never got into a price war with their competition, but instead focused on attracting customers that were tired of poor service, rude employees and a lack of respect from the other major rent-a-car companies. Guess what? It worked.

With a world full of sub-par or non-existent customer service out there to ruin our day, we as consumers have certainly learned to appreciate good customer service when we stumble across it.

In and Out Burger is a regional company where employees focus on providing their customers with a fine dinning experience at every one of their fast food location. Visit any In and Out Burger, (and believe you me, I've been to a lot of them up and down the West Coast), you will find that their employees take pride in providing the customer with good service to go along with a tasty Double-Double. From the counter help who initially greet you, to the service staff calling your number and delivering your food to the clean up crew working the dining area and restrooms, In and Out employees do their job efficiently, with a smile and a "thank you."

Recently my family and I were at Sugar Bowl Ski Resort and I'm here to tell you every employee of that company was friendly, polite, patient and accommodating. It is apparent that Sugar Bowl screens and hires only the best, using a positive attitude and personality as criteria. From the ski rental clerks to the chair lift operators and everyone in between they go out of their way to ensure their customers have a pleasant day at the ski park. Interestingly, a significant portion of their staff is from outside the U.S. which I hope doesn't mean they couldn't find qualified applicants within our border that could adhere to their rigid hiring standards. "We strive for consistency at every level by recognizing our employees for their performance and guest acknowledgements," says Greg Murtha, Director of Marketing and Sales for Sugar Bowl Resort. He adds, "It starts at the top by treating employees like we want them to treat our customers. We established a culture and address expectations very early on."

On a more local level, Bridges Restaurant and Forward Motion, both located in Danville, and Studio Blue Reprographics in Pleasanton, all seem to know the importance of Customer Service. Every employee of these family owned businesses goes out of their way to assist and respond to the customer's needs. Greg Betty of Studio Blue says, "We empower our employees to make customer service concessions to ensure our client's happiness. This usually translates into long term relationships and repeat business."

While the number of companies that seem to have lost their customer service pledge are too numerous to count, there are several that seem to be making a better effort of late. Wells Fargo, Safeway and Comcast are all major companies that seem to be placing a greater emphasis on customer service. Yet, with the sheer number of employees that these companies employ, there's always the chance that you'll run into a malcontent on any given day. Just one ultra-sensitive employee that didn't get their break on time or was reprimanded by a superior can derail a company's best efforts to turn the ship around. If you think the Republican's presidential primary debates can get nasty, just try to return an item without a receipt. If you catch the wrong person on the wrong day you may end up feeling like if you don't back down you might get a smack down. At the risk of trying to over simplify a solution to one of our nation's biggest problems (right after this potential recession thingy), wouldn't it behoove companies that have employees dealing with the public, especially in a customer service capacity, to instill in them a few basic phrases that were at one time commonplace? How can I help you; We'll be with you in a minute; Thank you for waiting, We appreciate your business and, please come again. It's like teaching our children manners. How many times have we all told our children, "say please and thank you when you're at someone's home or you're never leaving this house again." The key is for management to incorporate a level of expectations in the interview and training process, then to provide said employee with positive reinforcement for good behavior (a paycheck should suffice) and consequences for failing to comply with the preset standards (as Donald Trump says on his popular television show The Apprentice, "You're Fired!")

Several years ago I entered a contest to be a "regular viewer" panel member on the show *Politically Incorrect* with Bill Maher. They required applicants to submit a 100 word essay on what bugs you about America. My subject was a condensed version of this article about the lack of customer service in America. While I wasn't selected to participate in the television broadcast I did get a call from the producer saying that she and Mr. Maher enjoyed my entry and agreed with my comments. At its very core customer service is all about...servicing the customer. Come on, work with me. Whether it's responding to a problem, providing assistance or graciously accepting payment for a transaction, the customer's satisfaction is critically important to the success of any company's business. By recognizing the problem, and with a moderate amount of direction, it's not unfathomable to think we could see the resurgence of customer service in America? Thank you for reading.

47 The Obsession with Swim Teams along I-680

Contra Costa County is Fanatical About its Swimmers

If anyone out there thinks Tri-Valley families along the I-680 corridor have an unhealthy fixation with soccer, especially girls soccer, trust me when I say, soccer's got nothing on swim team. I can objectively make this statement because our family is involved with both. Swimming, like soccer, is a fanatical obsession in the suburban sprawl situated along the base of Mt. Diablo. Families in the communities of San Ramon, Danville, Blackhawk and Alamo are especially religious about their swim teams. You've undoubtedly seen hundreds of vehicles driving around town with colorful graffiti supporting their clubs throughout the summer months. During the late spring/early summer months, bold and boastful swim slogans such as; "We Rule the Pool," "Eat My Bubbles," "We Rock the Blocks," and "Catch Me If You Can," are painted on the windows of every third SUV and minivan in Contra Costa County, as a display of team pride, club spirit and competitive intimidation. Think high school football in Texas and you can get an image in your mind of the frenzy that swim team mania generates in this part of the East Bay.

Recently, my nine year old daughter, Claire, and I compared our impressions of the whole swim team experience. She and her sister are active members of the two time VSA and Contra Costa County Champion Crow Canyon Country Club ("CCCC") Sea Lions. Growing up, I always enjoyed my time at the Mountain View Parks and Recreation's Rengstroff community pool taking swimming lessons, jumping off the high dive and playing Marco Polo with my buddies. However, I've come to realize there's a colossal difference between swimming and swim team. It would've taken me about one swim team training session to realize I had it easy playing football. Swim team workouts are sadistic. I am incredibly impressed with the commitment our kids make for the love of the sport and exhilaration of competition. I assume it's either that or parental pressure. Personally, I'm hoping my kids can get a full ride scholarship to one of the Pac 10 colleges, considering what goes into a typical swim team season.

Workouts:

Claire: They're hard, but it makes us better swimmers. This season I go to two lappers and that makes me nervous. A 50 yard butterfly is going to be tough. (The transition from the 7/8 year old division to 9/10 essentially means that swimmers double their workouts to account for the increase in competitive distance from 25 yards to 50 yards). Friday isn't as hard as the rest of the week and it can be fun when we get to compete against each other. A lot of times the girls relay teams can beat the boys.

Dad: I get tired just watching practices. They are gut-wrenching workouts of endurance, conditioning and technique training. The coaches really push the kids hard, but the results are impressive. When I jumped in the pool at the age of nine or ten years old I often heard someone yell, "Whale in the water," as I flopped around trying to tread water like my boat had just been capsized in the middle of the ocean. It wasn't easy being a "husky" youth. If I was asked to perform a typical CCCC swim team workout, at that age, I probably would've: A) Puked, B) Cried or C) Quit. The answer would be, D) All of the above.

Competition:

Claire: There are nine teams in the Valley Swim Association ("VSA"): Crow Canyon Sea Lions, Blackhawk Hox, Diablo Sharks, Roundhill Heat, Del Amigo Dophins, San Ramon Aquacats, Sycamore Stingrays, Club Sport Marlins and Danville

Sea Devils. We swim against each one of them. I like swimming in the first heat and against girls I know. Last year our team went undefeated in league, then we won the league meet and then we won the county meet. It's awesome to be the champions. This year is going to be harder because a lot of our top swimmers went to year-round swimming.

Dad: Only nine teams? Aren't we typically tied up twice a week for like four months? If my math is correct, that's like 16 teams. As much as I like watching my daughters swim their races, it's a little daunting watching 23 heats of backstroke. It took me three seasons to figure out if my kid was in the IM, free or medley relay. The kids all look alike once they're in the water, so you really have to pay attention before a race. It's easy to lose your little one when every person under 18 at the pool is wearing swim caps, goggles and sporting Sharpie penned markings on their backs and hands (identifying them and their races).

The Swim Meet:

Claire: I love the meets. It's like a big picnic. It's fun hanging out with your friends, but I wish we didn't have to wait so long between races. I love when it's my turn to race. There are different kinds of meets too. Club time trials, pre-season challenges, league meets, Woodland's Invitational, the Blackhawk Relays, the league championship, a county "last chance" qualifier and the big Contra Costa County meet.

Dad: There's a common misconception that a swim meet usually lasts approximately eight hours and eats up an entire Saturday. It's actually only seven hours and 55 minutes, but because you have to arrive at the pool at 7:00 am, you're typically heading home (for a nap) around 3:00. Swim meets are an incredibly fun and entertaining social event. It's a party twice a week, hanging out with the families on our team or sharing some good natured smack talk with school and neighborhood friends from the other teams.

> *The social aspect of swim team is huge considering at any given four to five hour swim meet my kids are only actually in the pool competing for about 1 minute and 45 seconds.*
> —John Murphy, swim team parent

League Championships:

Claire: I love the league meet because everyone is all together except that everyone has their own little area for their teams. You get to see all of your friends and it's really crazy. There's like a hundred heats of every race and you have to leave for your heat about an hour before you swim. Some teams dress in costumes, everybody's car is decorated and they have the best snow cones there.

Dad: The league championship meet takes place every July hosting most of the league's 1,500 swimmers competing in 82 events over two days. The VSA board members work hard to create a fun, competitive and spirited atmosphere for the swimmers representing the nine league teams. Approximately 500 volunteers set the stage, allowing every swimmer to participate in three individual events plus relays. The last couple of years, the VSA league meet has taken place at the San Ramon Olympic Pool complex at California High School. Pop Ups, tents, lounge chairs and towels are visible as far as the eye can see. The high school grounds are so overrun by tanned bodies, painted faces, beach balls and festive music that it resembles a Bill Graham Day on the Green from the late 70's. You can usually find a good parking place in nearby Dublin.

County Championships:

Claire: The County meet is scary, but you feel like you've really accomplished something just qualifying. All the best swimmers are there and you really have to be focused. Last year, I was DQ'd (disqualified) twice for leaving early, which I totally didn't. I don't think I did. Okay maybe I did.

Dad: The Contra Costa County meet brings together the top swimmers from the County's 56 recreational swim teams. Similar to the VSA league meet, the county two-day meet assembles over 1,400 swimmers. The difference is that participating swimmers are among the elite 7% of the roughly 20,000 swimmers county-wide who have recorded a qualifying time to compete at the county meet. There's a food court, swim apparel vendors, professional sport action photographers and Henna tattoo artists. Swimmers love to be tatted up. It's so big time that NBC-3 covered it last year, highlighting the success of past swimmers such as Matt Biondi, Natalie Coughlin and more recently, Madison White.

> *This area is one of the top 5 swimming regions in the country. We have a wonderful swim team culture in Contra Costa County with fantastic coaches, great facilities and dedicated families.*
> —Ken Harmon, President of the Crow Canyon Country Club Sea Lions swim team

Coaches:

Claire: I like our coaches. They're tough, but they make us better. Our coaches were friends from U.C. Santa Barbara. Dan, Ethan, Jake and Dave all had different personalities, but one goal. They wanted us to win the league and county, which we did. This year we're going to have a woman coach. I hope she's nice. Sometimes girl coaches are tougher than the boy coaches.

Dad: The coaches are brutal. They don't let the kids get away with anything. They lay down the law from day one and oddly enough the kids respond to the challenge. Whining is not an option. I would never expect the coaches to know every kid by name, let alone remember how they performed at the previous meet, yet somehow they do. The coaches are unbelievably perceptive about how each individual kid practices, what motivates them and their level of competitiveness. It's not surprising that they get such impressive results. I think Mike Singletary could learn something from swim coaches.

Apparel:

Claire: Some team colors are cool and some are dorky. I like our suits, but I want a fast skin this season. I also have a team parka and flannel sweats that keep me warm on cold mornings. Sometimes I wear my parka around the house during the winter because it's so cozy.

Dad: You would think a swim suit is a swim suit. You would be wrong. There are a variety of technical suit options and Speedo has a monopoly on the market, although Nike is eating into their market share. If you watched last summer's Olympics, you saw how advancements in the swim suit industry have affected the sport. There is incredible demand from the elite swimmers to find a competitive edge wherever they can. I don't know if they make a $500 Laser Racer suit in XXL, but if it would allow me to swim like Michael Phelps and communicate with dolphins, I'm buying one.

I loved the league and county meets growing up, not to mention the invitational events. I have great memories of camping out at the venue to night before to secure a good spot. Swim team was such a big part of my summers and me and my family loved being part of it.
—Sarah Andrews, former Woodlands team member

Swimming requires a huge commitment from not only the swimmers, but the entire family. Beginning in March with pre-season stroke clinics and conditioning all the way through to the county meet in August, it's a six day a week job. That adds up to a lot of hours at the pool. In addition to the weekday workouts, there are the two competitive meets per week (Wednesday nights and Saturday mornings) and the occasional private "stroke specific" lesson. Over and above the routine swim stuff, there are also fundraisers, socials, and spirit rallies. Having never been exposed to swim team growing up, I reluctantly agreed to sign our daughters up at the urging of my wife (a former swimmer). I can now honestly say that I look forward to the start of the upcoming season. The physical maturation, team camaraderie and goal setting accomplishments my girls have achieved have been incredibly rewarding for all of us. The close friendships we've developed, the fun and excitement we've shared and the overall "swim team" experience has been truly rewarding for our family. I have to believe this is probably the case for a majority of the team families at most of the area's swim clubs along I-680. Call it fanatical or an obsession, but it's what we do. Now eat my bubbles.

This article is dedicated to the memory of Dave "Pooh" Maddan. Coach Dave was a treasured member of the Crow Canyon Country Club swim team family. Sadly, at the conclusion of last season, Dave lost his battle with cancer. He will be dearly missed by every member of the team, all of us parents and his fellow coaches.

48 Dad's Night Out
The Personification of a Dad's Social Networking Group

I love being a dad. It's the greatest job in the world with perhaps the one exception being Howie Mandel's sweet gig as the
host of *Deal or No Deal*. Since the day my children were born, I
thought nothing of rushing home from a hard day's work to put
in another five or six hours as the newly defined "active dad."
Active Dads are those of us who, in addition to earning a living,
enthusiastically assume our 50% share of the child rearing duties
by participating in such rituals as play time, bath time and bed
time. Once the kids are a little older, those activities transcend
into coaching sports, helping with homework, making lunches,
monitoring TV/computer/video game/cell phone usage and ref-
ereeing UFC-style disagreements. Those chores are on top of
helping our wives around the house with the cooking, cleaning
and laundry. That's in addition to my regular responsibilities of
garbage emptier, lawn mower, car washer, bill payer and spider
killer. Fifty-nine days out of 60, it's all about the wife and kids,
but on that 60th day/night, I think I deserve a little "me time."

My "me time" is defined as a night out with the fellas. One
night, every other month, when I can get together with a few of
my closest buddies in a relaxed and comfortable setting to chat,
commiserate and share our inner most thoughts and fears about
the rigors of being a working husband and dad. It's a chance to
bond and develop relationships with other men going through a
similar phase in their lives. We often talk about the economy,
sports, religion, politics, the environment or more often than not,
just how to be better husbands and fathers. The "Dads Night
Out" was a direct take off of the similarly themed, "Moms Night
Out," possibly made popular by the Iron Horse Mother's Club.
The fact that we hold our meetings every other month at Danville

Bowl is irrelevant. Sure, we've been known to over indulge in festive libations made of hops and barley, hoot and holler like frat boys, smack talk like pro athletes, wager like degenerate gamblers and be worthless at work the next day, only reinforces my amateur sociology theory. After extensive research, I've concluded that, for the good of the family unit, husbands/fathers need an occassionaly harmless night out with the boys. Dating back to cavemen, the head of the clan occasionally needs to blow off some steam and recharge the battery. Instead of hunting parties or sweating it out in a mud hut, suburban men of our day need to do something indigenous to our area, like playing poker, joining a softball team or bocce ball league, attending a sporting event or go bowling.

> *I wish Dad's Night Out was every week. I need more "me" time and DNO embodies everything good in our world— friends, beer and bowling. Everyone needs to relieve stress.*
> —Anonymous

Shortly after my wife gave birth to our first child she informed me that she was joining the Iron Horse Mother's Club. In my typical role as loving husband and father my response was probably, "What's for dinner?" It didn't take me long to find out how valuable the Iron Horse Mother's Club (IHMC) was going to be in our lives. The IHMC was formed in 1996 to serve as a resource to mothers (especially new moms) in the San Ramon, Danville, Dublin and Alamo communities. This wonderful network of mom's with young children meet regularly to socialize, share, learn, vent and, above all else, to get out of the house. While many mothers join to find a playgroup for their children, it's not uncommon to develop long lasting friendships. Since merging with the Mother's Club of San Ramon Valley, the group now has over 400 members and is involved in a variety of local activities, parenting issues and support endeavors. One of the most popular activities amongst its sleeper cells is "Mom's Night Out." MNO usually takes place one weekday night a month to allow moms the opportunity to enjoy an evening out with their girlfriends, but more importantly, an evening without her beloved children. The mommies congregate in a relaxed and comfortable environment to chat, commiserate and share their inner most thoughts and fears about the rigors of being a wife and mother usually over a glass of white wine (Rombauer typically). As the children get older (or the moms do, I'm not sure which), women gradually move on from the IHMC, but Mom's Night Out remains a constant and book club is added to the monthly schedule of must attend activities.

> *My wife goes out at least once a week for Bunco, PTA or some type of Cabi/BodyShop/ Pampered Chef/Southern Living show. Half the time I don't even know where she is, but that's my trade-off for DNO, and it's worth it.*
> —Anonymous

During a casual conversation with a few of the neighborhood dads, a little over four years ago, the following thought provoking question was raised, "Hey, why don't we have a dad's club?" and like that, Dad's Night Out was born. What started out as a mere six dad's getting together for one evening on the town has blossomed into upwards of twenty four dads rearranging their business travel schedules to avoid missing our every-other-month night out of bowling. Initially, we thought about meeting at someone's home or utilizing a room at a local church. We even considered an HOA clubhouse or having coffee at a book store, but ultimately we chose bowling to avoid any clique accusations. As everyone knows, bowling is a form of exercise and with our busy schedules it's hard to always get in a workout. A bowling alley also has a certain intrinsic social networking appeal. It comes with wearing rented shoes. An executive decision was made to not begin our gathering until 9:00 p.m., allowing each of us to spend ample quality time with our families before we went out. We didn't want to be accused of neglecting our "active dad" duties and depriving our wives of the night time assistance they've come to expect.

> *This may sound a little corny, but with everyone's busy schedule this is one thing on the calendar we can all depend on to get together...perfectly timed to start at 9pm, so dinner's complete, homework done and kids are on their way to being asleep and, because it's only every other month the wife can't complain (too much).*
> —Anonymous

There are seven simple rules of Dad's Night Out. 1) Never talk about Dad's Night Out. It's a lot like fight club. 2) Be on time and never flake on the group. If you say you'll be there and don't show up that would be disrespecting the group and grounds for expulsion. 3) Don't take the game too seriously. We're there to have fun, relax and verbally attack the weakest bowler. Nobody should be trying to roll a 300. 4) Don't forget to buy beer. Each participant is required to purchase one six pack of beer from the alley bar at some point during the evening. You can always tell a newbie by the fact that they purchase a premium beer while the grizzled veterans are content sucking down Bud or Coors Light. Even if you have an important meeting the next morning and are limiting your alcohol intake, you are still expected to contribute to the group. 5) The stakes are $2.00 per game and $1.00 if you throw a gutter ball. Winning team shares the pot. The gaming angle is because most men have some form of ADHD and money keeps us focused. 6) Make sure your bowling brothers get home safely. Be safe and responsible. Finally, #7. What happens at DNO stays at DNO. It's a lot like Vegas.

When my wife asks me how bowling was I usually just grunt
and say, "fine." There's no way she could appreciate how
important Dad's Night Out is to me. Women just don't get
the joyful appeal of guys ridiculing each other, drinking a few
brews, swearing, scratching and competing at a game that
most of us suck at. It's just guys being guys and we love it.
— Anonymous

We've recently determined that Dad's Night Out is even more fun if we establish a theme for the evening. Much like Rotary, Kiwanis or the Bloods and Crips, our gang likes to rally around a designated theme at our gatherings. What started with a Loud Hawaiian shirt night theme a few summers ago and has since morphed into a plethora of zany themes such as; employer logo night, support your favorite (baseball/football) team night, college alma mater night and we even threw one guy a baby shower. We all dressed head to toe in the color blue to send the expectant father of three girls a rush of male testosterone. They had a boy. One former member suggested cross dressers night which explains why he's a former member. Fortunately, we can always count on one of our more passionate brothers to take our designated theme a bit too far, as evidenced by his spandex Santa outfit last December. It was festive and yet disturbing.

Every DNO I'm running around the house like a madman
looking for something "theme appropriate" right before I'm
scheduled to leave. I know my wife thinks I'm a dork, but the
kids think it's hilarious.
— Anonymous

The employees of the bowling alley have come to appreciate the energy our Dad's Night Out brings to the lanes. Sam, the youthful senior who mans the front desk, looks forward to our visits and is ever ready with a recycled dirty joke and repeatedly asking if we're an "alternative lifestyle" social group. The bartender warmly says she "hits the jackpot" every time we come in. Thursdays, our night of choice thanks to the emergence of Casual Friday's, is country music night at Danville Bowl and the music starts blasting at ten o'clock. Oddly, our game scores actually seem to improve the later it gets. Collectively we attribute this to the abundance of liquid performance enhancing supplements we consume. It must be the beer because none of us can see more than 15 feet down the lane once the lights go down and the lasers and strobes kick on. It's like Wii on steroids.

> *I take the same approach as a closer in baseball. After a bad outing, I have a short memory. I respond to the bi-monthly e-mail announcements as if I were Earl Anthony re-incarnated...calling out everyone on the list and letting them know that this is my night to take home the top score and big money.*
> —Anonymous

At the end of the night, the conclusion of three games, it truly doesn't really matter who won, except for bragging rights and a little pocket change (money won is always sweeter than money earned and more than a few of the group are currently unemployed). We all shake hands or give each other a manly bro hug and go our separate ways until the next meeting in exactly 8 weeks, which is approximately 56 days or 1,343 hours, not that we're counting. As our neighborhood carpool group climbs into the SUV (with our designated driver) we've come to expect a rowdy ride home with more than a few distasteful jokes at the expense of wives, careers or the kids athletic or academic shortcomings. Good times are good times and Dad's Night Out (bowling and beer) is a great time.

DNO reminds me a lot of college except now we have money and a designated driver. Maybe it's more like the movie Old School. It's our own little fraternity for guys in their 40's. Phi Bowla Frama. I can't wait for rush week in the fall.

— Anonymous

With June being the month we celebrate Father's Day, we implore the mothers and children reading this article to not only embrace, but encourage Dad's Night Out for the men you love. It doesn't have to be a bowling group that they join, just some type of regularly scheduled social outing with a select group of their male friends. Men need to cut up, cut loose and hang out with their bros. Since real men don't Twitter or blog, hell we can barely text, DNO is the personification of a dad's social networking group. We encourage all men reading this Public Service Announcement to align yourself with a group of your buddies and implement a Dad's Night Out in your life.

The anonymous quotes throughout this article can be attributed to the men of our group not wanting to anger or upset their wives by speaking out. There's safety in anonymity.

49 The Economy is Killing My Lawn
Desperate Times Demand Desperate Measures

Virtually every family in the East Bay, the state and country is reducing their monthly overhead (aka cutting back) due to the troubled economy. It's no secret that our nation is experiencing a fiscal meltdown of biblical proportions, not seen since the Great Depression of the 1930's. Many Americans are out of work, companies are closing; the residential real estate lending and sales markets are in shambles, the stock market has decimated our retirement plans, the price of gas is on the rise again and my lawn is dead. That's right, my lawn is dead. This turf catastrophe is the direct result of the failing economy. Granted, millions of Americans have much bigger worries than their lawn care maintenance, but in an attempt to reduce my monthly expenses I've cut back on irrigation and mowing. Sadly, the economy has gotten so bad that I've had to sacrifice the curb appeal of my home to make ends meet. What's next, a soup line? Day labor? Crime? Before I go to extreme measures, I've come up with the few cost saving ideas that may just get us over the hump.

House Bills: First, I've decided stop paying my mortgage. Call me crazy, but given the amount of home loan defaults the mortgage industry is experiencing it will be six months to a year before they figure out I'm a little behind. By the time I get my first notice, I'll have saved up a nice little nest egg. Of course, I'll cure my default, but in the meantime I'll be able to keep my country club membership current. Next, I'm going to send my PG&E payment to Visa and the Verizon payment to EBMUD. Additionally, I won't actually sign any of the checks. This type of bookkeeping chaos comes across like an innocent overwhelmed homeowner doing his best to keep his head above water. Once I eventually hear from a friendly customer service rep or collection agency, I'll blame the bank and promise everyone that it will just be a matter of four or five months until I get everything sorted out.

Food: Many Americans have gardens in their yards where they grow fruits and vegetables for the family's personal consumption, but I plan to take it one step further and raise my own beef. Not just beef, but fowl, pork and lamb too. I've raised dogs, cats and rodents, so how hard could it be to raise a few cows, chickens and sheep? Hell, if I could turn the pool into a saltwater pond, I would stock it with swordfish and shrimp. Granted, the homeowners association may have restrictions against certain elements of my plan, but I have to assume there's a hardship clause. It's not so much the farm aspect I'm worried about, it's the slaughterhouse. I'm relatively confident that I could explain away a "moo" here or there, but the stench a slaughterhouse puts out is pretty recognizable. I wonder how hard it will be to get a garbage collection company to drop-off an extra large can for carcass pick-ups?

Additionally, piggybacking the popularity of local wineries, I plan to bottle my own brand of alcohol (think rain water, potatoes and corn syrup). If Jed Clampett and a cell block of locked up prisoners can distill a little moonshine, why can't I? I'm thinking of calling it, "Mt. Diablo Hooch, Spirits for All Occasions."

Transportation: What good is having access to all this wonderful public transportation if we're not going to take advantage of it? I need my car for work, but I'm thinking my wife can get rid of her SUV and start taking the bus. There's a comfortable and convenient bus stop just two short miles from our house. In addition to alleviating ourselves of car payments, gas bills, insurance premiums and costly automobile maintenance, the family will be getting valuable exercise (see Health and Fitness below). Think how cool it would be for the kids to show up at the Mustang Soccer complex or Crow Canyon Country Club in a Contra Costa County Transit bus. We could take the entire team out for ice cream and only need one vehicle and one driver, Hank—the bus driver. A run to Costco might be a challenge for the Mrs., but isn't necessity the mother of invention? Maybe we could save the big shopping for the weekend assuming it doesn't interfere with my golf game or "me" time.

Healthcare: One word...witchdoctor. Plenty of villages around the world utilize the services of a medicine man or shaman. With the cost of college, medical/dental school, office space, advertising and malpractice insurance, it's no wonder doctors and dentists charge so much for their services. If you're fortunate enough to have good insurance, that obviously offsets a lot of your medical/dental costs, but let us not lose sight of the absurd amount of money we pay for PPO coverage these days. I pay more annually for medical/dental insurance than my parents paid for their first house. For years, witchdoctors compassionately treated sick or injured patients with tried and true remedies that included spells, potions and leeches. In some cultures, witchdoctors are revered as holy men. I'm just glad I've already had my vasectomy procedure.

Entertainment: It's expensive to be entertained these days. We live in one of the most amazing areas in the world, but it costs an arm and a leg to do anything. It cost $10.00 to see a movie. Concerts have become so outrageously priced that I've lost all hopes of seeing Def Leppard's next tour. The theatre has always been pricey and I had to apply for a line of credit to take my family to a Warriors game last season. Forget going out for a fancy dinner, nowadays an expensive meal is when we dress up for an evening at Applebee's. It costs $5.00 just to cross the Golden Gate Bridge, the national parks charge at least $40.00 per car just to drive around and skiing has become so insanely expensive it's become an activity only the Vanderbilt's, Rothschild's and Gate's can afford. I long for simpler days of picnics in the park, sunburns at the beach and making our own popcorn for the drive-in.

Health and Fitness: Health club memberships go up every year. I like my Pilates classes as much as the next guy, but if I replace my office chair with an oversized beach ball I can twist and stretch while I get my work done. And if I'm going to run on the treadmill, in theory, I guess I could venture outside and run in the street? Although, I will miss the air-conditioned gym and multiple flat screens to distract me while I crank out the miles, so perhaps I'll just run in-place in our family room so I can still enjoy the amenities available to me at home. Now, if I can just get my kids to give up their cell phones, iPods and Wii to play hop-scotch, tag, or hide and seek in the front yard, we can get their fitness routines started. Fat chance that will ever happen, but a man's gotta dream.

Let's face it, life today is complicated and expensive. It's going to be interesting to see how this financial crisis shakes out in the long run. There's no telling how bad it could get. They say everything is cyclical, but could this generation actually experience our own Great Depression? I, for one, am going to start making adjustments in my spending and come up with a plan for generating additional income. I have no reservations about picking up a second job, but is anyone hiring? You may just see me riding my bike around East Danville delivering papers or pushing my lawn mower up and down streets looking for lawns to mow. Oh, who am I kidding? The economy will have killed everyone's lawn in a couple of months. Maybe I'll buy up all the eco-friendly/non-toxic green paint in town and an air sprayer to start a new business. Mr. Mike's Insta-Green Lawn Service. Call for a free quote.

50 What does "Going Green" Mean?

When the editor of Alive Magazine, Eric Johnson, told me the April issue was going green I naturally assumed the obvious. Once our readers finished perusing the magazine's monthly standard of entertaining and informative articles, colorful ads and community news they would then be able to recycle our topical issue. Recycle, meaning they could mulch it, smoke it or use it as a replacement for their Charmin bathroom tissue. I truly hoped no one had tried these "green" options with previous editions as those issues were not "eco-friendly."

The country's obsession with "going green" sure makes the early green pioneers look ahead of their time. No one thinks the band name *Green Day* is lame anymore. The Green Giant Food Company's *Jolly Green Giant* and *Little Green Sprout* are now the kings of the ACSA—Animated Commercial Spokesperson Association. The Broadway musical *Wicked* has audiences nationwide wanting to be green, thanks to the lovable and misunderstood character, Elphaba. As a kid, I always thought the *Incredible Hulk* and *the Green Hornet* were very cool. Finally, how about the Martians? Mars has apparently always been eco-friendly. So much so that the planet's inhabitants have green pigmentation which is evidence of every Martian who ever appeared on television or in the movies. Martians were at the party long before the ten foot blue Na'vis from the planet Pandora, (showcased in the movie Avatar) ever materialized in the mind of James Cameron. Have I mentioned *Shrek*?

I recently tracked down a random sampling of our population to find out what "Going Green" actually means. It didn't surprise me that there were recurring themes such as recycling, water conservation and energy reduction. Many of the participants actually had practical suggestions to reduce our carbon footprint. Below are the actual responses I received in my study;

> *Everyone should pick-up garbage and when you leave a room, unplug things.*
> —Regan B., 3rd grade

> *We need to cut back on gas and have more battery operated cars. It's also important to save the polar bears and other endangered animals so I would pick up trash at the beach*
> —Nicole C., 5th grade

> *It's important to save electricity and make our world a better place so we can be happy.*
> —Lauren H., 3rd grade

> *People should help the environment by recycling bottles, paper and cans. Everybody can do it.*
> —Santiago M., 3rd grade

> *I think people need to quit smoking and for everyone to start picking up their litter and throwing it in the garbage.*
> —Gianna C., 5th grade

> *Pick up your trash and water your plants.*
> —Michael M., 1st grade

> *We can help the Earth by recycling and planting trees. Trees make our neighborhoods more beautiful.*
> —Jules M., 4th grade

> *Conserving water is a good idea. I'm not exactly sure why, but I know it's important to the environment. We did a water conservation chart in school, but it didn't work out so well.*
> —Cecily K., 5th grade

I would be like Johnny Appleseed and go around planting plants everywhere.
—Hudson P., 3rd grade

We should all recycle, turn off lights and don't litter.
—Tyler G., 2nd grade

Everyone should turn down the heat in their homes and wear sweaters when they're cold to save energy.
—Claire C., 5th grade

I'm not going to tell you because you're a stinky head.
—Kylie K., 2nd grade

I actually think the last response, while hurtful, may have been the most insightful. Young Miss Kylie may be on to something if by stinky she was actually referring to my breath or post workout funk smell. Perhaps, if people focused more attention on their personal hygiene there might be a greater sharing of information. Groups of people might actually come together in think tanks and share ideas or information they have previously been keeping to themselves. Wouldn't it be incredible if out of this collaborative effort came some breakthrough idea? Perhaps some type of innovative solution to the global environmental problem that faces our generation. The possibilities are endless.

Looking back, I may have been doing this green thing for years and just never realized the relevance of my actions. When I was a youngster, Going Green used to be an expression my parents used to describe me after a ride on the Big Dipper Rollercoaster at the Santa Cruz Beach Boardwalk. Mean Joe Greene of the Pittsburg Steelers was my favorite football player back in the 70's. In college, my entire fraternity unwisely decided to Rock the Green (aka green body paint, everywhere) on St. Patrick's Day 1984, before we all headed down to the Shamrock Bar in Van Nuys, California for a night of green beer chugging.

I'm green with envy whenever someone in my office closes a large sale or lease transaction. I wish my lawn would go green instead of brown like it usually does every summer. My wife has an aversion to green vegetables and green tea, but oddly loves Green Appletinis, green M&Ms and Trader Joe's Salsa Verde. I may just send my kids to Green Valley School, move to Green Gables Court or read from the Dr. Suess book, Green Eggs and Ham.

This Going Green phenomenon make take some getting used to, but it is definitely the wave of the future. We all need to get on board or be run over...by a Prius Hybrid.

51 Dad University
Continuing Education in the Course of Fathering 101

Welcome to Dad University. My name is Mike and I'll be your instructor for this summer school continuing education class which is designed to help Dads reconnect with a few of the basics and fundamental concepts in the course of Fathering 101. My outline is less structured than say, a community college, where you might have lectures and tests. This refresher course is more like a tutorial session stressing the implementation of common sense practices. Consider this article our course syllabus, this magazine your text book and ALIVE our school motto. Dad University rocks!

Virtually all men have the capacity to be a dad, but it takes an innate ability to be a good father. It's not an easy job. It is a constantly evolving task which demands commitment, hard work and a desire to improve. To be a truly involved Dad, you've got to want to do more than Preside, Provide and Protect (The three P's of fathering). Given the day-to-day financial stress we all contend with to live in such a beautiful and affluent community, it's easy to lose track of our priorities and responsibilities when it comes to the act of interacting with our children. "Kids spell love T-I-M-E," says Dr. Ken Canfield, Founder of the National Center for Fathering. My Fathering 101 course outline is divided up into four quarters, each focusing on a distinct phase in the lives of our children and how we can better serve them.

First Quarter: This is when we learn how to assimilate ourselves with the new alien life form that has invaded our lives, otherwise known as the newborn/infant introduction through the toddler stage. I can't be the only Dad that didn't get an instruction manual when I brought the kid home from the hospital, so don't feel bad if you're not sure what to do right away?

While a father can't do much when it comes to nursing, we can be the one who responds to their cries and brings the baby to their mothers. In the middle of the night, regardless of the hour, be the one to respond to their cries. When the transition to bottle feeding occurs, help out there too. Also, don't avoid changing diapers. What doesn't kill you will make you stronger. Once you're feeling brave and confident, encourage your wife to take a night off and get out of the house. You will be amazed at what you're capable of when it comes to caring for your child.

To this day, my daughters call out for me in the middle of the night if they have a bad dream or aren't feeling well. That's not always an easy bell to answer, but it's certainly a feeling of being needed.

Second Quarter: As our toddlers grow to pre-school age, right up into their elementary school years, our role takes on a variety of mentoring applications. We are essentially Yoda to our young Jedi Knight prospects. I read somewhere that family is a place of training, instruction and discipline. Take manners for example. My parents were manners crazy. If we ate with our mouths open, put our elbows on the table or, God forbid, used our fingers as a fork, spoon or knife there was hell to pay. Appropriate table manners are a critical life training exercise, but raise your hand if you've been a little relaxed lately in the rules department. Now raise your hand if your own manners have taken on the traits of a band of marauding Huns, Vikings or pirates. You get my drift. Manners say a lot about an individual's character and upbringing. There was a recent article in the Contra Costa Times entitled, Good Etiquette is Good Business, in which students learn how important manners are to college graduates interviewing with potential employers. People will assuredly notice when visiting children have good manners, but they notice more when they don't. Motivation comes from both compliments and constructive criticism, but it also doesn't hurt to set a good example.

Don't be afraid to set high standards. Kids will often surprise us with what they're capable of when it comes to meeting parental expectations. If there are significant consequences for not towing the line, kids will typically rise to the occassion.

Third Quarter: This is typically our least favorite quarter at DAD U, the one dealing with "tweens" and teenagers. This demographic needs us to be fair parents who will lay down the law and enforce it. As our children are given more freedom and responsibilities they should be rewarded, not for doing what's expected of them, but instead for exceeding expectations. I would tell my 13 year old this, but she's rarely disconnected from a phone or iPod long enough for me to have a heartfelt sit down conversation. She tweets, texts, emails and sings, but she's not a real big talker. Middle school sets the stage for high school, so it's critically important that we establish a strong set the rules and boundaries. Take communication as an example. When we were young our parents simply eavesdropped on our phone conversations. Sadly, we now live in a world of cyber-talk where kids are handed a cell phone at their fifth grade commencement ceremony. It's not unreasonable to demand random access to their email and text for a review of the content and context of their communications. Whenever I watch one of those Today Show or 20/20 stories on cyber bullying or online sexual predators, I vow to uphold my position as an IT cop at home, even if it makes me unpopular.

Dr. Amy Chambliss, a psychologist with a private practice in Danville, states, "Kids need boundaries and limits to feel safe and secure. Rules and regulations send them the message that their parents care and are invested in them. From this, kids develop self-respect and a sense of worthiness."

Fourth Quarter: The last quarter of the year is spent on our children as young adults. This should be a peaceful and enjoyable time to observe the fruits of our labor. Ideally, what we taught our children in the early stages of their development has established a strong foundation for the choices they make once they are 18 and essentially adults. That's not to say we can't still be retained as consultants.

Post Graduate Degree: There is undoubtedly a Grandpa University, but it will hopefully be a lot of years before I attend classes there or even contemplate joining the staff.

Not every man had a good "father" role model. A lot of our father's either didn't attend or dropped out of Dad University. A lot of old school dads left child rearing up to the graduates of Mom University. My father was raised in a poor farming community and lost his father at a young age. He got his high school GED and enlisted in the Navy. After the Korean War he started his own company and traveled a lot. I always loved my dad, but didn't always understand him. I was often told, by his friends and co-workers, how proud he was of me. Sadly, he rarely spoke those words to me himself. While my sisters and I always appreciated how hard he worked to provide for us, we all would have preferred that he was around more. I thought that by succeeding in school and excelling in sports he would choose to be more involved. Unfortunately, my father died before I was mature enough to learn more firsthand about the man he was and what he had endured growing up. It may have made a difference in our relationship. I also regret that he never got to meet his two granddaughters, because they are pretty amazing.

According to Dr. Chambliss, "missing fathers or emotionally unavailable fathers are a contributing factor to the acting out we see in our kids today. Kids can go through what psychologists call "Father Hunger," defined as an intense desire for emotional connection with dad. When that connection doesn't happen, kids will try to force it. They may engage in exhausting perfectionist behavior or self-destructive behavior."

I know that I'm not a perfect father and there's a lot I can improve upon. Considering that our nation just celebrated Father's Day last month, this may be an ideal time to delve deeper into the role and responsibilities of being a good dad. We have another 12 months to better ourselves for the sake of our children. Class dismissed.

52 Who Couldn't Use a Million Dollars?

Given how the economy has devastated us financially over the past few years, and with tax day right around the corner, and because those *%)@!& Pittsburg Steelers didn't cover the point spread at the Super Bowl last month, who couldn't use a little money right now? By little, I'm talking about a round number like $1,000,000.00? Granted, a million dollars doesn't go as far as it used to, but it's not like any of us wouldn't bend over and pick up a $1,000,000 bill if we saw it lying in the gutter. It's a healthy enough sum that it would legitimately make a substantial impact in our lives as we scratch and claw our way out of the pit of financial despair. In the 1967 movie, *How to Succeed in Business without Really Trying,* the opening voice-over states that if someone placed $1,000,000 in a standard federally secured bank savings account, the bearer would receive $50,000 annually. In 1967, at the financially savvy age of five years old (think E*Trade baby in kindergarten), I determined that if one could accumulate one million $1.00 bills one would never have to work or ever worry about money. So, I started collecting George Washington's and hoping that savings accounts would always pay a 5% interest rate. Sadly, somewhere along the way, (candy, baseball cards, comic books or girls), my plan was derailed.

The popular musical artists, Travis McCoy and Bruno Mars recently wrote and performed the catchy little ditty called, *Billionaire,* which to me seems a little greedy, but given that Mr. McCoy and Mr. Mars are likely already millionaires (thanks to that one song) a billion would obviously be their next goal. Me, however, I would be more than happy with a million smackers. The question is: How do I get me a million smackers (or dollars)? Oh sure, I could work really hard, but I'm almost fifty. Let's face it, my best days are behind me. The only people "killing it" at work are hedge fund managers, app designers and internet brainiacs. For me to accumulate real wealth in my career, I would have to work 26 hours a day in a real growth industry. Let's see, what's hot right now? Anything solar, cloud computing; social networking; electronic gaming and porn are probably my best bets. Just to be prudent, I better come up with a few more ideas.

Game shows: There are game shows that pay the contestants $1,000,000 if they win the grand prize. *Who Wants to be a Millionaire* is the obvious choice, but shouldn't it be called Who Doesn't Want to be a Millionaire? I've watched it a few times and can occasionally get some of the questions correct, but you have to answer all of the questions correctly if you want to be in the big money. They've got these things called Lifelines, Phone-A-Friend and 50/50 to help "hook a brother up," but some of the questions are really hard. How do I know who invented internet, Al Gore? Maybe I stand a better chance at Minute to Win It. I could totally rock those baby games. You know what else I could rock, *Deal or No Deal*. The objective apparently is to hook-up with one of those smoking hot models holding a briefcase and out-smart Howie Mandel and some anonymous banker? I would select case number one and start picking off briefcase-toting hot-ties, numerically, starting with numero dos. Maybe I could create my own game show, Mail Mike One Million $1.00 Bills or Else I Start Dancing. That show would have to be on cable. Truth be told, my game is really *Wipeout.*

Crime: Probably not. White collar crime maybe? I wouldn't want to actually hurt anyone or steal anything, but crime does seem like easy money if you have half a brain. The problem is, most criminals are idiots. Too many criminals use the "smash and grab" approach which never works. The movies such as Ocean's 11 and Sneakers, come up with incredibly complicated and complex crimes. That's way too much work. My Robin Hood crime spree would include getting really wealthy people to each give me just a little bit of money. It's a pyramid scheme essentially, where one million of the world's wealthiest people each send me $1.00. That's not really a crime and I likely wouldn't go to jail. I'm confident that I wouldn't like jail. Three squares and a cot is a nice concept (like camp), but in reality there's a lot more involved than just crafts and games. Besides, I've heard those prison jobs don't pay much.

Gambling: The World Series of Poker has a huge payday and a nice bracelet to boot. Guys like Phil Ivy, Johnny Chen and Annie Duke seem to be doing pretty well for themselves. I don't want to brag, but I've faired nicely at the annual Sycamore Valley Elementary School Texas Hold'em tournament. I haven't actually ever won, but I've finished in the top 25 (out of 25) every year. As alternatives, there's roulette, horse racing and I have heard there's an interesting line brewing on next season's Dancing with the Stars finale. Obviously, betting "sure thing" football games didn't work out too well for me.

Inventions: I've been noodling on a few ideas that might be patentable. People love their animals and hybrid vehicles, so I have this crazy idea about energy efficient cars for cats. The Catmobile is in its infant stages, but last I checked the former Nummi assembly plant is empty. There are obviously plenty of qualified auto workers looking for a job and I doubt if they care who the end-user is, they just want to work. There's also sure fire ideas like tuna-flavored chewing gum, bullet-proof hoodies and musical i-pod shoes (for spontaneous dancing). Brilliant, right? All of my inventions are available for sale at the low, low price of $1,000,000.00.

Writing: For Sale, one unpublished collection of children's bedtime stories written and autographed by a talented Danville resident. Price: $1,000,000.00. Additionally, for sale, one finished screenplay entitled *Hungerlight Twigames*—a script ready for big budget production by a major motion picture studio. Also written and autographed by an acclaimed Danville resident. Purchase price: $1,000,000.00. Finally, get your limited collection of humor lifestyle articles written and autographed by a handsome and charming Danville author. Purchase Price: $20.00, but I need to sell 50,000 copies. Did I mention I have a concept for a new autobiographical comic strip? Think Calvin and Hobbes meets Garfield and you'll love, The Adventures of Mike, Mr. Whiskers and Bobo. Purchase price: $1,000,000.00. Isn't this how Scott Adams started?

It's been said that money is the root of all evil. You know who said that? Probably someone who had a bunch of money and blew it all. If you read business magazines, listen to the business news stations, follow economic blogs or just have an inkling of common sense, you've probably figured out that the economy is going to remain stagnate for the foreseeable future. All we can do is keep working hard and hope we come into a little extra cash somewhere. As one of my friends likes to say, "I'm only six numbers away from retirement every Wednesday and Saturday. I'm playing the Lottery baby!"

53 I Am a Dinosaur

Dinosaurs were a diverse group of animals and the dominant terrestrial vertebrates for over 160 million years, from the late Triassic period (about 230 million years ago) until the end of the Cretaceous (about 65 million years ago). Dinosaurs freely roamed every continent on earth and while generally known for the large size of some species, most were human-sized or even smaller. While most of the scientific community believed these ancestors of today's lizards to be sluggish, complacent, relatively unintelligent, predominately carnivorous, cold blooded and methodical they actually had numerous adaptations for social interaction. Wait one darn second! Couldn't those detailed adjectives easily be used when describing my buddies and me? I'm talking about guys I work with, play softball with, hang-out with at our kids sporting events and, dare I say, my bowling group? It used to be that a man with a receding hairline or some grey (salt and pepper) in his temples was seen as dashing or distinguished. Today, any guy over forty-five is considered a prehistoric dinosaur; impractically large, slow-moving, slow to adapt, obsolete and bound for extinction. Sadly, I'll be forty-nine this year which makes me part of the dinosaur demographic.

Before he hosted the popular game show, *Are You Smarter than a Fifth Grader,* Jeff Foxworthy (also a dinosaur) was a very successful stand-up comedian. His most popular bit was called, "You Might Be a Redneck." For instance, "If you have more cars parked on your front lawn than people living in your house, you might be a redneck." For the sake of this article, I would like to offer up a series of like minded ideas related to Dinosaurs.

If you don't maintain an active Facebook account, You Might Be a Dinosaur.

If you've never read or sent a Tweet, You Might Be a Dinosaur.

If you routinely fall asleep during episodes of "Law and Order," You Might Be a Dinosaur.

If you think spelling your name with a symbol (Ke$ha, Cope!and) is $illy, You Might Be a Dinosaur.

If you think Bieber Fever is a new strain of the flu, You Might Be a Dinosaur.

If you complain of aches and pains the day after a slow pitch softball game, You Might Be a Dinosaur.

If you're optimistic Martin Sheen will eventually talk some sense into his son Charlie, You Might be a Dinosaur.

If the last adult website you visited was to read up on Obamacare, You Might Be a Dinosaur.

If your idea of exercise is bowling or golf, You Might Be a Dinosaur.

If you think Angry Birds is a reference to the nesting doves on your front porch, You Might Be a Dinosaur.

If you have to ask your elementary school age kids to program your mobile phone, You Might Be a Dinosaur.

If you think owning a hybrid vehicle is for hippies and employees of Greenpeace, You Might Be a Dinosaur.

If you think the money professional athletes are paid is absurd (because you would've played for free given the chance), You Might Be a Dinosaur.

If you still pay your bills with conventional checks instead of on on-line bill pay, You Might Be a Dinosaur.

If you watch the popular television show "Glee" for the sensible dialogs of Sue Sylvester and the Journey tunes, You Might Be a Dinosaur.

If you still wash your own car, mow your own lawn, have less than a 50 inch, flat screen television and make your kids lunches, You Might Be a Dinosaur.

If you shook your head in agreement at five or more of the above referenced "Ifs...," You are a Dinosaur!

Dinosaurs remember the good old days, when it was totally acceptable in society to see a suave and debonair older gentleman in the company of an attractive younger woman? My, how times have changed. Now that "Dinosaur" relationship is frowned upon. My favorite new recording artist, Ke$ha (what, you thought I would say Justin Bieber?) even has a song out detailing the "creepiness" of my peer group appreciating the cutting edge look or her and her songstress contemporaries, such as Katy Perry, Fergie and Rhianna. Appropriately the song is called D-I-N-O-S-A-U-R. On the other hand, an older woman/younger man soirée is now in vogue with women being assigned the cool moniker of "Cougar." What's wrong with the term Lady Dino? Again I point out, how times have changed.

Back in the Jurassic era of our youth, life was so different from today. We often rode in the back bed of a pick-up truck and never wore seat belts in the car. When traveling by planes, trains or automobiles, we read books and listened to whatever music was available on AM radio. Portable DVD players, laptop computers and iPods were crazy space age ideas no one had the capacity to even imagine, except maybe Will Robinson or Scotty on *Star Trek*.

We had three national television networks to choose from — NBC, ABC and CBS — and an antenna strapped to our fireplace chimney for reception. Now there are 600 channels available through an underground cable. There was once only one type of gasoline (regular) and it cost under $1.00 per gallon. We sat in the car while friendly service station attendants pumped it and even checked under the hood. Now we pay almost $5.00 a gallon and have no communication with anyone.

We went to drive-in movie theatres, carnivals and picnics. No one ever wore a helmet while riding a bike or skating. We talked with our friends over the phone, used the Encyclopedia to do our homework and I had a Pterodactyl as a pet.

All of my dino-contemporaries are feeling a sense of gloom, knowing that we either adapt to the new environment (quickly) or face eventual extinction. Fossil records do indicate that birds evolved from theropod dinosaurs, which are the ancestors of all modern birds, so perhaps there is hope for us old guys.

If we ever-so-slightly modify our lifestyle and expand our comfort level, mainly by observing our children, we can hope-fully preserve our existence. We'll either adapt trying or sponta-neously combust from environmental overload, not unlike the asteroid theory that wiped out the real dinosaurs 65 million years ago. Sadly, I feel very old right now.

54 Another Election Year Is Coming

By the time you read this we'll be just a year away from the Presidential Election. President Barrack Obama versus the last man standing in the GOP Battle Royale. Every election year, I feel like I've had the sense beat out of me by the time I got to my designated polling place to vote, and presidential elections are the worst. The negative campaign ads, the "no holds barred" style debates and the dinner hour interruptions from pollsters and candidate call centers make my head hurt. Someone said, "Politics is a dirty business," and if that's the case then elections are like rolling around in a mud puddle after a litter of puppies has just "done their business."

Politicians spend so much time campaigning that they can't possibly be doing their actual job and where does that leave us as constituents? It leaves us unrepresented. The guy or gal we hired is not showing up for work because he or she is out of the office trying to get rehired. Here's a real world example: Imagine if all of the cashiers at Safeway, Lucky, Whole Foods, Lunardi's, Drager's, etc. left their registers to go door-to-door, asking for support to keep their job. Chances are, we would all be annoyed by their visit and then we'd all head to the grocery store to stock up on free stuff because no one would be there to ring us up and check us out. Could it be that the rest of the world knows we're our most vulnerable during an election year because no one is minding the store?

It doesn't matter which political affiliation you have these days—whether you're a Democrat, Republican, Libertarian, Communist, Vegetarian, Independent, New Union, Peace, Reform, American Populist, Citizens United, Daughters of the American Revolution or Sons of Anarchy—you're inundated with television ads, phone calls, banners, radio spots and town hall assemblies. It's a case of total sensory overload when it comes to our right to vote.

In the spring of 1975, when I was in the seventh grade at Isaac Newton Graham Junior High School, I ran for Student Body President. This was the ultimate in prestigious titles for anyone transitioning to the eighth grade. I watched in awe as students stepped aside anytime Charlie Passentino, the reigning Student Body President, roamed the corridors. Like many aspiring politicians, I was seduced by the power the office held. Once I submitted my application, with the required thirty signatures (I'm not afraid to admit that I cozied up to the band geeks and drama freaks), I hit the campaign trail. I plastered the hallways of our school with campaign posters, that would eventually be defaced with obscene drawings. I didn't so much defend my position on issues as much as make a lot of false promises I had no intention of keeping. At the candidate debate, which took place before the entire seventh grade class in the school's multi-purpose room, all of the candidates did their best just not to throw-up on stage during our first public speaking experience. Ultimately, I lost the election. I think I came in sixth and there were only five candidates running. The charismatic and dashing Russell Kevin Peoples (or was it Kevin Russell?) won in a landslide victory. To his credit, Russ was a born politician and did an admirable job during his term. He managed to create new jobs, balance the budget, reduce our international debt, stabilize the stock market and secure a jukebox for the cafeteria. Russ was eventually succeeded by Jack Vandervork. Sadly, Jack's administration was rocked with scandal during the fall of 1976 when he arrived stoned at the annual Sadie Hawkins Day dance.

The University of Akron conducted a study entitled, *Trends in Federal Campaign Spending,* which charts a ten year history of campaign spending. Not surprising, the peak was during the last presidential election in 2008. The findings recorded total campaign spending that year at just under $600 million dollars. As I recall, the average American couldn't escape the onslaught of ads. Our home phone message recorder had five to seven political related calls every day. Granted, I did feel popular, but it became so over-the-top that I just wanted it to stop. I kept thinking that all that money could've been spent more wisely or philanthropically.

Elections are good for the economy, but bad for the environment. Perhaps President Obama's jobs plan will coincide with the election year by pumping $600,000,000 into the economy. Smart. However, the post election disposal of 1000 tons of bulk mailers and one million lawn signs could actually melt the polar icecaps and dry out a rain forest. The Green Party won't like that one.

My own personal political views fall somewhere between Liberal Republican and Conservative Democrat. My Republican vote is usually cancelled out by my wife's Democrat vote, however knowing that every vote counts I try and vote early and often. Prior to every election, my wife and I sit down and go over our sample ballots cover to cover. We typically see eye-to-eye on Bonds, Measures and Referendums, but truthfully I couldn't tell you the difference between a bond, measure or referendum. Aren't referendums the guys wearing stripped shirts doing the officiating at basketball and football games? The Mrs. elects to mail her ballot in where I prefer to get the full election experience, and the *I Voted* sticker, at my local polling place.

The right to vote is a privilege we should not take lightly. People all over the world have fought long and hard for that right and many countries today still do not have that form of democracy. Our country was built by people (fondly know as Pilgrims) who left England to establish a country where citizens had a right to choose their officials and representatives. Initially it was just white male citizens, but we've come a long way since the mid-1700s. Every U.S. Citizen, 18 years old and older, should feel a need to exercise their right to participate in the electoral process. Each and every one of us has a voice. Our vote does count. Rock the Vote... or it might rock us!

55 My Interview with Me

It was a wet and dreary Saturday afternoon when I finally got a chance to sit down with author Mike Copeland, on the eve of the release of his first book, *Alive and Kickin': Sideways Views from an Upright Guy*—a collection of his humor lifestyle essays. Although I had been warned that Mr. Copeland could be a naracistic "DB," I actually found him to be relaxed and jovial, perhaps he was even mildly inebriated. While we sat in the den of his Danville home, he sipped a piping hot mug of Chamomile tea, likely mixed with bourbon, based on the whiskey scent of his breath. He seemed to be enjoying his new found celebrity status.

Mike is both heavier and balder in person than his photo in ALIVE Magazine would lead one to believe. My guess is that the head shot, found on the Contributing Writers page, is at least ten years old. Mike has spent the last five years writing monthly humor lifestyle articles and personality profiles for ALIVE Magazine and is the self-proclaimed master of bathroom writing. I was curious how the partnership with ALIVE Editor, Eric Johnson, began and what led to the creation of the soon to be released Toilet Tank Book by ALIVE Book Publishing. For those of you unfamiliar with the term "Toilet Tank Book," it is a similar concept to the hugely popular coffee table books, but without the pretty photos and prestige. A Toilet Tank Book contains writings that a reader can get through in the amount of time it takes them to "do their business" in the bathroom. Mike tears up when he proudly recants the time Mr. Johnson told him that his literary contributions to ALIVE were the perfect bathroom ready material, both in length and substance. Once Mike changed into his pajamas, UGG® boots and fedora hat our interview began.

MC: Mike, where did you and Alive Magazine Editor Eric Johnson first meet?

Mike: First, please call me Mr. Copeland. I believe it was a MENSA meeting (Tri Valley chapter) back in the winter of 2004. We both quickly realized we were way smarter than everyone else so we snuck out and started our own exclusive secret society of the USD&Cs- Uber Smart Dudes and Chicks. Our first meeting was at Forli Ristorante on Danville Boulevard in Alamo. We choose Forli because really smart people love Osso Buco.

MC: How did you gain inspiration for your monthly humor pieces that make up the Alive and Kickin' book?

Mike: Did you not hear me say USD&Cs? Say it with me, G-E-N-I-U-S. However, when I do need the occasional idea it often comes from my kids, my friends, memories of growing up, things that are relevant to living in the East Bay or the local and national media. I suppose my medical marijuana induced dreams are also helpful. JK—Just kidding. I don't use drugs, unless they are prescribed by my chiropractor for treatment of a gluteus maximus strain, but I digress. Inspiration can be found anywhere, anytime if you're truly gifted. I'm inspired right now.

MC: Why did you decide to publish a collection of your favorite humor pieces from your magazine writings of the last five years?

Mike: The money of course. People have the misperception that you get rich writing monthly 1,200 word essays for a regional magazine with a circulation of about 40,000. Not so. After my screenplay, *Allen and Allen,* wasn't purchased by a major motion picture studio and my collection of children's bedtime stories entitled, *"Would Someone Please Read Me a Story"* was rejected by every publishing company south of the Mississippi River, I decided to release a book that I could strategically peddle through a combination of network marketing, direct mail ads and garage sale book signings. Can you say, "Cha-Ching"?

MC: Who are your favorite humor magazine writers?

Mike: Rick Reilly is boss. He writes for *Sports Illustrated* and other two-bit rags. Dave Berry used to be crazy talented, but now I think he's just crazy. I still enjoy Tony Hicks, although he still works for a newspaper which is nowhere near as prestigious as a magazine. Just check out the paper stock. I am also a big fan of Scott Osler, but no one knows who he is other than me. I may one day invite these gentlemen to a swanky conference of brilliant writers, but since it would be a no host bar they probably wouldn't come.

MC: Do you remember the first humor piece you ever had published?

Mike: The year was in 1980 and I collaborated with my buddies Jeff Morales and Derek Sousa on a gritty (and hilariously sarcastic) expose for the *Mountain View High School Eagle Gazette* entitled, The Future of the Around the Tree Gang. The three of us were part of a really dangerous scholastic gang being forced to dissolve by the administration, the police and our parents. Or was it summer vacation? The article chronicled our rise to power and each member's blood oath to give up gang-banging in pursuit of higher education at a variety of community colleges and universities. I think it won a high school Pulitzer Prize.

MC: What other publications have you written for before you were signed exclusively with ALIVE East Bay Magazine?

Mike: Too many to name really, but let me try. Going back to the beginning it was the *MVHS Eagle Gazette*, followed by the *Foothill Community College Gazette* and the *Sigma Chi Fraternity Gazette*. I loved those Gazettes. Over the years I've scribed for the *San Jose Business Times*, the *California Real Estate News*, the *Country Music News*, *Floyd's Ordeal Newsletter*, *Valley Lifestyle* and *The Patch*. I must say that my best work may have been the intensely hard hitting reporting I did by having total access to the incredibly popular rock cover band *Floyd's Ordeal*. Their wildly popular newsletter (pre blog) allowed me to expand into areas such as show reviews, the Up Close and Personal expose` and an advice column. Our readership was up to eleven when the band broke up amidst rumors of eating disorders and necrophilia.

MC: How do you respond to critics that categorize your writing style as juvenile, sophomoric, lame and sucky. It's been said that your articles are filled with grammatical errors and factual inaccuracies?

Mike: I don't. Next question. Who says that? I want names. Was that you? Let me just say to my detractors that the writers of the Simpsons, Family Guy and South Park have made a fortune utilizing that style and my writing is much better. Wait one second. I just realized I've been wasting my time all these years. I should have been writing for an animated network show not print magazines. I feel so deflated, so empty, so broke. You'll have to leave now. I need to be alone with my thoughts.

I never have understood why pseudo celebrities insist on bidding farewell to their guests with a two-handed handshake and air kisses on both cheeks, but I'm not one to judge. For all his eccentricities and egotism, Mr. Copeland does have some talent. From time to time, his wordy ramblings have even given this hardened reporter a chuckle. I wish Mike well with his book and encourage everyone reading to contact ALIVE Magazine at www.aliveeastbay.com to order an autographed copy today.

About The Author

Michael S. Copeland has been a contributing writer for ALIVE Magazine since June 2007. Over the past 25 years, Mike has written humor, lifestyle and personality profile articles for a variety of publications including: *The San Jose Business Times, California Real Estate Journal, Country Western News* and *Valley Lifestyles.* Mike is a Managing Partner with Cassidy Turley, Northern California. He lives with his wife and two daughters in Danville, California.

ABOOKS

ALIVE Book Publishing and ALIVE Publishing Group
are divisions of Advanced Publishing LLC,
3200 A Danville Blvd., Suite 204, Alamo, California 94507

Telephone: 925.837.7303 Fax: 925.837.6951
www.alivebookpublishing.com

CPSIA information can be obtained
at www.ICGtesting.com
Printed in the USA
FSOW02n1232261216
28746FS